SONNY MAGAÑA

ROBERT MARZANO

Enhancing the Art & Science of Teaching With Technology

MARZANO
—Research—

THE **CLASSROOM** STRATEGIES **SERIES**

555 North Morton Street
Bloomington, IN 47404
888.849.0851
FAX: 866.801.1447

email: info@marzanoresearch.com
marzanoresearch.com

Visit **marzanoresearch.com/classroomstrategies** to download the reproducibles in this book.

Printed in the United States of America

Library of Congress Control Number: 2013952335

ISBN: 978-0-9858902-4-7 (paperback)

18 17 16   8 9 10

Editorial Director: Lesley Bolton
Managing Production Editor: Caroline Weiss
Production Editor: Rachel Rosolina
Proofreader: Sarah Payne-Mills
Text and Cover Designer: Amy Shock
Compositor: Laura Kagemann

MARZANO RESEARCH DEVELOPMENT TEAM

Director of Publications

Julia A. Simms

Production Editor

Katie Rogers

Marzano Research Associates

Tina Boogren

Bev Clemens

Jane K. Doty Fischer

Jeff Flygare

Maria C. Foseid

Mark P. Foseid

Tammy Heflebower

Mitzi Hoback

Jan K. Hoegh

Russell Jenson

Jessica Kanold-McIntyre

Sharon V. Kramer

David Livingston

Pam Livingston

Sonny Magaña

Beatrice McGarvey

Margaret McInteer

Diane E. Paynter

Debra J. Pickering

Salle Quackenboss

Laurie Robinson

Ainsley B. Rose

Tom Roy

Gerry Varty

Phil Warrick

Kenneth C. Williams

Visit **marzanoresearch.com/classroomstrategies**
to download reproducibles from this book.

CONTENTS

Italicized entries indicate reproducible forms.

CHAPTER 3

ESTABLISHING CLASSROOM RULES AND PROCEDURES 39

CHAPTER 4

INTERACTING WITH NEW KNOWLEDGE 47

CHAPTER 5

PRACTICING AND DEEPENING KNOWLEDGE 67

CHAPTER **6**

GENERATING AND TESTING HYPOTHESES 91

CHAPTER **7**

ENGAGING STUDENTS 105

CHAPTER 8

RECOGNIZING LEVELS OF ADHERENCE TO RULES AND PROCEDURES 125

CHAPTER 9

MAINTAINING EFFECTIVE RELATIONSHIPS WITH STUDENTS . . 133

CHAPTER 10

COMMUNICATING HIGH EXPECTATIONS 141

ABOUT THE AUTHORS

Anthony J. "Sonny" Magaña, EdM, is an associate vice president of Marzano Research and director of the Educational Technology Division. He works with teams of teachers and leaders to support, enhance, and expand powerful instructional strategies with technology. Sonny has served in the field of education for thirty years as a classroom teacher, building principal, district administrator, state technology project director, author, speaker, and trainer. Sonny created and served as director of Washington's first CyberSchool, a successful blended learning program that continues to meet the needs of at-risk students in Washington State. He received the Milken National Educator Award in 1997 and the Governor's Commendation for Distinguished Achievement in Education in 1998. Sonny received a bachelor of science degree in biology from Stockton College in New Jersey and a master's degree in educational technology from City University of Seattle and is completing a doctorate at Seattle University.

Robert J. Marzano, PhD, is the cofounder and CEO of Marzano Research in Denver, Colorado. During his forty years in the field of education, he has worked with educators as a speaker and trainer and has authored more than thirty books and 150 articles on topics such as instruction, assessment, writing and implementing standards, cognition, effective leadership, and school intervention. His books include *The Art and Science of Teaching*, *Leaders of Learning*, *On Excellence in Teaching*, *Effective Supervision*, *The Classroom Strategies Series*, *Using Common Core Standards to Enhance Classroom Instruction and Assessment*, *Vocabulary for the Common Core*, and *Teacher Evaluation That Makes a Difference*. His practical translations of the most current research and theory into classroom strategies are known internationally and are widely practiced by both teachers and administrators. He received a bachelor's degree from Iona College in New York, a master's degree from Seattle University, and a doctorate from the University of Washington.

ABOUT MARZANO RESEARCH

Marzano Research is a joint venture between Solution Tree and Dr. Robert J. Marzano. Marzano Research combines Dr. Marzano's forty years of educational research with continuous action research in all major areas of schooling in order to provide effective and accessible instructional strategies, leadership strategies, and classroom assessment strategies that are always at the forefront of best practice. By providing such an all-inclusive research-into-practice resource center, Marzano Research provides teachers and principals the tools they need to effect profound and immediate improvement in student achievement.

INTRODUCTION

Enhancing the Art & Science of Teaching With Technology is part of a series of books collectively referred to as *The Classroom Strategies Series*. This series aims to provide teachers, as well as building and district administrators, with an in-depth treatment of research-based instructional strategies that can be used in the classroom to enhance student achievement. Many of the strategies addressed in this series have been covered in other works, such as *Classroom Instruction That Works* (Marzano, Pickering, & Pollock, 2001), *Classroom Management That Works* (Marzano, 2003), *The Art and Science of Teaching* (Marzano, 2007), and *Effective Supervision* (Marzano, Frontier, & Livingston, 2011). Although those works devoted a chapter or a part of a chapter to particular strategies, *The Classroom Strategies Series* devotes an entire book to an instructional strategy or set of related strategies.

Enhancing the Art & Science of Teaching With Technology represents a shift in thinking about educational technology. Educators who only know how to operate new technologies are insufficiently prepared to use these powerful tools to improve classroom instruction. Teachers must also understand and apply effective pedagogical principles in order to wield technology tools with maximum impact. We believe that educational technology is best used in conjunction with research-based instructional strategies that already have a high probability of enhancing learning outcomes. This book offers practical guidance for supplementing effective instruction with technology.

We begin with a brief but inclusive chapter that reviews the research and theory on educational technology. Although you may be eager to move right into those chapters that provide recommendations for practice in schools, we strongly encourage you to examine the research and theory, as they are the foundation for the entire book. Indeed, a basic purpose of *Enhancing the Art & Science of Teaching With Technology* and others in *The Classroom Strategies Series* is to present the most useful strategies based on the strongest research and theory available.

Because research and theory can provide only a general direction for classroom practice, *Enhancing the Art & Science of Teaching With Technology* goes one step further to translate that research into applications for educational technology use in schools. Specifically, this book addresses how technology can help teachers enhance their current effective instructional practices.

How to Use This Book

After a chapter on the research and theory behind technology use in classrooms, we explore *The Art and Science of Teaching* framework. Each chapter begins with a design question that asks the reader to consider how technology can be applied to enhance the elements of the framework. Next, we describe instructional strategies for each element under that design question. Then, we detail practical ways teachers can enhance each strategy using educational technology tools. Finally, each chapter concludes with a classroom-based vignette that shows how teachers can integrate these tools into their classroom practice. To conclude the book, we've provided a glossary of helpful terms regarding technology in the classroom.

Educators can use *Enhancing the Art & Science of Teaching With Technology* as a self-study text that provides an in-depth understanding of educational technology. As you progress through the chapters, you will encounter comprehension questions. It is important to complete these questions and compare your answers with those in appendix A (page 151). Such interaction provides a review of the content and allows a thorough examination of your understanding. Groups or teams of teachers and administrators who wish to examine the topic of educational technology in depth may also use *Enhancing the Art & Science of Teaching With Technology*. When this is the case, teams should answer the questions independently and then compare their answers in small- or large-group settings.

Chapter 1

RESEARCH AND THEORY

In 1913, American inventor Thomas Edison boldly predicted what has since become a familiar claim: education in the United States, he said, would never be the same again. In an interview with *The New York Dramatic Mirror*, Edison proclaimed, "Books . . . will soon be obsolete in the schools. . . . Our school system will be completely changed inside of ten years" (as cited in Smith, 1913, p. 24). This statement may sound similar to modern predictions, but Edison was not foretelling the influence of ebooks, laptop classrooms, or even the Internet. Instead, he believed, textbooks would be replaced by motion pictures.

Rapid Increase in Educational Technology

While Edison's prediction has not, as of yet, come true, the availability of educational technology continues to increase. The rise in classroom computer use serves as a particularly clear example. According to the National Center for Education Statistics (NCES), the average number of instructional computers in public schools more than doubled in the thirteen-year period between 1995 and 2008, rising from 72 to 189 computers per school (Snyder & Dillow, 2012). In 2009, 97 percent of teachers had at least one computer in the classroom every day, and 69 percent of teachers reported using these computers either often or sometimes (Gray, Thomas, & Lewis, 2010). The Internet provides another example of the increasing use of technology. According to the Federal Communications Commission (FCC), in 2010, 97 percent of schools across the United States were able to connect to the Internet. As these statistics show, new technologies are increasingly pervasive in U.S. schools.

Mobile devices have also made their way into education. In 2007, Apple's iPhone arrived on the digital scene. Less than five years later, more than 25 percent of all parents had downloaded mobile applications (commonly called *apps*) for their children (Rideout, 2011). An analysis of Apple's multibillion dollar market for apps showed that "over 80% of the top selling paid apps in the Education category of the iTunes Store target children" (Shuler, 2012, p. 3). The Speak Up research project (2013) reported that over one-third of principals (36 percent) believe that a "bring your own device to school" policy for students will be implemented within the next few years.

The Center for Digital Education (CDE) corroborated the finding that technology use is increasing (Halpin & Muth, 2012). As shown in figure 1.1 (page 4), between 2011 and 2012, U.S. school districts saw a 5 percent increase in online classes, a 13 percent increase in virtual field trips, a 15 percent increase in allowing educators to use Web 2.0 tools with students, and a 43 percent increase in social networking presence.

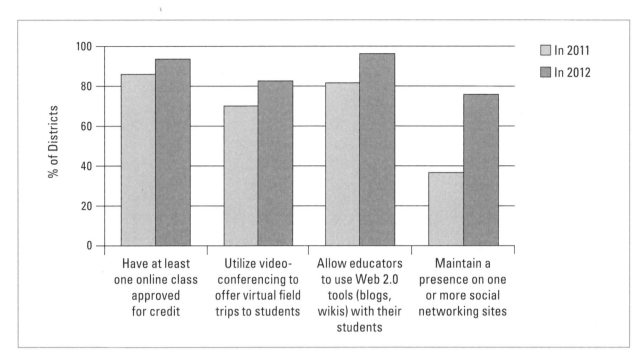

Figure 1.1: Technology growth by percent in K–12 districts from 2011 to 2012.

Source: Halpin & Muth, 2012, p. 6. Used with permission.

Furthermore, as figure 1.2 shows, many districts have already adopted (or are in the process of implementing) various classroom technology supports, including new technology standards, data dashboards, and digital content strategies.

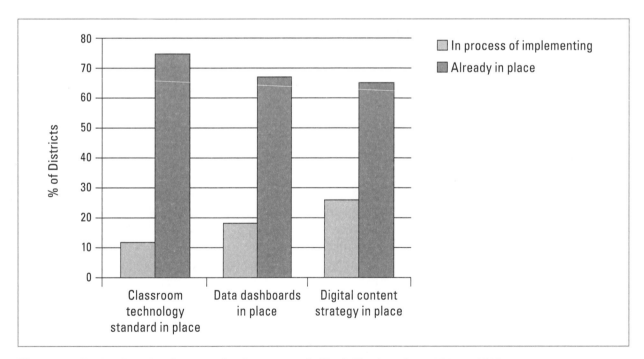

Figure 1.2: Technology implementation by percent in K–12 districts from 2011 to 2012.

Source: Halpin & Muth, 2012, p. 6. Used with permission.

Clearly, the use of technology is increasing in K–12 classrooms, and educator attitudes toward this increase vary from unbridled enthusiasm to extreme skepticism. While all teachers can learn to use technology, they generally require extensive training, schoolwide support, and scheduled time for independent learning in order to feel confident and competent enough to use new technology effectively and frequently (Demetriadis et al., 2003; Gray et al., 2010; Inan & Lowther, 2010; Staples, Pugach, & Himes, 2005). Despite all of the additional support necessary for the effective use of technology, however, many believe it has the power to restructure education.

Potential Restructuring of Education

Allan Collins and Richard Halverson (2009) believed that U.S. education must undergo a structural change to accommodate new digital technology. New technologies like mobile devices are having "profound effects on the ways we learn" (Collins & Halverson, 2009, p. 5) because they allow people to readily acquire knowledge outside of a school building: "There are deep incompatibilities between the demands of the new technologies and the traditional school. . . . Even as schools rush to incorporate technologies into their buildings, the traditional school classroom is very uncomfortable with these new subversive technologies" (p. 7). Terry Anderson (2012) agreed that the incompatibility of traditional schooling (*closed systems*) with new technology leads to disruptive effects in schools:

> The culture and customary use of these closed systems [in traditional learning] runs contrary to Web 2.0 applications, which are usually open, participatory, connected, persistent, and controlled by individual users (not by school administrators or teachers). Thus, they create disruptive effects. (p. 305)

Many others have supported the notion that technology may lead to fundamental changes in education (Christensen, Horn, & Johnson, 2008; Cuban, Kirkpatrick, & Peck, 2001; Gee, 2011; Squire, 2005). Educational technology researcher Christopher Dede summarized this perspective: "You can't just sprinkle 21st century skills on the 20th century doughnut. . . . It requires a fundamental reconception of what we're doing" (as cited in Walser, 2011, p. 45).

Collins and Halverson (2009) explained that before the early 19th century, children in the United States were not required to attend school. Instead, parents decided what trade skills their children ought to know and taught them as apprentices. With the rise of the Industrial Revolution, manufacturing technologies dramatically reduced the need for children to learn skilled labor, but labor laws prohibited children's employment in factories. These changes left children relatively unoccupied and unsupervised, which led to "a shift that occurred in education, from a family responsibility to a state responsibility" (p. 55). Instead of learning practical trade skills as they did in the era of apprenticeship, children in the universal education era began learning the sorts of disciplinary knowledge—reading, writing, and arithmetic—meant to help them succeed in a democratic society. The act of learning became associated with compulsory attendance in physical institutions called schools.

According to Collins and Halverson (2009), the United States is going through "another revolution on the same scale as the Industrial Revolution" (p. 4). This new *Knowledge Revolution*, as they called it, will be "fueled by personal computers, video games, the Internet, and cell phones" (p. 4) and, like the Industrial Revolution, will completely transform our lives and the structure of our schools. As a result, the rigid structure of traditional schools will become more pliable in order to impart what Collins and Halverson called *lifelong learning*, which "requires moving away from highly structured schooling institutions" and instead focuses on teaching "the skills to judge the quality of learning venues and the kinds of social networks that provide guidance and advice" (p. 130). Two ways by which technology is changing the traditional approach in classrooms are (1) flipped classrooms and (2) new literacies.

Flipped Classrooms

One classroom-level example of the power of technology to restructure the old paradigm is the flipped classroom. A *flipped classroom* is one in which students listen to online lectures at home at night and then use that content at school the next day. Table 1.1 compares a traditional classroom to a flipped classroom.

Table 1.1: Comparison of Class Time in Traditional Versus Flipped Classrooms

Traditional Classroom		Flipped Classroom	
Activity	*Time*	*Activity*	*Time*
Warm-up activity	5 min.	Warm-up activity	5 min.
Go over previous night's homework	20 min.	Q & A time on video	10 min.
Lecture new content	30–45 min.	Guided and independent practice and/or lab activity	75 min.
Guided and independent practice and/or lab activity	20–35 min.		

Source: Bergmann & Sams, 2012, p. 15.

In the flipped model, students listen to a short lecture (ten to fifteen minutes) and take notes as homework the evening before they cover the information in class. As shown in table 1.1, this frees up class time that would traditionally be spent introducing new content and resolving student confusion about the previous day's homework. Therefore, students in the flipped model still complete the same amount of independent practice work as students in a traditional model, but they do it during class instead of as homework. Rather than complete assignments without teacher guidance at home, students complete them in school, where teachers are there to offer help or answer questions.

Jonathan Bergmann and Aaron Sams (2012) asserted that, among other things, flipping a classroom allows teachers to help busy and struggling students with their assignments, increases student-teacher and student-student interaction during class, gives teachers the time to provide more individualized differentiation, alleviates classroom management issues that might otherwise occur during direct instruction, educates parents who actually watch the video lectures with their children, and makes absences easier to mitigate—students simply need to watch the videos from the days they've missed. In its mission statement, Knewton (2013), an organization that advocates for flipped classrooms, echoed the argument that technology will inevitably restructure education: "Education is right now undergoing a monumental shift, from the one-size-fits-all factory model to a digital, personalized model" (para. 3).

New Literacies

More than two billion people across the globe have Internet access (Internet World Stats, 2013). NCES (Snyder & Dillow, 2012) reported that the percentage of schools with Internet access increased from 8 percent in 1995 to 98 percent in 2008, meaning that if students do not have access at home, most of them have access at school. In response, an educational movement has emerged around what are considered the new literacies of the Internet.

Donald Leu, Charles Kinzer, Julie Coiro, and Dana Cammack (2004) defined these new literacies as "the skills, strategies, and dispositions necessary to successfully use and adapt to the rapidly changing information and communication technologies and contexts that continuously emerge in our world and influence all areas of our personal and professional lives" (p. 1572). Leu and his colleagues argued that successful use of the Internet requires a set of new literacies and that students need explicit instruction in those new literacies. Four points support their claim.

First, the Internet gives students an unprecedented opportunity to freely publish content as quickly as they can write it. Donald Leu, Ian O'Byrne, Lisa Zawilinski, Greg McVerry, and Heidi Everett-Cacopardo (2009) commented on this inextricable link between reading and communicating in an online context:

> Online reading and writing are so closely connected that it is not possible to separate them; we read online as authors and we write online as readers (Huffaker, 2004, 2005; McVerry, 2007; Zawilinski, 2009). Thus online reading comprehension includes the online reading and communication skills required by texting, blogs, wikis, video, shared writing spaces (such as Google Docs), and social networks. (p. 266)

This close connection between reading and writing on the Internet requires that students possess a unique set of skills that is more varied and multidimensional than the skills required for traditional print-based reading and writing activities. For example, a printed text is a finite resource; all of the information is contained between the covers of the book, pamphlet, magazine, or journal, and the organization of the text is usually designed to guide the reader through the content. In contrast, Raven Wallace (2004) explained, the Internet is "unbounded and large," and its organization "does not readily lend coherence to a topic" (p. 474). Finding information in a printed text usually involves consulting the table of contents or the index, two structures that may be hidden or absent from most web pages. Research shows that when students cannot perceive the organizational structure of a text, they remember less of its content (van Dijk & Kintsch, 1983). Therefore, students must be taught to read texts that lack a clear organizational structure, as well as how to formulate keyword searches, use Boolean operators, identify characteristics of reputable journal articles, and distinguish library catalogs from bibliographic databases (Mittermeyer & Quirion, 2003).

Second, evaluating sources on the Internet is categorically distinct from evaluating sources in traditional print materials. According to Christopher Weare and Wan-Ying Lin (2000), the Internet "is rapidly becoming the largest repository of information ever known" (p. 276). As we know, however, not every piece of information in that repository is equally useful, and some of it is either misleading or factually incorrect. A study by Nielsen (2013) found that teenagers had a low tolerance for websites they thought were boring and generally found visually appealing websites more plausible than others. As Jane David (2009) pointed out, such misconceptions create the need to teach students basic critical-thinking skills that "reflect the open-ended, continually changing online context" (p. 84).

Third, as of 2013, the knowledge and skills necessary to efficiently use the Internet are still overlooked in assessments and curriculums. State reading standards and assessments in the United States—including the Common Core State Standards (CCSS)—do not include or test any standards that distinguish between online reading comprehension and print reading comprehension (Leu et al., 2009; National Governors Association Center for Best Practices [NGA] & Council of Chief State School

Officers [CCSSO], 2010a, 2010b). Because of this oversight, educators may neglect to provide formal instruction in the literacy skills most crucial to navigating, reading, using, and evaluating information on the Internet.

Fourth, teaching new literacy skills may have positive effects for low-income students. Digital technology tools, such as laptops and academic software, have been shown to help low-income students develop proficiency and confidence in literacy, cultivate strong independent work habits, decrease disciplinary issues in class, and build skills and self-efficacy related to technology (Blachowicz et al., 2009). In a study by Kelly Shapely, Daniel Sheehan, Catherine Maloney, and Fanny Caranikas-Walker (2011), "economically disadvantaged students in treatment schools [with technology] reached proficiency levels that matched the skills of advantaged students in control schools [without technology]" (p. 310). Shapely and her colleagues pointed out that while these increased technical proficiencies "may not raise [students'] standardized test scores, new competencies could have long-ranging effects on students' future academic and career options" (p. 310).

Despite the demonstrated effects of teaching new literacy skills in low-income schools, U.S. public policies fail to provide incentives for teaching them. Consequently, these policies "may serve to increase achievement gaps, not close them" (Leu et al., 2009, p. 267). Leu and his colleagues (2009) elaborated on the effects of this digital divide:

> Children in the poorest school districts in the United States have the least amount of Internet access at home (Cooper, 2004). Unfortunately, the poorest schools are also under the greatest pressure to raise scores on tests that have nothing to do with online reading comprehension (Henry, 2007). There is little incentive to teach the new literacies of online reading comprehension because they are not tested. Thus students in the poorest schools become doubly disadvantaged: They have less access to the Internet at home, and schools do not always prepare them for the new literacies of online reading comprehension at school. (p. 267)

For some low-income students, school may be the only place where they have the opportunity to interact with the Internet and other technologies. If schools fail to teach the new literacies that students need to meaningfully interact with and use those technologies, they may continue to fall behind their more affluent peers.

Research on Educational Technology

Along with an increased use of technology in K–12 education, and the discussion and opinions that accompany this increase, there has been heightened interest in the research on the effects and utility of educational technology. However, researchers, theorists, and educators have not clearly and unanimously defined the terms *technology* and *educational technology*. We define *technology* as electronic, digital, or multimedia tools used to achieve a goal more efficiently or effectively. This definition is broad enough to accommodate the wide variety of innovative tools and strategies included in this book, yet narrow enough to exclude tools that already enjoy universal use in schools, such as the chalkboard or the pencil. In keeping with this definition of technology, we define *educational technology* as the use of technology tools in the classroom to improve learning.

Several meta-analyses (along with numerous independent primary studies) have addressed the general effects of educational technology on student achievement, motivation, and behavior. A *meta-analysis* is a method of statistical research that involves gathering a large number of studies on a particular topic or strategy in order to calculate its average effect. Basically, a meta-analysis aims to quantify the general effectiveness of a certain strategy or topic by combining the results from numerous individual studies.

The strategy's level of effectiveness is frequently conveyed using a number known as an effect size. In educational research, effect sizes near 0.15–0.20 are considered small, sizes near 0.45–0.50 are considered medium, and sizes near 0.80–0.90 are considered large (Cohen, 1988; Lipsey, 1990). The greater the effect size, the more effective the strategy. Table 1.2 reports the findings from several meta-analyses that examined the effect of technology on student achievement.

Table 1.2: Selected Meta-Analyses for the Effects of Technology on Student Achievement

Authors and Date	Focus	Number of Studies	Number of Effect Sizes	Number of Participants	Average Effect Size	Percentile Gain
Waxman, Lin, & Michko, 2003	Effect of technology on cognition, affect, and behavior	42 primary studies	282	7,000	0.41 across all three; 0.45 for cognitive	16 across all three; 17 for cognitive
Schmid et al., 2009	Effect of technology on achievement in higher education	231 primary studies	310	25,497	0.28	11
Tamim, Bernard, Borokhovski, Abrami, & Schmid, 2011	Effect of technology on student achievement	25 meta-analyses (1,055 primary studies)	574	109,700	0.33	13

In his book *Visible Learning*, John Hattie (2009) combined the results from more than 800 meta-analyses, including over 52,000 studies and over 145,000 effect sizes, to pinpoint the elements that have significant correlations with student achievement. Some of the elements that Hattie analyzed pertained to the use of educational technology as defined in this book. Specifically, Hattie found that when used as a *supplement* to the teacher's instruction, computer-assisted instruction had an effect size of 0.45, but when used as a *replacement* for the teacher's instruction, it had an effect size of 0.30. In other words, computer-assisted instruction is likely to result in a 12 percentile point gain in achievement when it replaces the instruction of the teacher, but this gain is likely to rise to 17 percentile points when the technology is used as a supplement to the teacher's instruction. Table 1.3 reports the findings for computers used as supplements versus replacements for teachers.

Table 1.3: Summary of Effects From Studies of Computer as Replacement vs. Supplement to the Teacher

Authors and Date	Replacement			Supplement		
	Number of Effect Sizes	Average Effect Size	Percentile Gain	Number of Effect Sizes	Average Effect Size	Percentile Gain
Cohen & Dacanay, 1992	28	0.36	14	9	0.56	21

Continued on next page →

Authors and Date	Replacement			Supplement		
	Number of Effect Sizes	Average Effect Size	Percentile Gain	Number of Effect Sizes	Average Effect Size	Percentile Gain
Kuchler, 1998	17	0.28	11	42	0.51	19
Bayraktar, 2000	27	0.18	7	81	0.29	11
Yaakub & Finch, 2001	19	0.32	13	8	0.49	19
Hsu, 2003	9	0.35	14	22	0.44	17

Source: Based on results reported by Hattie, 2009, p. 223.

As shown in table 1.3, technology is best used as a supplement to effective instruction rather than a replacement for teachers. For the purposes of this book, we have categorized the research on using specific types of educational technology as a supplement (as opposed to a replacement) into four basic categories: (1) computers (including computer-assisted instruction and one-to-one laptop instruction), (2) the Internet (including distance learning and blended learning), (3) interactive whiteboards, and (4) mobile devices (such as smartphones or student response systems [SRS; also known as clickers]).

Computers

Perhaps the greatest concentration of educational technology studies has focused on the general use of computers. Since the 1960s, "thousands of comparisons between computing and noncomputing classrooms, ranging from kindergarten to graduate school, have been made" (Tamim et al., 2011, p. 5). The research on computers can be broadly organized into two categories: (1) computer-assisted instruction (CAI) and (2) one-to-one laptop instruction.

Computer-Assisted Instruction

The most common focus for computer-related research has been computer-assisted instruction. CAI is typically defined as "a method of instruction in which the computer is used to instruct the student and where the computer contains the instruction which is designed to teach, guide, and test the student until the desired level of proficiency is attained" (Jenks & Springer, 2002, p. 43). Table 1.4 reports the results of a number of meta-analyses on computer-assisted instruction.

The meta-analytic findings in table 1.4 indicate that CAI generally yields a percentile gain ranging from 6 to 14 points. Other studies have shown CAI to produce small to moderate gains in achievement in mathematics (Barrow, Markman, & Rouse, 2008; House, 2002; Huang & Ke, 2009), science (Azevedo, 2005), and beginning reading (Chambers et al., 2008). While the general results of the CAI studies are positive, research indicates that at least three factors mediate the effects of CAI: (1) individual teaching practices, (2) fidelity of teacher implementation and technology use, and (3) degree of student collaboration while using technology. We consider each mediator briefly.

Table 1.4: Selected Meta-Analyses for the Effects of Computer-Assisted Instruction on Student Achievement

Authors and Date	Focus	Number of Studies	Number of Effect Sizes	Number of Participants	Average Effect Size	Percentile Gain
Christmann & Badgett, 1999	Effect of computer-assisted instruction on science achievement	11 primary studies	24	2,343	0.27	11
Soe, Koki, & Chang, 2000	Effect of computer-assisted instruction on K–12 reading achievement	17 primary studies	40	Not stated	0.26	10
Lou, Abrami, & d'Apollonia, 2001	Effect of collaborative (rather than individual) use of technology on student learning and task performance	122 primary studies	178	11,317	0.15 for student learning; 0.31 for task performance	6 for student learning; 12 for task performance
Blok, Oostdam, Otter, & Overmaat, 2002	Effect of computer-assisted instruction on beginning reading achievement	42 primary studies	75	Not stated	0.25	10
Christmann & Badgett, 2003	Effect of computer-assisted instruction on K–6 student achievement	39 primary studies	68	8,274	0.34	13
Hattie, 2009	Effect of computer-assisted instruction on student achievement	4,875 primary studies; 81 meta-analyses	8,886	3,990,028	0.37	14
Li & Ma, 2010	Effect of computer-assisted instruction on K–12 mathematics achievement	46 primary studies	85	36,783	0.28	11

Several researchers have postulated that individual teaching practices influence the effects of CAI in the classroom. Rana Tamim, Robert Bernard, Eugene Borokhovski, Phillip Abrami, and Richard Schmid (2011) reported a mean effect size of 0.33 in their meta-analysis on digital technology use in various settings and learner groups. Tamim and her colleagues (2011) wrote: "The average student in a classroom where technology is used will perform 12 percentile points higher than the average student in the traditional setting that does not use technology to enhance the learning process" (p. 17). Still, the authors emphasize mediating variables like instructional goals and individual teacher practices:

> It is arguable that it is aspects of the goals of instruction, pedagogy, teacher effectiveness, subject matter, age level, fidelity of technology implementation, and possibly other factors that may represent more powerful influences on effect sizes than the nature of technology intervention. (p. 17)

Likewise, Qing Li and Xin Ma (2010) found that mathematics students who used computer-assisted instruction generally had higher achievement, but the authors were quick to point out that these results "should not diminish the importance of good teaching. . . . To achieve maximum benefit, the way to use CT [computer technology] matters" (p. 232). Similar findings have also been reported by Sara Dexter, Ronald Anderson, and Henry Becker (1999) and Barbara Means (2010).

Researchers have also cited fidelity of technology implementation as critical to the success of technology. For example, Kelly Glassett and Lynne Schrum (2009) drew such conclusions from a two-year investigation of MINTY, a schoolwide project designed to build technology-equipped classrooms, create a learning community for educators, and mandate teacher participation in trainings that prioritized instruction. They concluded:

> Positive effects of technology . . . are mediated by the fidelity of implementation. Even if schools and teachers are provided with enough access to appropriate instructional technology, and teachers receive proper professional development in the use and integration of educational technology and technology is integrated in curricula, course objectives, and assessment, the outcomes are fundamentally grounded in self-reflective processes in human adaptation and change. (p. 148)

In short, Glassett and Schrum found that while the technology produced positive effects, ensuring that all teachers use it to its full potential could be challenging.

Students' degree of collaboration while using technology also mediates its impact. For instance, Yiping Lou, Phillip Abrami, and Sylvia d'Apollonia (2001) found that students may get the most out of computer-assisted technology when they collaborate in small groups. In their meta-analysis, they reported an average effect size of 0.15 for the effect of collaborative technology use (as opposed to individual learning with one student per computer) on student achievement. They also reported an average effect size of 0.31 for the effect of collaborative technology use on task performance. Lou and her colleagues wrote, "When working with CT [computer technology] in small groups, students in general produced substantially better group products than individual products and they also gained more individual knowledge than those learning with CT individually" (p. 476). Multiple studies have corroborated the finding that collaborative use of technology may yield higher achievement gains than individual use (Gallardo-Virgen & DeVillar, 2011; Hattie, 2009).

One-to-One Laptop Instruction

Put simply, one-to-one (or 1:1) laptop use means that every student has access to his or her own laptop in the classroom. As laptop technology advances and becomes more affordable, there is a growing push to implement one-to-one laptop classrooms on a national and even global scale. As an example, consider One Laptop per Child (OLPC), a nonprofit organization that seeks to put a laptop into the hands of every child in the world. The program has already provided over two million students and teachers with laptops (OLPC, 2013a). OLPC's mission statement is:

We aim to provide each child with a rugged, low-cost, low-power, connected laptop. To this end, we have designed hardware, content and software for collaborative, joyful, and self-empowered learning. With access to this type of tool, children are engaged in their own education, and learn, share, and create together. They become connected to each other, to the world and to a brighter future. (OLPC, 2013b)

OLPC was founded by Nicholas Negroponte, the chairman emeritus of the Media Laboratory at the Massachusetts Institute of Technology (MIT) and current member of the board of directors for Motorola (OLPC, 2013d). Since its inception, the OLPC initiative has also partnered with Google, eBay, and Citigroup (OLPC, 2013c) and gained widespread recognition through organizations such as TED (Technology, Entertainment, Design), which promotes "ideas worth spreading" (TED, 2013) through a set of global conferences and online videos.

According to Negroponte (2006), OLPC teachers reported declines in truancy to almost zero, declines in discipline problems, increases in student engagement, and practically universal attendance of parent-teacher conferences. These findings notwithstanding, this information on the effects of OLPC is only anecdotal. Negroponte himself explicitly stated that he considers research on the effectiveness of OLPC to be unnecessary:

This is not something you have to test. The days of pilot projects are over. When people say, "Well, we'd like to do three or four thousand in our country to see how it works," [we say,] "Go to the back of the line, and someone else will do it, and then when you figure out that this works, you can join, as well." (Negroponte, 2006)

The first randomized research evaluations on the program were carried out in Peru, OLPC's largest deployment country with over 8,300 involved schools. Julián Cristia, Pablo Ibarrarán, Santiago Cueto, Ana Santiago, and Eugenio Severín (2012) found that while "the intervention generated a substantial increase in computer use both at school and at home" and "positive impacts on cognitive skills and competences related to computer use," the results "indicate limited effects on academic achievement" (p. 21). Furthermore, they stated:

To improve learning in Math and Language, there is a need for high-quality instruction. From previous studies, this does not seem the norm in public schools in Peru, where much rote learning takes place (Cueto et al., 2006; Cueto, Ramírez, and León, 2006). Hence, our suggestion is to combine the provision of laptops with a pedagogical model targeted toward increased academic achievement by students. Our results suggest that computers by themselves, at least as initially delivered by the OLPC program, do not increase achievement in curricular areas. (p. 21)

Other studies on one-to-one laptop use have produced mixed results, as well. According to Colleen Gillard (2011), Maine's $35 million laptop program for middle school students sometimes "floundered" in its implementation as a result of "poor execution, tepid leadership, or inadequate teacher training" (p. 84). Program director Bette Manchester said, "People don't realize it's more about teaching and learning than technology" (as cited in Gillard, 2011, pp. 84–85).

Likewise, a study by Shapely and her colleagues (2011) suggested that "large-scale one-to-one laptop programs are difficult to implement, and, as a result, programs may produce either very small or no improvements in test scores" (p. 312). They added, "If improved standardized test scores is the primary justification for investments in one-to-one laptop programs, then results probably will be disappointing" (p. 312). However, Shapely and her colleagues found other positive effects of one-to-one laptop programs that are congruent with the benefits discovered by Cristia and his colleagues (2012) in Peru. For example, they pointed out, "Individual laptops and digital resources allowed middle school students to develop greater technical proficiency and reduced their disciplinary problems in classes. . . . Especially noteworthy was the positive immersion effect on students from lower socioeconomic backgrounds"

(Shapely et al., 2011, p. 310). Mark Windschitl and Kurt Sahl (2002) also reported positive effects; students "uniformly acknowledged a sense of pride in having their own computers" and reported that they were "more organized because most of their schoolwork was stored on the laptops" (p. 201). In sum, while one-to-one laptop programs may increase students' technological skills and technological confidence, effective teaching is required to produce meaningful gains in student achievement.

The Internet

The Internet is considered the most efficient system for distributing new reading, writing, and communication tools in the history of civilization (Lankshear & Knobel, 2006). Between 2000 and 2012, global Internet usage increased by 566 percent, and in 2013, over 2.4 billion people, or 34 percent of the world's population, had access to the Internet (Internet World Stats, 2013). In the United States, nearly all public schools have access to the Internet (Snyder & Dillow, 2012). Most educational research on the Internet is focused on two areas: (1) distance learning and (2) blended learning.

Distance Learning

In *distance learning*, students do not attend a physical school, but they take lessons remotely on the Internet or via broadcast technologies. The broader category of distance learning encompasses earlier technologies like correspondence courses, educational television, and videoconferencing. A number of meta-analyses have reported relatively small effect sizes for distance learning (defined in this broader sense) versus regular classroom learning, prompting debate over the efficacy of distance learning (see Bernard et al., 2004; Cavanaugh, Gillan, Kromrey, Hess, & Blomeyer, 2004; Jenks & Springer, 2002; Zhao, Lei, Yan, Lai, & Tan, 2005). For example, Hattie (2009) reported an average effect size for distance education of only 0.09 (equivalent to a 4 percentile point gain).

However, a report by the U.S. Department of Education's Office of Planning, Evaluation and Policy Development (Means, Toyama, Murphy, Bakia, & Jones, 2010) called for a fresh perspective on distance learning, since its manifestations are changing rapidly:

> The question of the relative efficacy of online and face-to-face instruction needs to be revisited, however, in light of today's online learning applications, which can take advantage of a wide range of Web resources, including not only multimedia but also Web-based applications and new collaboration technologies. These forms of online learning are a far cry from the televised broadcasts and videoconferencing that characterized earlier generations of distance education. (p. xi)

The sentiment expressed by Means and her colleagues—that manifestations of distance learning are changing—is echoed by others (see Bernard et al., 2004; Jenks & Springer, 2002; Sitzmann, Kraiger, Stewart, & Wisher, 2006; Tallent-Runnels et al., 2006; Waxman et al., 2003; C. Zirkle, 2003).

Means and her colleagues' (2010) optimistic perspective may be due to the fact that their meta-analysis focused on web-based instruction, a relatively new format for distance learning. Hattie (2009) reported an average effect size of 0.18 for web-based learning (equivalent to a 7 percentile point gain). A meta-analysis by Traci Sitzmann, Kurt Kraiger, David Stewart, and Robert Wisher (2006) found that web-based learning was most effective for declarative knowledge (understanding of facts, details, principles, and generalizations), as opposed to procedural knowledge (strategies and processes).

Blended Learning

Instruction that combines online and face-to-face elements is known as *blended learning*, or hybrid learning (Means et al., 2010; Schulte, 2011). The aforementioned meta-analysis by Means and her colleagues (2010) compared blended learning to face-to-face instruction and reported an average effect size of 0.35 in favor of the blended approach. Similarly, Sitzmann and her colleagues (2006) examined the effects of web-based instruction as a blended supplement to classroom instruction and reported a mean effect size of 0.34 for declarative knowledge and 0.52 for procedural knowledge. David Pearson, Richard Ferdig, Robert Blomeyer, and Juan Moran (2005) examined the impact of digital literacy tools on middle school students through a synthesis of studies published between 1988 and 2005. Most of the digital literacy tools they examined were used in a blended approach. They found an overall effect size of 0.49, indicating a 19 percentile point gain. Finally, Hattie (2009) reported a number of specific uses of digital media that indicated a blended approach. For example, he reported an average effect size of 0.52 for interactive video, an average effect size of 0.22 for audiovisual methods (including television, film, video, and slides), and an average effect size of 0.33 for simulations. As with the research on computer use, this research seems to indicate that using technology in tandem with effective instruction may provide the most benefits.

Interactive Whiteboards

The basic distinction between interactive and noninteractive technology tools is that interactive technologies are two-way systems: they provide output in response to a user's specific input. To illustrate, a film is *noninteractive* because the response from the audience does not change the trajectory of the plot. An audience member cannot click on the screen, for instance, to elicit different reactions from the characters. On the other hand, a video game is *interactive* because what happens on the screen is a direct result of the way in which a player manipulates the controls.

In his meta-analysis of the effectiveness of audiovisual methods in general, Hattie (2009) reported a relatively small effect size of 0.22, indicating a percentile gain of 9 points. However, in a synthesis of research on the effectiveness of *interactive* video methods, Hattie found a medium to large effect size of 0.52, indicating a percentile gain of 20 points. From this difference, one might reasonably infer that interactive technologies are more likely than noninteractive technologies to lead to positive gains in student achievement.

In schools, interactive whiteboards (IWBs) are a common form of interactive technology. IWBs use projectors to display a computer desktop onto a large, wall-mounted surface. Using a stylus or a fingertip, users can write, select, move, and interact with objects on the screen. Two studies conducted by Robert Marzano and Mark Haystead (2009, 2010) focused specifically on IWBs. They found an average effect size of 0.44 for 85 independent quasi-experimental studies involving 3,338 subjects. This means that on average, teachers who used IWBs saw student achievement gains of 15 percentile points over what was expected when teachers did not use IWBs. Analysis of video recordings of teachers in the studies provided further detail about the effects of IWBs. Marzano and Haystead (2010) found that teachers whose students exhibited higher achievement integrated the technology better with research-based instructional strategies. Their findings suggested that "substantial increases in student achievement would be predicted with improvements in teacher behavior" (p. 70), particularly with respect to chunking, scaffolding, pacing, progress monitoring, clarity of content depicted on the IWB, and student response rates. All six of these instructional variables were found to correlate with the size of the IWB effect. In summary, when teachers used these strategies more effectively, student achievement gains were greater.

Other studies on IWBs include Omar López's (2010) analysis of English learners' (ELs) academic achievement with and without IWB technology. His results strongly suggested that IWBs increased student achievement among ELs compared to ELs in traditional classrooms without technology. He also found that IWBs narrowed the achievement gap between ELs in IWB-enhanced classrooms and non-ELs in traditional classrooms. IWB technology has also been found to increase student engagement (Beeland, 2002; Smith, 2000), improve student retention of content (M. L. Zirkle, 2003), and enhance teacher planning and organization (Latham, 2002).

Mobile Devices

Any pocket-sized, handheld computing device, such as a smartphone, tablet, or e-reader, can be classified as a mobile device. In 2013, Grunwald Associates published the results of a U.S. survey on student use of mobile devices. Of K–12 parents surveyed, 56 percent said they'd "be willing to purchase a mobile device for their child to use in the classroom if the school required it" (p. 3). However, the authors found that only 16 percent of schools allow students to use personal mobile devices in the classroom. Nevertheless, a quarter of all middle school students (28 percent) and half of all high school students (51 percent) carry a smartphone with them to school every day.

In a review of trends in research, Wen-Hsiung Wu and his colleagues (2012) defined *mobile learning* as "using technology as a mediating tool for learning via mobile devices accessing data and communicating with others through wireless technology" (p. 818). In other words, the learner does not have to be in a fixed, specific location to engage in mobile learning. The authors reported that 86 percent of the 164 mobile learning studies in their literature review present positive outcomes, although they did not offer an average effect size for these outcomes or define whether these outcomes are related to achievement, motivation, behavior, or some other variable entirely. More specific research on mobile devices can be organized into two categories: (1) smartphones and (2) student response systems.

Smartphones

A smartphone is a mobile phone that uses a computer operating system to connect the user to online data. Modern smartphones often have recognizable features such as compact digital cameras and touch-screen interfaces that allow a user to scroll with a finger through a web page or a document. Research by Christopher Sanchez and Jennifer Wiley (2009) and Christopher Sanchez and Russell Branaghan (2011) on the effect of scrolling textual interfaces on cognition and memory has direct implications for the use of smartphones for learning. Sanchez and Wiley (2009) reported that text displayed in a scrolling format is not only harder to understand but also harder to remember than text displayed in a print format, especially for individuals with low working memory: "Nonscrolling interfaces produced significantly better comprehension overall than did scrolling interfaces. . . . Whereas scrolling did lead to worse performance overall, there was a more pronounced effect for those individuals who had lower WMC [working memory capacity]" (p. 734). Furthermore, the learners in the study "were less able to develop a causal understanding of a complex topic when presented with a scrolling interface than when presented the same information units in discrete pages" (Sanchez & Wiley, 2009, p. 737). In sum, scrolling text is more difficult to read than stationary text.

Two years later, Sanchez and Branaghan (2011) conducted a similar set of studies to determine whether the small, scrolling displays on mobile devices affect a reader's ability to reason or remember facts. They found that while "factual recall is relatively unaffected," there is a significant decrease in performance when readers must use the factual information "to make appropriate decisions or otherwise reason about a given situation" (p. 796). The authors elaborated:

> Small displays produced lower overall reasoning performance, and also increased the amount of time it took to solve the problems relative to a full-size display. This suggests that while factual information gathering is unaffected when done [on] a small device, reasoning performance is negatively affected when done on a small device. (p. 796)

These results indicate that reading scrolling text or text on a small screen may have negative effects on students' comprehension and reasoning abilities.

Student Response Systems

A *student response system*, often called a clicker, is a small, handheld mobile device that allows students to respond to teacher questions in real time. The students' responses are then "immediately displayed on a screen for all to see (usually in the form of a graph), allowing students to receive corrective feedback on their answer as well as compare their answer to peers' answers" (Blood & Gulchak, 2013, p. 246). While there are several competing clicker devices and corresponding software systems available for purchase, a number of websites—such as Poll Everywhere and Socrative—offer free services that can be used with smartphones or other mobile devices.

As described by Steven Ross, Gary Morrison, and Deborah Lowther (2010), some instructional advantages of clickers include: "(a) valuable immediate review and feedback for students, (b) immediate data on student progress for teachers to examine and use as a basis for making instructional adaptations, and (c) high engagement and interactivity by students during teacher-led instruction" (p. 21). The capacity of clickers to "give students frequent, integral access to new representational forms and communication options" has the potential to "enable students to better express what they know and can do," which could make clickers useful for formative assessment (Roschelle, Penuel, Yarnall, Shechtman, & Tatar, 2004, p. 5). Clickers have also been found to increase student engagement (Bojinova & Oigara, 2011).

Perspectives on Educational Technology

As research on the impacts of educational technology expands, numerous theories and perspectives have emerged regarding the general utility of educational technology. One perspective views technology through a *value-positive* lens, meaning technology has the capacity to constructively transform education. The value-positive approach maintains that, when used for education, technology will almost always have a positive effect, regardless of other variables. A conclusion typically following this viewpoint is that schools can improve the achievement of their students by increasing their usage of technology as quickly as possible.

A second perspective views technology through a *value-negative* lens, meaning that technology cannot impact teaching and learning in any positive way and does not belong in the classroom. These theorists often allege that technology is a waste of time, money, and public policy initiative, since the same achievement goals can be accomplished with and without technology.

A third perspective views educational technology as *value-neutral*, meaning that technology is neither inherently good nor inherently bad by its nature but is only as beneficial as the teaching practices it enhances. When used in tandem with effective instructional practices, technology is likely to have a number of positive impacts in the classroom including gains in student achievement, engagement, and motivation. We consider each perspective briefly.

The Value-Positive Lens

The rise of educational technology in the late 20th and early 21st centuries resulted in a call for transformational change in U.S. public policy. In their review of twenty years of educational technology policy, Katie Culp, Margaret Honey, and Ellen Mandinach (2005) wrote:

> In 1995 the tone of policy reports changes noticeably. In part this is a response to the emergence of the Internet as a major force driving changes in business, civic life and, to some extent, education. During this period, policy reports begin to present education technology as a *driver* of school reform, rather than as a class of tools and resources that, to varying extents, could be matched to educational challenges already recognized by educators. In these reports technology becomes a

tool of *transformation,* which promised, simply by its presence and capabilities, to cause changes in how teachers teach, how schools are organized, and how students work together and learn. (p. 301)

These policy changes reflect a value-positive view of educational technology. Initial expressions of the value-positive view took place prior to the advent of the Internet, however. In 1980, educational technology advocate Seymour Papert published the first edition of *Mindstorms*, his groundbreaking book about the first student-friendly computer programming language. Papert (1993) theorized that this computer language—called *LOGO*—would help students learn mathematics "in a context which is to learning mathematics what living in France is to learning French" (p. 6). Papert made two central claims in *Mindstorms*: (1) children can learn to master computer skills, and (2) once children learn to use computers, it will change the way they learn everything else. The second claim, that computers would fundamentally revolutionize the way children learn, inspired many efforts to put computers into children's hands, including the aforementioned OLPC initiative, with which Papert was principally involved. OLPC founding members also included Google, eBay, Quanta, Red Hat, and Marvell. Partners of the nonprofit include companies such as Citigroup, Pentagram, Underwriters Laboratories, United Nations Development Program, Foley Hoag, and fuseproject. By 2013, more than two million students and teachers in the developing world had received OLPC's patented XO laptop, despite little to no research in support of its effectiveness (Cristia et al., 2012). These organizations share the common perspective that technology has the power to fundamentally and positively change the way children think and learn.

The Value-Negative Lens

Retrospective analyses reveal that value-positive conjectures may have been overly optimistic. Educational technology, it seems, has not revolutionized education, at least to the extent originally imagined. Judi Harris (2005) commented, "Despite more than two decades of effort, technology as 'Trojan horse' for educational reform has succeeded in only a minority of K–12 contexts" (p. 120), and Richard Noeth and Boris Volkov (2004) stated that "despite schools flooded with computers, the evidence is mixed as to whether overall student achievement has notably increased or the achievement gap has visibly narrowed as a result" (p. 7). The U.S. Department of Education (2004) lamented, "We have not realized the promise of technology in education. . . . Computers, instead of transforming education, were often shunted to a 'computer room,' where they were little used and poorly maintained" (p. 10). In a policy review, Culp and her colleagues (2005) observed that "education technology experts, who have largely been responsible for guiding and informing policymakers' understandings of the potential role of technology in education over the past 20 years, have provided energizing, exciting visions of how technology could potentially 'change everything'" (pp. 302–303). However, they noted that the technological uses policymakers and researchers hoped for are not yet reflected in widespread instructional practice: "What begins to surface in these policy documents is a widening gap between the promise and potential of technology and the ways in which technology actually gains traction in school settings" (p. 302).

Indeed, qualitative data show that most teachers use new forms of technology primarily to accomplish the same tasks they were already accomplishing (such as lesson planning, information presentation, and personal productivity) rather than to restructure their practice to facilitate higher-order thinking skills (Culp et al., 2005; Ottenbreit-Leftwich et al., 2012). Furthermore, when teachers *do* make changes to their practice, technology is not the primary catalyst for those changes (Dexter et al., 1999). Research by Dexter and her colleagues (1999) illustrated that:

The primary reason [for change in instructional practice] was of internal origin and agency: Change was the consequence of reflecting on teaching practice, its goals, and its efficacy. . . . [Teachers also] mentioned specifically a catalyst of external origin: schoolwide expectations and instructional emphases, such as performance assessment, or a new instructional focus adopted at their school, like cooperative learning. (p. 227)

Iliana Snyder (1998) wrote that "no technology . . . can guarantee any particular change in cultural practices simply by its 'nature'" (p. 140), and Robert Branch and Christa Deissler (2008) agreed that "the use of technology merely for technology's sake is ineffective and often a misuse of resources" (p. 210). Technology, it seems, cannot yield achievement gains in a vacuum. Technology, on its own, is not enough.

The Value-Neutral Lens

Theorists who see technology through a *value-neutral* lens attempt to reconcile competing value-positive and value-negative arguments to create a third viewpoint. They concede that both value-positive and value-negative theorists make valuable points. For instance, Collins and Halverson (2009) stated, "We think that the skeptics are correct in that there are deep incompatibilities between technology and schooling but that the enthusiasts are correct in that education must change to stay relevant in the wake of the Knowledge Revolution" (p. 7). Educational technology may not have revolutionized and transformed education, such theorists admit, but that does not mean it has no place in a classroom. Despite an unrealized technological miracle, Culp and her colleagues (2005) described the preceding two decades' increases in technological infrastructure—including a move to widespread computer and Internet access in public schools—as "major accomplishments" (p. 299).

Rather than endorsing or openly rejecting the potential of educational technology, Harris (2005) distinguished between using technology and using technology well. She encouraged educational technologists to modify the value-positive view of technology as a vehicle for education reform in favor of a more neutral view of technology integration. Harris defined *technology integration* simply as "the pervasive and productive use of educational technologies for purposes of learning and teaching" (p. 119). She wrote:

I urge us to consider seriously whether it is more appropriate to try to change the nature of teaching and learning through the integration of educational technologies—or to help teachers and learners use appropriate curriculum-based technological applications more pervasively in all their varied forms. (p. 121)

Rather than viewing the lackluster results from technology-fueled reform efforts as failures, Culp and her colleagues (2005) were optimistic about the gradual increase in technology use. They believed it allowed educational technology advocates to "understand with more nuance that technology needs to work in concert with other factors like effective leadership, instructional priorities, and the day-to-day demands of classroom practice" (p. 303).

Punya Mishra, Matthew Koehler, and Kristen Kereluik (2009) agreed that, due to the belief that technology would rescue education, "most innovations have focused inordinately on the technology rather than more fundamental issues of how to approach teaching subject matter with these technologies" (p. 49). Mishra and his colleagues (2009) summarized the value-neutral perspective well: "If technology is truly to be beneficial to education, the power and potential of educational technology must be acknowledged to reside within educators and not within objects" (p. 52).

Our Perspective in This Book

For the most part, our perspective in this book is that educational technology has a slight tendency toward being value positive. We believe that when considered as a whole, the aforementioned categories of educational technology use—computers, the Internet, interactive whiteboards, and mobile devices—will produce a slight positive effect on student learning. However, when combined with effective use of specific instructional strategies, the positive effects on student learning are greater than the effect of the technology used in isolation or the instructional strategies used in isolation. To use a well-worn phrase, the whole is greater than the sum of its parts. Both authors of this book have had concrete experience to this end.

As mentioned previously, Marzano Research conducted a series of studies on the effects of IWBs on student achievement (Marzano & Haystead, 2009, 2010). These studies involved over 130 teachers who used IWB technology with one group of students and IWB-free methods with a second group of students. In both classes, teachers took the same amount of time to teach the same content and used the same assessments to measure student growth and learning. However, in one class, they used IWB technology and in the other they didn't. The overall effect size for the use of IWBs was 0.37, which translates into a 14 percentile point gain. This finding would seem to support the notion that the use of a specific type of educational technology, in this case the use of interactive whiteboards, has a moderate positive effect on student learning. However, when video recordings of the teachers were analyzed to see how well they used specific instructional strategies—such as chunking content, scaffolding information, and monitoring student progress—the researchers found a strong relationship between the execution of the strategies and the effect of IWB usage on student achievement. Specifically, when teachers used IWB technology and executed strategies well, the effect size was 1.60, indicating a 45 percentile point gain. The average effect of these strategies without IWB technology has been shown to be about 0.64, indicating a 24 percentile point gain. Essentially, the combined effect of IWB technology and the effective execution of instructional strategies was greater than the independent effect of either variable in isolation.

One School's Experience

Action research was conducted in an elementary school in California to examine the use of technology to support or enhance specific instructional strategies (Haystead & Magaña, 2013). This low-performing elementary school served a very diverse, high-needs population of students. Most of the students attending this school lived at or below the poverty level and qualified for the free or reduced lunch program. Nearly half of the students in the school were English learners, and many were considered highly mobile, meaning they had changed their place of residence at least twice during an academic year. Prior to the introduction of technology professional development and tools in 2009, the school had failed to attain adequate yearly progress, as measured by the California Academic Performance Index (API), for five consecutive years. Student behavior and attendance issues were also major concerns in this school.

Beginning in the 2009–2010 academic year, the school received focused professional development about using their existing technology tools to support specific instructional strategies. The teachers and the school instructional coach were trained to use IWBs, IWB software, and student response systems in combination with effective instructional strategies (such as previewing, chunking, scaffolding, pacing, monitoring student progress, identifying similarities and differences, using nonlinguistic representations, and using questioning strategies).

As described previously, the school had failed to meet API standards for five years before the beginning of the study. In 2010, however, the school received a Growth API score of 804, achieving adequate yearly progress for the first time. This was followed by two more years of growth. Furthermore, the school outperformed the median Growth API score, which includes one hundred other California schools with similar demographic characteristics (for example, socioeconomic status, ethnicity, English learner population, and so on). Figure 1.3 compares this school's API scores with the median Growth API scores from 2004 to 2012.

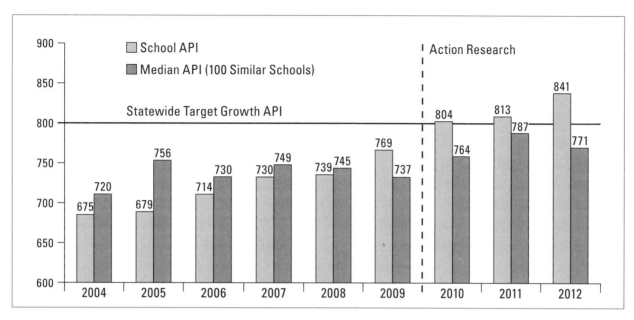

Figure 1.3: Comparison of median academic growth and growth of the test school as measured by the California API.

Source: Haystead & Magaña, 2013, p. 8.

The percentage of students in the school achieving proficient or advanced levels of achievement in English language arts (ELA) and mathematics on the California Standardized Testing and Reporting (STAR) Program increased during the first year of the study, as well as in each consecutive year (see figure 1.4). Additionally, the school's principal reported a decrease in student behavioral issues and increases in student attendance and teacher morale.

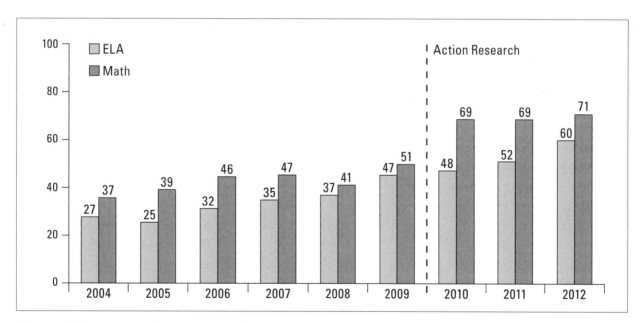

Figure 1.4: Percentage of students scoring at the proficient or advanced level in ELA and math on STAR.

Source: Haystead & Magaña, 2013, p. 11.

Other factors may have contributed to the school's gains in achievement (for example, effective school leadership, district management, and instructional coaching in the building). Still, a reasonable inference can be made that the guidance provided to teachers on using existing technology tools to enhance instruction was a contributing factor to academic growth.

Our Instructional Model

Throughout this book, we discuss a variety of types of educational technology. However, we do so in concert with specific instructional strategies. That is, we do not discuss technology in isolation, nor do we discuss instruction in isolation. Rather, we discuss how specific technology tools can be used with specific instructional strategies.

We use the instructional framework articulated in *The Art and Science of Teaching* (Marzano, 2007) and further detailed in several additional books, including *A Handbook for the Art and Science of Teaching* (Marzano & Brown, 2009), *Effective Supervision* (Marzano et al., 2011), and *Becoming a Reflective Teacher* (Marzano, 2012). This framework presents three lesson segments, which signify the main types of procedures used in the classroom (routine events, content, and on the spot). Each lesson segment is further categorized into design questions, which organize the forty-one elements (or forty-one categories of specific classroom strategies and behaviors) that correlate with teacher proficiency in the classroom. Table 1.5 lists the forty-one elements of the framework presented in *The Art and Science of Teaching*.

Table 1.5: Forty-One Elements of *The Art and Science of Teaching* Framework

Lesson Segments Involving Routine Events
Design Question: What will I do to establish and communicate learning goals, track student progress, and celebrate success?
Element 1: Providing clear learning goals and scales (rubrics)
Element 2: Tracking student progress
Element 3: Celebrating success
Design Question: What will I do to establish and maintain classroom rules and procedures?
Element 4: Establishing and maintaining classroom rules and procedures
Element 5: Organizing the physical layout of the classroom
Lesson Segments Addressing Content
Design Question: What will I do to help students effectively interact with new knowledge?
Element 6: Identifying critical information
Element 7: Organizing students to interact with new knowledge
Element 8: Previewing new content
Element 9: Chunking content into digestible bites
Element 10: Helping students process new information
Element 11: Helping students elaborate on new information
Element 12: Helping students record and represent knowledge
Element 13: Helping students reflect on their learning

Design Question: What will I do to help students practice and deepen their understanding of new knowledge?

Element 14: Reviewing content

Element 15: Organizing students to practice and deepen knowledge

Element 16: Using homework

Element 17: Helping students examine similarities and differences

Element 18: Helping students examine errors in reasoning

Element 19: Helping students practice skills, strategies, and processes

Element 20: Helping students revise knowledge

Design Question: What will I do to help students generate and test hypotheses about new knowledge?

Element 21: Organizing students for cognitively complex tasks

Element 22: Engaging students in cognitively complex tasks involving hypothesis generation and testing

Element 23: Providing resources and guidance

Lesson Segments Enacted on the Spot

Design Question: What will I do to engage students?

Element 24: Noticing when students are not engaged

Element 25: Using academic games

Element 26: Managing response rates

Element 27: Using physical movement

Element 28: Maintaining a lively pace

Element 29: Demonstrating intensity and enthusiasm

Element 30: Using friendly controversy

Element 31: Providing opportunities for students to talk about themselves

Element 32: Presenting unusual or intriguing information

Design Question: What will I do to recognize and acknowledge adherence or lack of adherence to rules and procedures?

Element 33: Demonstrating withitness

Element 34: Applying consequences for lack of adherence to rules and procedures

Element 35: Acknowledging adherence to rules and procedures

Design Question: What will I do to establish and maintain effective relationships with students?

Element 36: Understanding students' interests and backgrounds

Element 37: Using verbal and nonverbal behaviors that indicate affection for students

Element 38: Displaying objectivity and control

Design Question: What will I do to communicate high expectations for all students?

Element 39: Demonstrating value and respect for low-expectancy students

Element 40: Asking questions of low-expectancy students

Element 41: Probing incorrect answers with low-expectancy students

Lesson segments involving routine events include procedures that teachers use on a day-to-day or otherwise regular basis. As indicated by the two design questions that make up this category, routine events include communicating learning goals, tracking student progress, celebrating success, and establishing and maintaining classroom rules and procedures. *Lesson segments addressing content* pertain to helping students explore, digest, and retain new information. These segments include helping students effectively interact with new knowledge, practice and deepen their understanding of new knowledge, and generate and test hypotheses about new knowledge. Finally, *lesson segments enacted on the spot* involve procedures that teachers use as necessary. As shown by the design questions, these procedures include engaging students, acknowledging adherence or lack of adherence to rules and procedures, maintaining effective relationships with students, and communicating high expectations for all students. Figure 1.5 illustrates the interconnected nature of these segments and design questions.

As depicted in figure 1.5, lesson segments enacted on the spot lay the foundation for a classroom environment that facilitates learning. In order to build such an environment, a teacher should consider the four design questions positioned around the perimeter of figure 1.5. A teacher does not necessarily plan these on-the-spot segments ahead of time; instead, he or she utilizes them as needed in response to various classroom situations. For instance, upon noticing that a student is not engaged in the lesson, a teacher may use nonverbal gestures to correct the behavior of that student in the moment.

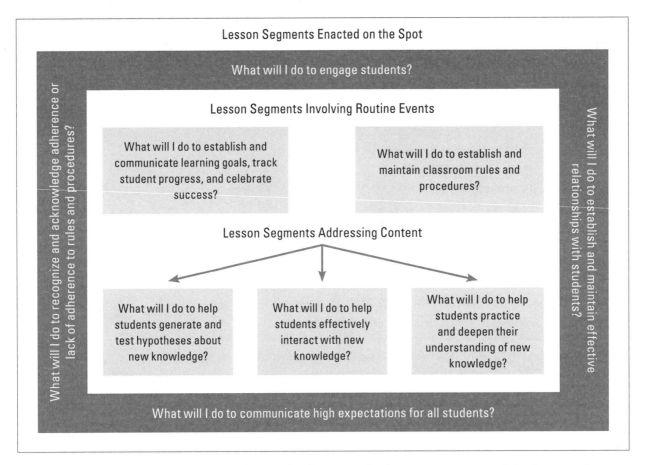

Figure 1.5: Visual representation of the interaction between the lesson segments and design questions.

Source: Marzano & Simms, 2013, p. 22.

When a teacher uses on-the-spot segments to create an effective classroom environment, the remaining lesson segments—involving routine events and addressing content—can operate within this environment. In figure 1.5, lesson segments involving routine events precede lesson segments addressing content because, in order to facilitate learning, teachers must first establish a safe, orderly, and predictable environment in which their students can learn comfortably. Unlike on-the-spot segments, teachers plan for routine event segments in advance (that is, in the weeks before school starts or before beginning a new unit). Once on-the-spot and routine event segments are firmly in place, a teacher has a strong foundation for addressing content.

To summarize, the framework for effective teaching includes three broad categories of lesson segments: (1) routine events, (2) content, and (3) on the spot. The corresponding design questions for each segment guide teachers in creating an effective classroom environment that facilitates learning.

Translating Research and Theory Into Practice

In the following chapters, we use the research and theory presented in this chapter and the research and theory from books such as *The Art and Science of Teaching* (Marzano, 2007) and *Becoming a Reflective Teacher* (Marzano, 2012) to create a unique approach to educational technology use. Our approach is grounded in a very comprehensive yet detailed model of effective teaching drawn from decades of research and thousands of studies. As mentioned in the introduction, throughout this book you will encounter comprehension questions to help you process the content presented as you progress through the remaining chapters. After completing each set of questions, you can check your answers with those in appendix A (page 151).

Chapter 2

COMMUNICATING LEARNING GOALS, TRACKING STUDENT PROGRESS, AND CELEBRATING SUCCESS

The first design question under lesson segments involving routine events is, How can I establish and communicate learning goals, track student progress, and celebrate success? As might be inferred from the design question itself, three elements are important to this question.

Element 1: Providing clear learning goals and scales (rubrics)

Element 2: Tracking student progress

Element 3: Celebrating success

Each of these elements is supported by specific research on the effects of setting goals (Lipsey & Wilson, 1993; Walberg, 1999; Wise & Okey, 1983), giving feedback to students (Bangert-Drowns, Kulik, Kulik, & Morgan, 1991; Haas, 2005; Hattie & Timperley, 2007; Kumar, 1991), reinforcing effort rather than innate talent (Hattie, Biggs, & Purdie, 1996; Kumar, 1991; Schunk & Cox, 1986), and the use of praise and rewards (Bloom, 1976; Deci, Ryan, & Koestner, 2001; Wilkinson, 1981). Additionally, specific strategies support each element and each of those strategies can be adapted and improved using technology.

Element 1: Providing Clear Learning Goals and Scales (Rubrics)

Element 1 involves the teacher providing and reminding students of specific learning goals for a lesson or unit. Strategies associated with this element include:

- Clearly articulating learning goals

- Creating scales or rubrics

Here, we explain each strategy and highlight various educational technologies and tools that can be used to support its use.

Clearly Articulating Learning Goals

It is important for the teacher to clearly articulate the learning goal to students. Learning goals can be stated in two ways. Declarative learning goals take the form "Students will understand _____." Procedural learning goals take the form "Students will be able to _____." Many times, teachers combine declarative and procedural knowledge to create a learning goal that might take the form "Students will understand _____ and be able to _____." Teachers can use a variety of technology tools to help them articulate and communicate learning goals to students.

With technology, teachers can expose students to the learning goals of a lesson prior to the start of the lesson itself. This allows students to begin making connections between learning goals, background knowledge, and personal experience before class begins. Prior to the lesson, post the learning goal on a class website (which may be a blog, a wiki, or a social media page) to stimulate student thinking about and discussion of the learning goal. Sharing a learning goal can be as straightforward as posting the comment, "Our learning goal for tomorrow's lesson is: Students will understand the causes and effects of early 20th century immigration in the United States."

Technology tools can also help a teacher draw students' attention to the important details of the learning goal. Type the learning goal as a large text object in IWB software. Using the fill tool, change the color of key words to deconstruct the learning goal into manageable chunks. Choose bright colors like orange, red, or purple to emphasize the critical components. Utilize this visual cue to start a class discussion about the learning goal to ensure student understanding.

Additionally, IWB software can be used to help students generate predictions about new content based on prior learning goals. Hide the new learning goal behind an image that relates to the learning goal of the lesson. During a lesson on early 20th century immigration, for instance, you might conceal the learning goal beneath an image of a family of immigrants traveling to the United States. Ask students to consider how the image might relate to the day's lesson and provide think time before erasing the top layer image to reveal the learning goal.

Intentional use of certain IWB features can also serve to remind students that classroom tasks always relate to a specific learning goal. Use the scrolling text function in your IWB software to make the learning goal scroll horizontally across the top or bottom of each page like a nightly news ticker on a television screen. Drawing attention to the learning goal at strategic points in your lesson can help students keep track of the ways in which their thoughts and activities relate.

Another way to provide clear learning goals for students is to have them paraphrase the goals in their own words, creating examples and analogies to deepen their understanding of them. Student response systems allow students to instantly share these restatements with the class. They can be sent via text message using clickers with text input or using polling software (such as Twitter, Socrative, TodaysMeet, or Poll Everywhere) on student mobile devices.

Finally, ask students to share their learning goals with the class. Technology tools can be used to encourage every student to participate. Assign each student a number in your gradebook, and use a random number generator online or in your IWB software to randomly select students to explain the learning goal. This tool allows you to select a range of numbers to match the number of students in your class (such as 1–30, if you have thirty students) and push a button or spin a dial to randomly choose a student to restate the learning goal. Alternatively, select students by name using a random name generator.

Creating Scales or Rubrics

Teachers can create scales for each learning goal to measure students' progression of learning. A scale should include the target learning goal, a simpler version of the target learning goal, and a more complex version of the target learning goal. Table 2.1 presents a generic scale that teachers might use.

Table 2.1: Generic Scale

Score 4.0	More complex learning goal
Score 3.0	Target learning goal
Score 2.0	Simpler learning goal
Score 1.0	With help, partial success at score 2.0 content and score 3.0 content
Score 0.0	Even with help, no success

Source: Marzano, 2010, p. 45.

As seen in table 2.1, the 2.0, 3.0, and 4.0 performance levels of the scale are the only ones that change depending on the content. The 1.0 and 0.0 levels stay the same. The following technology tools and techniques can be used to create and communicate scales or rubrics for learning goals to students.

Give students a clear idea of exactly what they need to do to achieve proficiency on the learning goal. Prior to the lesson, post the scale or rubric on a class website to stimulate student thinking about and discussion of the scale or rubric. Post comments that include the learning goal for the lesson and the proficiency scale associated with the learning goal. Students can then comment to demonstrate that they have read and understood the learning goal and the proficiency scale.

Expose students to proficiency scales in different ways to deepen their understanding and help them make progress on the scale. Create a page in your IWB software that clearly shows a scale or rubric. Use this prompt to initiate a class discussion to ensure understanding of the different levels of performance. You might also begin your lesson with an image of the proficiency scale, explain the differences in performance at each level, and invite students to commit to achieving the target learning goal.

Students can rephrase the language of the performance levels in their own words to deepen their understanding of them. Using clickers with text input or mobile devices with polling software, they can share their explanations with the class. They send a text response that explains what they think proficiency looks like at each of the different levels using concrete examples. Discuss these responses as a class to prompt whole-group thinking and interaction.

Using a random name generator, select students to explain their understanding of the target 3.0 learning goal, how their current activities relate to the learning goal, or the meaning of the other performance levels in the proficiency scale. Use the random name generator consistently over the course of a school year to ensure that every student has a chance to be chosen.

Element 2: Tracking Student Progress

Element 2 involves helping students chart both their individual and group (or class) progress on the target learning goal or goals. Strategies associated with this element include:

- Formative assessments

- Different types of assessments

- Charting student progress

Here, we explain each strategy and highlight a number of educational technology tools that can be used to enhance each one.

Formative Assessments

Teachers create assessment tasks that measure students' achievement on the 2.0, 3.0, or 4.0 content of a proficiency scale. These tasks might be multiple choice (usually most appropriate for 2.0 tasks), constructed response (usually most appropriate for 3.0 tasks), or extended response (usually most appropriate for 4.0 tasks) and may be given to students using a traditional pencil-and-paper format, demonstrations, or probing discussions.

Involve students in designing formative assessments to help them focus on critical information while introducing new content. Give students the opportunity to generate, consider, and discuss questions that may be used during formative assessment tasks or checks for understanding. They can submit these questions using clickers with text input or mobile devices with polling software.

You can also track and archive student formative assessment data during instruction using clickers with text input or polling software on student mobile devices. For instance, you might ask students to use clickers or their own mobile devices to respond to assessment questions at the 2.0, 3.0, and 4.0 proficiency levels. You might also ask students to rate their effort on each question, as well as what they think they need to do to achieve success at the target level.

Different Types of Assessments

Three types of assessments can be used with proficiency scales to track students' progress. *Obtrusive assessments* interrupt the flow of instruction in the classroom and are usually paper-and-pencil tests, demonstrations, or probing discussions. During *unobtrusive assessments*, the teacher simply observes a student performing the skills or demonstrating the knowledge from a specific level of the proficiency scale and records an appropriate score for the student in his or her gradebook. *Student-generated assessments* are a particularly effective way to help students track their progress, because students design the tasks that will allow them to demonstrate their knowledge and skill on a particular level of the scale. They then complete the tasks and deliver their products or performances to the teacher. The teacher and student confer about what score level the student has achieved, and the student's score is recorded in the gradebook.

Students can show their understanding using multimedia tools, which stimulate multiple senses at once and can provide new perspectives on content. Have students use screen capture software on laptops or computers (such as Jing) or apps on tablets (such as ScreenChomp, Educreations, or TouchCast) to capture and narrate student-generated assessment tasks that demonstrate knowledge and skill on a particular level of the scale. For example, students could use screen capture software to record and narrate the process used to solve a math problem. These screencasts can be archived and shared with other students.

Technology allows students to save various iterations of a file and monitor their progress on digital projects (such as essays, multimedia presentations, and so on). For example, students can give different file names—such as V1 (version 1), V2, V3, and so on—to the same project when saving. This convention makes it easy for students to compare several different drafts of the same project and see their progress throughout a lesson or unit.

Charting Student Progress

Teachers can help students measure their own progress by providing charts or tables that allow them to track their scores and progress on a learning goal over time. For example, a line graph (like the one in figure 2.1) can be used to show a student's gradual increase in knowledge and skill for a particular learning goal.

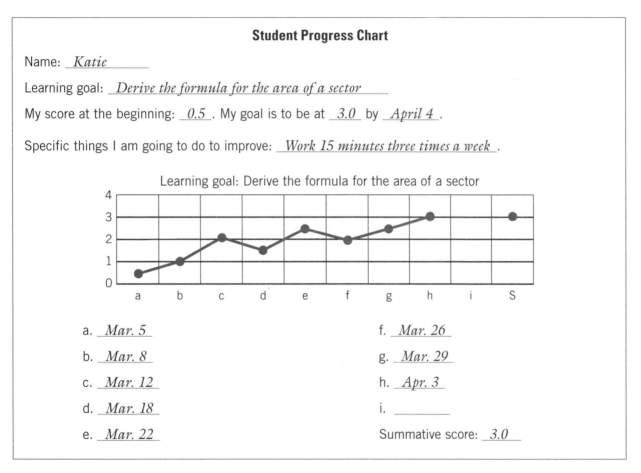

Figure 2.1: Student progress chart.

Source: Adapted from Marzano, 2010.

When students use technology to chart their progress toward target learning goals, it prompts them to take an active role in understanding the learning target, processing their current level of achievement, and planning action steps. For instance, students can keep a digital journal using Google Drive or Evernote. Establish a classroom procedure for students to reflect on their learning and track their progress digitally. In addition, ask students to self-assess their understanding of the learning content before and during instruction using clickers with text input or mobile devices with polling software. Pose preassessment questions prior to the start of the lesson, and capture students' responses. Then, ask the same questions again at strategic points during the lesson, and compare new responses with previous responses to ascertain knowledge gains.

Access students' digital journals to comment on their progress and offer suggestions, considerations, and encouragement. This type of feedback can motivate students to persevere in their learning efforts. Positive feedback in students' digital journals will prompt them to examine their progress toward the learning goal, evaluate the amount of time they have spent working on the content, and reflect on the level of effort they have exerted.

Students can also track their behavior at school using online behavior feedback services such as ClassDojo. This website allows students to create personal accounts, set behavioral goals, assess their daily behavior, and keep track of their progress toward their behavioral goals over time.

Element 3: Celebrating Success

For element 3, the teacher helps students acknowledge and celebrate two indicators of their success: current status and knowledge gain. A student's *current status* on a learning goal shows the level of achievement he or she has attained for that particular learning goal at the present point in a unit. At the end of a unit, teachers assign students *final statuses* (also known as summative scores) based on their pattern of scores during the unit. A student's *knowledge gain* for a particular learning goal shows how much growth he or she has made on the learning goal. For example, a student whose current status is 3.0 might have started at 1.0 for that particular learning goal. In that case, the student's knowledge gain would be 2.0. Strategies associated with element 3 include:

- Final status and knowledge gain celebrations
- Verbal or written feedback

Here, we describe each strategy and explain how technology can be used to implement it and enhance its effectiveness.

Final Status and Knowledge Gain Celebrations

While knowledge gain can be celebrated throughout the unit, the natural time to celebrate students' final statuses is at the end of a unit. Students can participate in these celebrations by highlighting products or performances that they completed to achieve their knowledge gain or final status.

Celebrations of academic success help students realize and acknowledge progress made during a lesson or unit. Use the class website to post examples of high-quality student work and exemplary knowledge gains. Post congratulatory comments on students' learning products, and provide links for other students to view the products. Encourage students to view and comment on these exemplars to celebrate peers' learning.

Students can also use technology to tutor other students about knowledge that they have recently gained. Have students record tutorials for other students using screen capture software on computers (such as Jing) or apps on tablets (such as ScreenChomp, Educreations, or TouchCast). Post these tutorials on the class website to share and celebrate students' work with their classmates. To make students' tutorials anonymous to their peers, have each class member create an unidentifiable username under which to post work. Keep a master list of students' usernames to avoid misattributing one student's work to another.

Use technology tools to monitor the work that students have published online and see how many views the work has received. Websites like ClustrMaps can show you who is accessing students' work on your class website. Begin by establishing a class website, and post exemplary student screencasts and tutorials on the site. Next, go to www.clustrmaps.com and obtain an HTML code to include the map on your site for free. ClustrMaps will create an interactive map on your website that tracks the number of visitors and displays their locations around the world. However, keep in mind that some schools may not allow student-created pages to be shared with the public. Take the time to review your school's Internet policies before publishing student work online.

Verbal or Written Feedback

Feedback is most effective when it highlights what a student did to achieve growth on a learning goal. Teachers can highlight specific cognitive behaviors that helped students learn or specific work habits that helped make them successful.

To incorporate technology, provide sharable forms of recognition for students' efforts toward achieving a learning goal. For example, use publishing software to create certificates and awards to celebrate student academic achievement and knowledge gains. Certificates can be personalized and then printed or emailed to students' parents. Recognition awards can focus on individual effort, knowledge gains, positive behavior, or contribution to the classroom learning environment.

Inspire students to continue positive efforts by celebrating their success online. Post positive feedback on the class website to acknowledge student achievement, effort, and knowledge gain. Encourage students to do the same. Comments can be as simple as, "Gregory has been working hard to improve his learning level and has just reached the 3.0 stage for this week's lesson! Effort pays off!"

Regular communication with parents can influence student effort and motivation as well, as it increases parental interest and involvement in student learning. However, regular communication with families can be challenging for teachers with many students and limited time. Technology helps teachers keep parents informed of their child's academic performance and work habits. Send short emails or text messages to parents acknowledging and celebrating student successes. Such messages can be as simple as, "Jane improved from a 2.0 to a 3.0 on her learning goal in just two weeks!"

Establish a classroom culture that celebrates contribution. A positive routine such as a unique classroom cheer, dance, or song can provide a feeling of celebration during moments of whole-class or individual success. For example, the class might chant, "On fire!" and make sizzling sounds when polling technology results show that a certain percentage of the class got a correct answer.

Teaching With Technology

The three elements of the first design question can all be enhanced and augmented using the technology tools and techniques explained in this chapter. The following vignette illustrates how a teacher might use technology to enhance the instructional strategies that pertain to these elements, as well as others.

Mr. Ensey teaches fourth-grade students in a suburban school district near a large U.S. city. He is beginning a lesson on immigration to the United States. The Neil Diamond song "America" (1980, track 1) plays through his computer speakers.

Students sit in table groups, and each student has a tablet that he or she uses to record notes and ideas during the lesson. Mr. Ensey turns on his IWB at the front of the room and displays a slideshow of digital images. A grainy photograph of the Statue of Liberty appears. The next image shows a group of people packed onto an impossibly crowded steamship's deck. Another photograph shows a woman in a tattered scarf holding an infant and two younger children carrying canvas sacks. The slideshow zooms in on the young boy in the photograph. He appears to be the same age as the students in the class.

When the music stops, Mr. Ensey navigates to a new page of his presentation that displays a black box in the center. The students seem aware of what comes next and are visibly excited as Mr. Ensey slowly moves the black box to uncover the following essential question (which is tied to the class's learning goal): *What are the things that would drive people to leave their families and the country of their birth to come to the United States?* He asks students to consider and respond to the question individually by submitting their text answers using an application on their tablets. He starts a countdown timer, showing students that they have two minutes to complete this task.

The sound of a ringing bell signals that two minutes have passed. Mr. Ensey tells the students to finish the sentence they are working on and submit their responses. On the IWB, he displays all of the ideas that the students have submitted as individual text objects. Then, he randomly selects a text object and moves it to the top of the board. He asks the student who submitted that particular idea to explain the thinking that led to her response. Mr. Ensey does this with several other text responses, randomly selecting students to expand on and share their thinking with the group.

Mr. Ensey then navigates to a new page of his presentation with an image of a newspaper printing press in the center of the page. Upon seeing the image, his students begin to type on their tablets. The students know that the printing press is a prompt to make a prediction about what they think the learning goal of the lesson is, based on the preview activity they have just completed.

After giving the students one minute to enter their ideas, Mr. Ensey asks, "Whose turn is it today?"

Maya raises her hand.

"OK, Maya," says Mr. Ensey. "You know what to do."

The class watches as Maya gets out of her chair and walks to the IWB at the front of the room. She clicks on a button, and the sound of an early 20th century ragtime song plays through the speakers.

Maya turns to class and says, "Extra, extra! Read all about it! The learning goal for today's lesson is . . ." and with that, she drags a digital newspaper headline into view from behind the image of the printing press on the screen. Maya reads the text to the class, "Students will understand the reasons why people immigrated to the United States in the early 20th century and the impact of immigration on American society."

The learning goal is a clear statement of the declarative knowledge students should be able to demonstrate at the end of the lesson. Mr. Ensey then asks the students to share the predictions they made about the learning goal with the rest of the class. He reviews the predictions and uses the results to prompt a discussion with the students to ensure their understanding of the learning goal. He asks students to keep track of how close their predictions came to the actual learning goal in their digital journals.

Mr. Ensey then shows a page with a proficiency scale that relates to the outcomes for the lesson's learning goal (see table 2.2).

Table 2.2: Proficiency Scale for 20th Century Immigration in the United States

History—Immigration	
4.0	The student will: • Generate in-depth inferences or unique insights about early 20th century immigration and modern immigration • Generate in-depth inferences or unique insights about the impact of immigration on American society in the early 20th century and in modern times
3.0	The student will: • Understand the causes of early 20th century immigration and its impact on American society
2.0	The student will: • Identify vocabulary, concepts, people, and events related to early 20th century immigration and its impact on American society • Identify or explain reasons for emigrating to the United States in the early 20th century, origins of immigrant groups, living conditions in their countries of origin, methods of transportation, travel conditions, and the symbolism of the Statue of Liberty
1.0	With help, partial success at score 2.0 content and score 3.0 content
0.0	Even with help, no success

As depicted in table 2.2, Mr. Ensey's proficiency scale clearly shows four different levels of proficiency. He explains each level to the class and identifies the 3.0 level as the target for all students to achieve. He then shows two example assessment items for this level: (1) Use vocabulary from our unit to write a cause-and-effect paragraph explaining why people immigrated to the United States and how immigration affected American society, and (2) create an interactive map or flowchart showing the sequence of events that led to various groups' immigration to the United States.

Mr. Ensey uses clickers to have students rate their level of understanding of both the learning goal and the proficiency scale. He then returns to the presentation on his IWB. He has built numerous references into the presentation prompting him to refer back to the learning goal and explain how the current activity relates.

Mr. Ensey uses clickers throughout the lesson to help his students think about the proficiency scale and reflect on their levels of performance. This periodic check-in keeps students thinking about the learning goal, how their current activities relate to the learning goal, and how much effort they need to invest in order to achieve the target proficiency level with the learning goal.

As the lesson progresses, Mr. Ensey launches a random name generator on his IWB to choose students to respond to questions. Rashad's name is selected first. Mr. Ensey asks Rashad if he sees any connections between the previous lesson's learning goal and the current learning goal. Rashad thinks for a moment and then says that he really enjoyed learning about Thomas

Edison's inventions during the previous unit. He adds that Edison's invention of the first commercially available incandescent lightbulb probably made life easier for immigrants because they had light to read by at night. Mr. Ensey thanks Rashad for contributing and adds that Rashad has earned several points for his group, which Mr. Ensey tracks using ClassDojo.

During the lesson, Mr. Ensey also uses clickers to ask students questions that help him determine their level of understanding. He uses the polling data to identify any gaps in student understanding. With this real-time learning feedback, he can specifically target any student misconceptions that need to be addressed during the instructional phase of his lesson. He also relies on this level of student feedback to help him monitor the pace of his instruction and adjust the pace accordingly. Mr. Ensey's response software records students' responses to all of the polling questions he asks the class. He uses these data to track each student's progress and analyze patterns of individual and group understanding. This helps him make sure his students have a clear understanding of the learning goal and their progress toward that learning goal.

To conclude the lesson, Mr. Ensey returns to the IWB page that contained student responses to the essential question: *What are the things that would drive people to leave their families and the country of their birth to come to the United States?* Mr. Ensey asks his students to work in their groups to create categories and organize all of the reasons shared by the class into corresponding categories for their interactive project work. Using tablets to create and share rough drafts of their ideas with other group members, the students organize the class results into categories, such as *to be less poor, to look for a new job,* and *to be free.*

Mr. Ensey prompts struggling groups by asking, "Think back to our unit on the Pilgrims—why did they travel to the United States?" and "Think about the things people need to survive and be happy—might any of these have been missing for immigrants in their birth countries?"

Students brainstorm and capture ideas for creating a digital representation of their new knowledge and the online resources they can use to find primary-source documents that will help them extend and deepen their learning.

A few days later, students in Mr. Ensey's class develop digital representations of their new knowledge on early 20th century immigration. Students save multiple iterations of their work on the class computers to show the progress they have made. Working collaboratively, they find many relevant primary sources, including audio files, digital images, and letters written by early immigrants.

Some students have decided to use Google Earth to create an interactive map representing various groups' journeys to the United States. Others have decided to create a blog to showcase their understanding. Still others are creating PowerPoint tutorials to teach other students about immigration. Each student selects the format that will help him or her best represent and share new understanding with others. Students also regularly record entries into their digital learning journals to reflect on their learning and to record ideas about representing and sharing their understanding. In addition, Mr. Ensey accesses students' online learning journals and provides feedback as well as encouragement, guidance, and support.

At the beginning of the school year, Mr. Ensey and his class agreed on a set of classroom rules and procedures. One element of this agreement pertained to celebrating student success. In addition to individual recognition for exemplary performance, current status, and knowledge gain (such as positive emails to students' parents and certificates for student of the week), the students agreed that it would be helpful to celebrate their collective performance as a class. They decided that if each student achieved a certain proficiency level for a unit, and that each group earned a certain threshold of points for citizenship and contribution, then the entire class would get to celebrate its learning achievement at the end of the unit. For this unit, the class decided that if it met its goals, students would conduct a videoconference with their sister classroom in Ireland to share their projects. Mr. Ensey's students interact with their sister classroom regularly and look forward to seeing their peers by videoconferencing through their IWB.

Unbeknownst to the students, Mr. Ensey has also arranged a surprise virtual field trip to the Statue of Liberty National Monument. Impressed with his students' level of effort, he has been secretly coordinating with the rangers at the Statue of Liberty National Monument to bring the experience of early 20th century immigration into his classroom.

As seen here, Mr. Ensey uses many technology tools, some of which relate to element 1, providing clear learning goals and scales (rubrics). Specifically, he provides students with a nonlinguistic representation of early 20th century immigration and, using this as a prompt, asks students to make a prediction about the learning goal. Next, he embeds the learning goal and proficiency scale into his IWB software, and students use classroom clickers to rate their understanding of both. He then uses IWB software to randomly select students to explain how their classroom activities relate to the learning goal.

Mr. Ensey also uses technology tools and techniques to support element 2, tracking student progress, throughout each lesson and unit. As seen in the vignette, he uses clickers to pose questions that everyone can answer. With this system, he can capture all of his students' responses to questions and monitor each student's progress throughout the course of the lesson. Mr. Ensey also tracks students' contributions in class using ClassDojo, an online behavior-tracking tool. Additionally, students keep track of their learning goals and their progress toward these goals by maintaining digital learning journals online.

Finally, Mr. Ensey uses educational technology to celebrate students' success, element 3, as he recognizes their knowledge gain and final status on the learning goal. He sends positive emails to parents and publishes certificates and awards for student effort, current status, and knowledge gain. When his students meet a threshold level of points for positive behavior and learning outcomes, he organizes a virtual field trip using videoconferencing software to celebrate.

Chapter 2: Comprehension Questions

1. Why is it beneficial to use technology to expose students to a learning goal before beginning a lesson?

2. Describe at least two benefits that come with using digital journals (as opposed to paper-and-pencil journals) to track student progress.

3. In what ways do online publishing and social media tools have the potential to enhance the process of celebrating success?

4. How do you use technology to provide clear learning goals, track student progress, and celebrate success in your classroom? Share your ideas by going to **marzanoresearch.com/classroomstrategies**, clicking on the *Enhancing the Art & Science of Teaching With Technology* link, and becoming a member of our virtual learning community.

Chapter 3

ESTABLISHING CLASSROOM RULES AND PROCEDURES

The second design question—How can I use technology to establish and maintain classroom rules and procedures?—addresses a crucial step toward a safe, orderly, and predictable learning environment for students. Two elements make up this design question, which falls under lesson segments involving routine events.

Element 4: Establishing and maintaining classroom rules and procedures

Element 5: Organizing the physical layout of the classroom

The idea that routines and procedures ought to be explicitly taught at the beginning of the school year, after which they are practiced and periodically reviewed, is well grounded in research (Anderson, Evertson, & Emmer, 1980; Brophy & Evertson, 1976; Eisenhart, 1977; Emmer, Evertson, & Anderson, 1980; Good & Brophy, 2003; Moskowitz & Hayman, 1976). The technology tools in this chapter facilitate teaching and review of rules and procedures, and they increase students' participation in generating rules and procedures and designing the physical layout of the classroom. This involvement gives students a sense of agency and belonging in the classroom.

Element 4: Establishing and Maintaining Classroom Rules and Procedures

Element 4 involves establishing a new rule or procedure for the classroom and reminding students of that rule or procedure. Strategies for this element include:

- Explaining rules and procedures to students

- Generating rules and procedures with students

- Class pledge or classroom constitution

- Vignettes and role playing

Clearly, engaging students in discussions about classroom rules and procedures requires more effort than simply posting the classroom rules and procedures and making sure that students understand and agree to abide by them. A number of technology tools can be employed to support and enhance this process, helping each student contribute to, access, and willingly abide by the classroom rules and procedures.

Explaining Rules and Procedures to Students

The teacher should take time at the beginning of the school year to address the importance of rules and procedures in the classroom and to establish a set of teacher-created rules, explaining the reasoning behind each one.

Technology offers engaging techniques for presenting these rules and procedures, as well as ways in which students can demonstrate their understanding of them. For instance, multimedia presentations that include text, images, sound, animation, and videos capture students' attention by simultaneously engaging different senses. Present new information like classroom rules and procedures in a multimedia format to take advantage of these benefits. For example, use IWB software or presentation software (such as Prezi) to create a multimedia presentation to share and discuss the classroom rules and procedures. Incorporate images, sounds, important text, and videos depicting examples of your classroom rules and procedures.

Technology also allows students to digitally represent their own interpretations of classroom rules and procedures. This can clarify students' understanding and elicit students' justifications for rules and procedures. Students can use screen capture software on computers or laptops (such as Jing) or apps on tablets (such as ScreenChomp, Educreations, or TouchCast) to explain the rules in their own words. For instance, you might divide your class into small groups and have each one focus on a single classroom rule or procedure. Students explain why the rule is important and act out what it looks like when students follow it.

Generating Rules and Procedures With Students

One way to establish and maintain classroom rules and procedures is to have students help generate them. Technology can help the teacher gather and compile student suggestions.

When students contribute meaningfully to the classroom rules and procedures, they may be more likely to choose positive behaviors in the classroom. Students can submit ideas for classroom rules and procedures using clickers with text input or mobile devices with polling software. Use the class-compiled list to stimulate discussions about the rules and procedures. For example, you might organize students into small brainstorming groups and assign each group an overarching category for classroom procedures (for example, entering the classroom, whole-class discussion, small-group collaboration, or individual work time).

Generate classroom consensus by asking students to vote for rules they think should be included on the final list using clickers with text input or mobile devices with polling software. You could use an agreement scale for this vote: (1) this rule should definitely be included, (2) this rule should probably be included, (3) I can live with this and support it, (4) this rule should probably not be included, or (5) this rule should definitely not be included.

Furthermore, technology tools can make it easy for students to take an active role in generating consequences for adhering or not adhering to a rule or procedure. Students contribute their ideas for positive and negative consequences using clickers with text input or mobile devices with polling software. Discuss these ideas with the whole class to agree on appropriate consequences.

Class Pledge or Classroom Constitution

Once the class has established a set of rules and procedures, the teacher and students use it to write a class pledge or classroom constitution. This strategy helps students understand the rules and procedures and prompts them to agree to adhere to them. Teachers can use technology to check student understanding and obtain student agreement to comply.

Giving students the opportunity to confirm their understanding of the class pledge or classroom constitution can encourage them to adhere to its tenets. Have students submit these confirmations using clickers with text input or mobile devices with polling software. You can also display the pledge using IWB software and ask questions to determine the class's degree of comprehension. Use the results of student polling as a prompt for classroom discussion to clarify unclear elements of the pledge.

Similarly, requiring students to put their signatures on classroom contracts can help students take ownership for their behavioral decisions. Use publishing or word processing software to create contracts that list the agreed-upon rules, procedures, and consequences. Have each student digitally sign and save the contract or print a personal copy. Websites like www.freebehaviorcontracts.com allow teachers to create their own behavior contract or use provided sample contracts.

Vignettes and Role Playing

A fun and engaging way to practice rules and procedures with students is through vignettes and role playing. Students create and perform skits that illustrate what it looks like to follow the rules and procedures. Technology can be particularly useful for students who do not wish to perform live in front of their classmates.

Students can demonstrate, record, or represent their understanding in interesting ways with technology. Using tablets, smartphones, or other devices, students record themselves acting out scenarios in which rules and procedures are or are not followed. Divide students into groups to script, direct, record, and edit these dramatic skits. You might even set aside time for a movie premiere, during which you air each group's video to the whole class. Facilitate a discussion of the videos to ensure whole-group understanding and appreciation.

Element 5: Organizing the Physical Layout of the Classroom

A classroom's physical layout sends a strong message to students about a teacher's beliefs and values regarding the learning process. In deciding the layout of a technology-enhanced classroom, teachers should consider the following aspects of classroom design:

- Learning centers
- Involving students in the design process

In element 4, technology helped teachers include students in the process of creating a classwide set of rules and procedures. Technology can be similarly used to include students in the process of designing the physical layout of the classroom. The layout should send the message to students that the classroom is a shared space for learning.

Learning Centers

As teachers consider where to locate technology and other resources in the classroom, a number of questions are useful to consider: How many learning centers are needed? Should some centers be close to particular books, materials, or other resources? Where should student desks face relative to the IWB? What is the best placement for computers and printers? What is the best placement for a technology cart (for charging tablets, transporting laptops, or storing clickers) to provide easy access but avoid traffic jams? To maximize the potential of technology tools, it is important to carefully consider how and when they will be used.

Teachers can use digital recording technology to determine the optimal location of centers and resources in the classroom. Set up a video recording device—such as a digital video camera, document camera, or tablet—to record students as they access the learning centers and technology resources in your classroom. Analyze students' traffic patterns as they enter and exit these areas to improve the organization of classroom resources. Share sample clips with your students to prompt their involvement in identifying and generating resolutions to any perceived problems or issues. Teachers who wish to use this strategy should bear in mind that some schools may have limitations on videotaping students. Take the time to review your school's policies.

Involving Students in the Design Process

Although many teachers arrange the classroom before students arrive for the first day of class, asking students to be involved in the design process can help them feel invested and comfortable as they work in and move around the classroom. Technology offers many tools that students can use to collaborate and model their ideal classrooms.

Use online group generators, such as Team Maker, to randomly assign students into small groups to design their ideal classrooms. Encourage students to include areas in their design that support whole-group instruction, small-group interaction, and individual learning centers. Have each group share its completed designs with the class to stimulate group thinking and discussion. Students can use clickers or polling software on their mobile devices to vote on the best design to fit the learning needs of the entire class.

Involve groups of students in relatable, authentic problem-solving tasks to increase student participation and collaboration. Students can browse the Internet to research, locate, analyze, and discuss examples of appealing classroom designs. Once students have considered the advantages and disadvantages of other classroom designs, they can illustrate and present their ideal classroom using a digital drawing program, IWB software, Google Drive, or Prezi. Students can even consider issues of space and organization of classroom resources by creating three-dimensional representations of their blueprints using design software (such as SketchUp). When all designs have been considered, students can use clickers or their mobile devices to vote on a design that will meet the learning needs of everyone in the class.

Teaching With Technology

The design question addressed in this chapter emphasizes how technology can be used to support the formation of rules and procedures in the classroom, as well as the organization of the classroom's physical layout. The following vignette depicts a teacher using technology to enhance these elements, as well as others.

> Ms. Kushner has been teaching sixth grade in an urban school district for nine years. Visitors to her classroom notice a relaxed, active, and orderly atmosphere. Students appear to be monitoring and regulating their own behavior, at times reminding each other to keep their voices quiet to avoid disturbing others. At the end of the day, each student tracks his or her progress on behavioral, contribution, and effort goals using an app.
>
> What a visitor wouldn't see is the work that Ms. Kushner has done with her students to create such an environment. Her students feel secure enough to take learning risks and regularly challenge themselves beyond what they think they can do. Ms. Kushner's students make mistakes,

but rather than perceiving their mistakes as failures, they perceive them as unique opportunities for reflection and new learning. Because each student contributes to a shared understanding of the classroom norms, each is invested in supporting, maintaining, and contributing to a classroom culture of respectful communication and collaboration.

One of the first things that Ms. Kushner does when she meets her students at the beginning of the school year is establish the classroom rules and procedures. But she does not do this alone. She uses technology—clickers and an IWB—to have students actively contribute their thoughts and ideas for the rules and procedures that they feel will help make their classroom a safe and orderly place. Using polling software, Ms. Kushner engages the class in a discussion about each student's ideas for classroom rules and procedures. She treats even partially formed ideas with respect and includes them in the brainstorming session to make all of her students feel involved.

Each student also contributes to the incentives for adhering to and the consequences for lack of adherence to the rules and procedures. Each student then digitally signs a classroom user license agreement, much like an end-user license agreement, acknowledging that he or she has read and agrees to abide by the rules and procedures. Digital copies of the agreement are stored on the school's shared drive and are also sent to each student's device, where they can easily be opened and referenced.

Ms. Kushner's students also helped design the physical layout of her classroom. First, they used measuring tapes to determine the square footage of the classroom, and then they worked in groups to create ideal designs. Using SketchUp on their tablets, students in each group created a rough outline of their ideas for the classroom. Then, they created a final design on a computer and submitted it to the whole class. Using clickers, the class voted on the design that it liked the best and then went about rearranging the desks, chairs, and tables to create three different work areas: an area for direct instruction in the front of the room, an area with collaborative workstations for group brainstorming and processing in the middle of the room, and an area for individual project work on computers in the back of the room.

Using her IWB, Ms. Kushner directly instructs a small group of students in the front of the room. She manipulates various digital learning objects on the board to demonstrate the process of dividing fractions while students in the group follow along and record notes on their tablets. She incorporates numbers, colors, and shapes to create visual patterns for students.

At various intervals, Ms. Kushner uses a random name generator to select students to solve problems at the board. Each student has the opportunity to choose a problem from the easy, moderate, or challenging level and earn a corresponding number of group points for a correct answer. Ely's name appears on the name generator, and he chooses to solve a moderate-level problem on the IWB.

Ms. Kushner enables a screen recorder tool to capture Ely's narration and annotations as he solves the division problem and explains his thinking. When he completes the problem, Ely reaches for an image of a smiling sun on the board. He drags it aside to reveal the correct answer beneath the image. Ms. Kushner congratulates Ely on answering correctly and prompts the group of students to perform the class cheer.

"Let's give Ely two claps on 'two!'" she says, and the group claps twice in unison.

More students are selected to solve problems, and each one comes up to the IWB to complete and record his or her work. The students know they can always ask for help from other students in the group, so they feel comfortable taking risks and trying challenging problems. Ms. Kushner has taught students to think aloud while solving problems at the board to explain the processes they use to their classmates.

Using the screen recorder tool, Ms. Kushner can save each student's individual problem-solving experience as a multimedia file in his or her digital "process-folio" on the school's cloud-based shared drive. The students can then access these files from tablets or devices anywhere in the school or at home to share with their parents. This allows them to review their problem-solving processes whenever they wish.

Meanwhile, another small group of students works on a project at a collaborative workstation in the middle of the room. The students are designing a podcast about fractions and are discussing the elements that will go into the final product. One student in the group has been assigned the job of group recorder and takes notes on a tablet. Another student uses a mind-mapping app on a tablet to organize the information the group has generated. The other students in the group contribute their ideas and volunteer to complete various tasks.

A third group of students works individually on laptops in the back of the room. Students wear earphones with built-in microphones and use screen capture software to record tutorials on adding, subtracting, multiplying, and dividing fractions. Later, Ms. Kushner will use a rubric to assess the tutorials and upload exemplary products to the class website.

Ms. Kushner uses many different technology tools, some of which are focused on element 4, establishing and maintaining classroom rules and procedures. As demonstrated here, she uses her IWB and set of clickers so that each student can contribute to the classroom rules and procedures. She also uses these tools to have all students generate potential incentives for adherence and consequences for lack of adherence. Students then use clickers to confirm their understanding of the classroom rules and procedures.

Ms. Kushner also uses technology tools and techniques to incorporate element 5—organizing the physical layout of the classroom—into the design of her classroom each year. She asks her students to use SketchUp on their tablets to design their ideal classrooms. Her students work in groups with tablets to generate the first draft representations of their classroom designs and then complete their finished designs on the classroom computers. The students can share their designs with the entire class and use the classroom set of clickers to vote on their favorites. All students know that they contributed to the creation of the classroom design. This sets them up for comfort and success in the learning environment.

Chapter 3: Comprehension Questions

1. Why is it important for students to create digital representations of classroom rules and procedures?

2. Describe how technology can be used to enhance vignettes and role playing.

3. Provide two examples that demonstrate your own intentionality regarding the planning and organization of learning centers in your classroom.

4. How do you use technology to establish and maintain rules and procedures in your classroom? Share your ideas by going to **marzanoresearch.com/classroom strategies**, clicking on the *Enhancing the Art & Science of Teaching With Technology* link, and becoming a member of our virtual learning community.

Chapter 4

INTERACTING WITH NEW KNOWLEDGE

The third design question—How can I use technology to help students effectively interact with new knowledge?—falls under lesson segments addressing content. This chapter emphasizes the identification of critical information needed to master the learning goal. Once that information has been identified, the teacher organizes students into cooperative groups and uses previewing, chunking, processing, elaborating, recording, and reflecting strategies to help them interact with the information. Eight elements are associated with this design question.

Element 6: Identifying critical information

Element 7: Organizing students to interact with new knowledge

Element 8: Previewing new content

Element 9: Chunking content into digestible bites

Element 10: Helping students process new information

Element 11: Helping students elaborate on new information

Element 12: Helping students record and represent knowledge

Element 13: Helping students reflect on their learning

These elements are drawn from an extensive body of literature on introducing new content, including research on presentation formats (Nuthall, 1999), previewing new content (Ausubel, 1968; Mayer, 1989, 2003; West & Fensham, 1976), organizing new knowledge for efficient processing (Linden et al., 2003; Rosenshine, 2002), summarizing new information (Anderson & Hidi, 1988; Hidi & Anderson, 1987), representing new knowledge in various ways (Alvermann & Boothby, 1986; Aubusson, Foswill, Barr, & Perkovic, 1997; Druyan, 1997; Newton, 1995; Sadoski & Paivio, 2001; Welch, 1997), questioning strategies (Pressley et al., 1992; Reder, 1980; Redfield & Rousseau, 1981), and student self-reflection (Cross, 1998). Each of the aforementioned elements can be augmented with the use of educational technology tools.

Element 6: Identifying Critical Information

When introducing new material to students, it is crucial for the teacher to identify and cue students about what information is most critical to their mastery of the learning goal, using strategies such as:

- Identifying critical-input experiences

- Visual activities

- Pause time

Here, we clarify each strategy and focus on a number of educational technology tools that can be used to enrich each.

Identifying Critical-Input Experiences

It is important for the teacher to clearly identify which segments of content are most critical to achieving the learning goal. There should only be two or three critical-input experiences per learning goal, and singling these out provides focus for students and the teacher.

Establish a multisensory routine to alert students that they are about to experience information that is critical to achieving the learning goal. Use IWB software or presentation software to create a slide with images, sound, and text to convey that you are about to introduce a critical segment of the content. For example, you might insert a linked image into a presentation that plays a particular sound (such as the sound of a trumpet or a drumroll) when you click on it. The sound alerts students to the importance of upcoming information.

Students can also use technology tools to rate their level of understanding of critical information using a four-point scale like the one in table 4.1, and you can use these data to guide your instruction.

Table 4.1: Four-Point Scale for Student Self-Assessment

4.0	I understand the simple and complex elements of the new information and can make inferences about how this new information relates to the learning goal.
3.0	I understand the simple and complex elements of the new information.
2.0	I understand the simple elements but need more help to understand the complex elements of the new information.
1.0	I need more help to understand both the simple elements and the complex elements of this new information.

Use the multiple-choice feature in polling technology to create four answer choices, one for each level. Students then send in their self-assessed level using clickers with text input or their mobile devices with polling software.

Visual Activities

Technology can highlight important information for students by providing visual cues that supplement the auditory cues provided by the teacher. IWBs, in particular, offer a variety of visual tools that clearly emphasize the most vital information in a presentation.

Stimulate students' visual and auditory senses to increase student engagement and understanding of important information. Use IWB software or presentation software to embed a visual, video, or nonlinguistic representation of the critical information into a presentation. During a lesson on cell division, for example, display an image of a scanning electron microscope slide to clearly show the different stages of mitosis. Alternatively, search the Internet for a video of bacteria binary fission to compare the rapid rate of the split with other forms of cell division. Have students consider the implications of these disease-causing bacteria on human health.

Use presentation software to provide visual cues that help students identify and focus on important information. Change the color of text using the highlighter or fill tools in your IWB software to draw attention to important information in classroom presentations. For instance, emphasize an important analogy in an excerpt from a work of literature that the students are reading. Be sure to use consistent patterns of color for important text and for the background field of important text to help accentuate important information for students. In a presentation on parts of speech, for instance, change the color of all nouns to blue, verbs to yellow, and adjectives to green. Randomly select students to use the IWB or document camera to annotate a sentence or text passage.

Hide or partially conceal diagrams or pieces of complex text to underscore important chunks of information and help focus students' attention on each chunk. Use the reveal tools in your IWB software to block critical information or portions of critical information from students' view, wait until the whole class is engaged, and then reveal the critical information. For example, during a lesson on Lincoln's presidency, use the reveal tool in your IWB software to display one line of the Gettysburg Address at a time. You can also use this tool as a pacing guide during the lesson to ensure that all students have time to consider and discuss key lines or phrases from the speech.

Hide critical pieces of information in layers beneath a visual prompt, such as an image or symbolic representation of information, to prompt students to make predictions about new knowledge. Then, slowly reveal important information to catch students' attention. During a geometry lesson on congruency, for example, hide the definition of congruent triangles beneath an image of an architectural structure filled with congruent triangles. Ask students to consider the attributes of the triangles in the image and make predictions about the new definition concealed beneath it. Then, remove the image in the top layer to reveal the definition.

Use visuals to help students understand the links between past content and new content and to contextualize new knowledge within a body of previously acquired knowledge. During a lesson on cellular respiration, for instance, use a graphic organizer or flowchart in IWB software to establish connections between the process of photosynthesis (previously acquired knowledge) and cellular respiration (new knowledge).

Pause Time

At key points during an introduction to new content, it can be very helpful for teachers to pause, indicate important points, and give students time to reflect. Technology tools can take these one step further, encouraging students to reiterate what they understand to be the most essential information as part of their reflection.

Give students pause time to reflect on their understanding of new information, connect new information to past knowledge, or generate analogies to deepen comprehension. Use a countdown tool to perform a ten-second countdown before stating critical information. Before introducing Spanish numerals above 100, for instance, use a countdown timer to give students ten seconds to reflect on what they already know about the Spanish words for numerals 1–100.

Element 7: Organizing Students to Interact With New Knowledge

Element 7 encourages teachers to organize students into pairs, triads, or small groups of four to discuss small chunks of content. Group interaction is beneficial because it exposes students to multiple points of reference. Strategies associated with this element include:

- Grouping for active processing

- Job cards

We briefly explain each strategy and describe technology tools that can be used to improve its efficiency and effectiveness.

Grouping for Active Processing

Processing new information in small groups gives students the opportunity to observe the different ways in which their classmates may be processing the same information. A student's exposure to other students' perspectives has the potential to enrich his or her own processing of new information. You can randomly organize students into pairs, triads, or small groups of four or assign groupings based on levels of understanding, heterogeneously mixing students who have a firm grasp on the material with students who do not. Prior to group processing, teachers should explicitly review their expectations for group behavior, such as expecting students to contribute to the discussion, respect other group members, and ask clarifying questions if they don't understand something.

Technology tools can be useful in the assignment of groups and facilitation of group discussion. For instance, organize students into random groups using software such as Team Maker. This method of creating groups is quick and easy for teachers. When organizing students to engage in laboratory work, for instance, enter students' names into Team Maker, establish the number of students that you wish to have in each team, and then let Team Maker randomly distribute the students into lab table groups.

Give students the opportunity to actively process their thinking by taking digital notes during group discussions using Evernote or iPad Notes. Such technology tools can enhance this process by making those notes readily available to the student at any time and through a variety of devices such as laptops, tablets, or students' mobile devices.

Technology also provides ways for groups to collaboratively record notes and contribute to the collective understanding of new information. Students can use tablets, laptops, or mobile devices to log in to word- or image-based collaboration tools while collectively processing new information. For example, students can use Pinterest to repin screenshots of digital notes captured during a group discussion or use Google Drive to revise and edit the notes. To illustrate the nature and direction of their group's thinking and conversation, students can even capture nonlinguistic or diagrammatic representations of the group's ideas. They can create diagrams or flowcharts using IWB software on laptops or drawing and flowchart apps (such as Mindjet) on tablets.

The process of questioning also helps deepen students' understanding of the important facets of new content. For instance, students can work in groups to craft a variety of simple and complex questions and then pose the questions to other groups. Other groups then respond using clickers with text input or mobile devices with polling software. For example, students who are processing their understanding of Zora Neale Hurston's novel *Their Eyes Were Watching God* could generate contextual questions about racial hostility in the early 1900s and share them with the class. Alternatively, you can post students' questions on the class website to prompt an extended group discussion. Providing time to consider and respond to questions can allow students to be more reflective and careful in their answers.

Job Cards

Distributing note cards to groups that designate jobs or roles for each member serves the dual purpose of guiding student groups in a particular direction and equalizing participation among the students in a group. Technology can improve this strategy by eliminating prep time for the teacher and increasing the randomization of job distribution.

Select students for jobs within each group—such as *recorder*, *summarizer*, and *questioner*—using random number or name generators. For example, give the role of recorder to the first student assigned to each group, the role of summarizer to the second student, the role of questioner to the third student, and so on.

Element 8: Previewing New Content

Previewing refers to any activity that initiates student thinking about the information students will encounter in class. This practice is beneficial even for students who do not have any background knowledge on the topic, because at the very least, they will be able to activate related knowledge, which will allow them to formulate crucial links between new and previously acquired content. Strategies associated with this element include:

- Preview questions

- Skimming

- K-W-L strategy (Ogle, 1986)

- Advance organizers

- Anticipation guides

- Word splash activity

Here, we briefly explain the strategies and illustrate how teachers can use technology tools to improve each.

Preview Questions

Preview questions highlight critical information to come and guide students in knowing what information they should be listening for. The teacher asks questions and shares information to catch the attention of the class and activate background knowledge students may have about new content.

Leverage technology tools to create and administer question sets or concept inventories to preview new knowledge for students. Create concept inventories using online survey tools (such as SurveyMonkey), and conduct these surveys with students before lessons in order to preview new academic content and stimulate background knowledge. During the course of the lesson, refer back to the concept inventory as the students process new information.

Polling technology is a great tool for drawing out students' understanding or misconceptions while previewing new content. Pose questions about new content to students prior to the lesson, and ask them to respond using clickers with text input or mobile devices with polling software. Display the results of the poll, but refrain from displaying the correct answer. Instead, use student answers to stimulate meaningful classroom discussions about the new content, and allow students to realize whether their answers were correct as the lesson progresses. Prior to a lesson on DNA replication, for instance, refrain from revealing correct answers to preview questions until the lesson is underway to help students anticipate potential causes of genetic mutation.

Use digitized primary-source documents to activate background knowledge and help students generate links between past knowledge, related knowledge, and new content. For instance, search for primary-source documents (audio, images, video, and text) on websites for the Smithsonian Institution, the National Archives, the Library of Congress, or PBS. When previewing a lesson on the Vietnam War, you could have students view video footage of protests at Kent State University and listen to archived audio recordings of speeches by Richard Nixon and Lyndon B. Johnson. Use these resources to prompt a discussion on nonviolent protest and the culture of the United States during periods of war.

Digital videos are also engaging resources for previewing new content and activating students' prior knowledge. For example, when previewing an ELA lesson about the distinction between satire and parody, show students video clips from *The Daily Show With Jon Stewart*, a television show with elements of satire, and *The Colbert Report*, which is primarily a parody (teachers should, of course, prescreen any video that will be used in class to ensure it is appropriate). Students then compare and contrast the clips and discuss the similarities and differences as a class.

Skimming

When modeling skimming, the teacher walks students through the process of glancing at headings, subheadings, and images to make inferences about the meaning of a text before reading. After skimming a passage, students can try to summarize the main ideas in the section, make predictions about what they might learn from reading the passage, or compose questions about the content.

Demonstrate skimming techniques using presentation software (such as Prezi or Google Drive) or IWB software to introduce new content. As you skim through the presentation, stop to point out major headings and subheadings, explaining how those major topics relate to the learning goal. When previewing a lesson on Newtonian laws, for example, design a presentation using Prezi that visibly links the major headings in the lesson together. Use this as a visual prompt to skim each heading and stimulate student discussion prior to the lesson.

K-W-L Strategy

Before and after presenting new content, teachers can guide the class through the K-W-L (Know, Want to Know, Learned) process using a chart divided into three columns (Ogle, 1986). First, the class brainstorms information it already knows about the topic. The teacher records this information in the *K* column of the chart. Second, students brainstorm information they want to find out about the topic during the lesson. The teacher records this information under *W* in the chart. At this point, the lesson begins, and the teacher presents the new content. At the end of the lesson, the class generates a list of information it learned throughout the lesson. The teacher records this information under the *L* in the chart. Students can create their own individual K-W-L charts on notebook paper or handouts once the class has become familiar with the K-W-L structure.

Use technology to create interactive, multisensory versions of the K-W-L elements. Students can use IWB software on laptop computers to add textual elements and nonlinguistic representations of K-W-L elements. They can also use hyperlinks to augment the K-W-L chart with supporting information and visual representations of connections between past content and new content. Finally, students can suggest elements for the K-W-L chart using clickers with text input or mobile devices with polling software.

Advance Organizers

In this strategy, the teacher distributes a blank graphic organizer that students fill in during the introduction of new content. This allows students to visualize the structure, organization, and flow of information, which makes the content more digestible. Advance organizers also help students make connections between new content and content they have previously learned in class.

Create a graphic organizer that previews new content, its connections, and its sequence using online presentation software (such as Prezi or Google Drive). Modify and archive the interactive visual elements of the presentation for students to retrieve later. Embed visual, textual, or auditory elements into the presentation to meet the needs of different learning styles. Leave space for students to contribute their own explanations of the new content, its connections, and its sequence. When previewing a lesson on the water cycle, for example, show a video clip that outlines the process. Distribute an advance organizer to students and have them label the parts of the process as the video plays, as well as contribute their own textual descriptions and visual elements to organize their thoughts about the water cycle.

Anticipation Guides

To pique students' interest and activate background knowledge, the teacher can create a series of statements and have students respond to them. Depending on the level of complex thought that the teacher wants to elicit, student responses can be as simple as *I agree* or *I disagree* with a given statement (use *true* or *false* for facts) or take the form of more open-ended constructs, such as a paragraph explaining the student's views on the U.S. criminal justice system. After giving students time to work through their anticipation guides, the teacher leads them in a whole-class discussion about their responses. In addition to provoking student curiosity and activating prior knowledge, the discussion exposes students to a variety of perspectives, opinions, and controversies about the topic.

To incorporate technology, pose anticipation guide questions to students at the beginning of the lesson, and ask them to respond using clickers with text input or mobile devices with polling software. Use the results of the polling to activate prior knowledge, make students' thinking visible, and generate group discussion about the content. Save the data generated, and refer to the polling results from the anticipation guides throughout the lesson.

Additionally, technology can be used to randomly select students to respond to anticipation guide questions, have students share their thinking, or get students to comment on a peer's response. For instance, use a random name generator to choose students to defend their answers on the anticipation guide or comment on other students' answers.

Word Splash Activity

To help students preview upcoming vocabulary concepts, the teacher can create a list of key words and phrases from the new content, present the list to students, and ask them to classify the terms into logical categories. After giving students time to categorize the terms, the teacher leads a whole-class discussion about the strategies students used to sort the terms, how the terms relate to one another, and what students already know about the topic.

Use technology to create visual representations of key vocabulary in a passage. Online tools like Wordle allow users to create a word cloud that represents the frequency of words used in a single text or passage. Use this visual prompt to stimulate class discussion about the new content. Simply select and copy the new content text from a digital source, and paste the copied text into the word-cloud generator on the Wordle website. Select Create, and use the image to begin a discussion on the nature and frequency of the terms used in the passage.

Element 9: Chunking Content Into Digestible Bites

Chunking content into digestible bites involves presenting content in small segments that are tailored to students' level of understanding. The work of Barak Rosenshine (2002), who calls this strategy "teaching in small steps" (p. 182), supports the importance of chunking, an assertion that has also been reinforced by others (Good & Brophy, 2003; Mayer, 2003). Strategies associated with this element include:

- Presenting content in small chunks

- Using preassessment data to vary the size of each chunk

We elaborate on each of these strategies and suggest methods for using it in concert with technology.

Presenting Content in Small Chunks

To help students absorb and digest new information, teachers can divide the content into small segments of information, or chunks, when presenting it to students. For declarative knowledge, chunks contain concepts and details that logically fit together. For procedural knowledge, chunks contain a series of consecutive steps in a process.

Digital presentation tools can enhance the process of chunking by incorporating multisensory media into related segments of information. Use presentation software (such as Prezi or Google Drive) or IWB software to create interactive graphic organizers that highlight small chunks of information. For example, when presenting a second-grade lesson on interdependence in an ecosystem, which can be a very complex topic for young students, use Prezi to segment the lesson into a series of smaller lessons: explain what plants and animals need to survive, provide examples of organisms that rely on others to survive in a given area, and describe a situation in which one type of plant or animal dies out. Represent each chunk with unique images, sounds, or animations. Provide students with ample time to consider or reflect on each segment and how it relates to the learning goal.

Technology tools allow students to process new chunks of information using multiple senses. For instance, use the interactive math tools in your IWB software (such as the ruler, protractor, or compass) to give students a hands-on feel for processing new information about angles and measurement. During a lesson on geometric reflections and transformations, students can use interactive math tools to manipulate increasingly complex digital shapes and explore these new concepts piece by piece.

Include digital representations of new content in lessons to help students explore the various attributes of the information. Use visual prompts such as drawings, diagrams, or photographs to help students identify similarities and differences between past knowledge and chunks of new information. When presenting new information about the carbon cycle, for instance, use images, diagrams, or pictures to represent the segments of the water cycle, and ask students to consider the similarities and differences between these two processes.

Preview multimedia representations of information from different chunks prior to the start of a lesson. Have students view preselected video tutorials focusing on new content knowledge. Alternatively, have students use tablets or laptops to search the Internet for video tutorials or relevant websites. For example, before a lesson on critically reading and annotating a text, provide links to premade video demonstrations of this process, or have students search for relevant videos on the topic.

Classify chunks of information to help students interact with new procedural knowledge. Students use clickers with text input or mobile devices with polling software to sort small chunks of information into containers in IWB software. For example, to help students explore the process of metamorphosis, create a series of containers in your IWB software, and display several out-of-order images of the various stages. Have students work individually or in groups to reorder the images and place them into containers that represent the correct life sequence for each organism.

Using Preassessment Data to Vary the Size of Each Chunk

To adjust instruction based on students' scores on a preassessment, the teacher can vary the size of each chunk of content. If most of the class attained high scores on the preassessment, the students can probably handle larger chunks of information. If the class demonstrated misconceptions or little prior knowledge about a concept on the preassessment, students will need information to be presented in smaller chunks accompanied by clarification of misconceptions.

Use polling technology to efficiently preassess student understanding of new knowledge. Polling technology can also help determine the best size for each learning chunk. To minimize scoring time, administer an electronic preassessment, or ask students to respond to preassessment questions using clickers or polling software on their mobile devices. Use the scores to determine the extent to which the content must be chunked to make it more manageable for students.

Element 10: Helping Students Process New Information

Even small chunks of information require active processing from students. Element 10 focuses on how teachers can stimulate that kind of processing by asking students to summarize and clarify their understanding of the content each time a new chunk has been presented. The benefits of group processing, in particular, are supported by research on collaborative interaction and knowledge development (Lou et al., 1996; McVee, Dunsmore, & Gavelek, 2005; O'Donnell et al., 1990). The strategy associated with this element is:

- Collaborative processing

Here, we explain collaborative processing and describe ways to enhance it with technology.

Collaborative Processing

To help students understand chunks of information, the teacher can ask them to work collaboratively in small groups of three. After presenting each chunk of information, group members summarize the chunk, the teacher takes questions about areas of confusion, and students make predictions about the content of the next chunk. To illustrate, the teacher presents the first chunk of information. Member A summarizes it, members B and C add to what A has said, and all three group members point out the pieces of the chunk that still confuse them. Next, the teacher responds to questions from the whole class and uses them to clarify the information contained within the first chunk. The teacher then prompts the students to make a prediction about the material in the next chunk. After presenting the second chunk of information, the process repeats. The only difference is that, this time, member B summarizes the material, and members A and C add to it. After the teacher presents the third chunk, member C summarizes, and members A and B add to it.

One way that polling technology can enhance collaborative processing is by increasing the number of students who can respond to questions and by making those responses visible. Have students work in groups to respond to questions prior to the lesson and submit their answers using clickers with text input or mobile devices with polling software. Students then use the polling data to summarize each chunk; add to, amend, or modify their understanding of each chunk; and generate predictions about the next chunk in the learning sequence.

Students can also summarize their understanding of each chunk by capturing and narrating screencasts. These multimedia files can then be tagged, archived, and shared to enrich the active processing of other students. Students can use screencasting software such as Jing on computers or ScreenChomp, Educreations, or TouchCast on tablets. Students can also use notes or diagrams in their recordings.

Have students review and analyze their peers' screencasts using a rubric, scoring guide, or scale to take note of new perspectives, opinions, background knowledge, and problem-solving strategies. They can provide feedback using clickers with text input or mobile devices with polling software. Encourage students to share constructive comments to foster a sense of contribution in the classroom.

Publish student-created screencast tutorials online to motivate students to produce high-quality work. Share these screencasts via online publishing and hosting software or on the class website. Use ClustrMaps to track access to the tutorials.

Element 11: Helping Students Elaborate on New Information

Element 11, helping students elaborate on new information, involves the teacher asking questions that require students to make and defend inferences about the content. Redfield and Rousseau (1981) stressed the importance of questions that require students to use higher-order cognition skills, such as those that prompt students to elaborate or make inferences. Strategies associated with element 11 include:

- General inferential questions
- Elaborative interrogation

We briefly explain each strategy and give examples of ways in which it can be modified with technology.

General Inferential Questions

General inferential questions are designed to elicit inferences about the content from students. Teachers can use two types of these: (1) default questions and (2) reasoned inference questions. A *default question* requires a student to draw upon, or default to, his or her background knowledge to find the answer. A *reasoned inference question* asks a student to use his or her reasoning to draw conclusions or make predictions about information based on evidence found in the information presented by the teacher.

Polling technology enables teachers to ask general inferential questions of an entire classroom of students and display the answers. Students use clickers with text input or mobile devices with polling software to make and submit inferences. View the results of the polling data as a class to stimulate group discussion on the attributes of the responses. Use a random name generator to call on students to explain their answers and reasoning.

Ask an unusual or intriguing question to prompt students to make inferences. For instance, use a document camera to magnify a content-related object to the point of unrecognizability. Use this visual prompt to pose two questions to your students: (1) What does this object look like? and (2) What do you think this object is? For example, magnify the pistil or stamen of a flower. Students then use polling technology to respond to inferential questions about the object or make predictions about the nature of the object. Next, students share the reasoning behind their answers based on previously learned information.

Elaborative Interrogation

Elaborative interrogation has been found to help students comprehend new knowledge (Fishbein, Eckart, Lauver, Van Leeuwen, & Langmeyer, 1990; Ozgungor & Guthrie, 2004). After a student answers a question, the teacher probes for clarification to get a more accurate picture of the student's understanding. Questions might ask students to provide evidence to support their assertions (for example, How do you know that is true? or Why do you think that?); to classify and sort people, places, and events into categories (for example, What are some traits you might expect from a _____?); or to understand cause and effect (for example, What do you think would happen if _____?).

Technology can enhance group elaborative interrogation by enabling students to capture, archive, and retrieve multimedia representations of evidence for their ideas. Students work in groups to respond to questions or capture interesting ideas using screen capture software such as Jing on computers or ScreenChomp, Educreations, or TouchCast on tablets. Finally, students review the screencasts of other groups to gain insight into alternative types of evidence.

Also, students can create multimedia representations of historical events using primary sources from the Smithsonian, the National Archives, or the Library of Congress. Students can use such sources to gather supporting evidence for assertions as well. Alternately, students use presentation software, IWB software, or screen capture software to generate narrative movie clips—in the style of a documentary—using still images, photographs, and primary-source documents from historical events. For example, students can use images from the Smithsonian online database to generate claims about historical people, places, or events and then find evidence for their claims from other primary-source documents. Students can also use online collaborative documentation tools like Google Drive to generate and store the scripts for their narrative movies.

Students can distribute their recorded screencasts or narrative movies using online publishing and hosting software such as blogs, wikis, or websites. ClustrMaps can help you track global access to students' screencasts or narrative movies. Encourage viewers to post comments or offer suggestions for further explorations or elaborative interrogations.

Element 12: Helping Students Record and Represent Knowledge

Helping students record and represent new content knowledge involves the teacher asking students to summarize, take notes, or use nonlinguistic representations. Such techniques give students practice in differentiating between critically important information and supplemental information. Strategies associated with element 12 include:

- Informal outlines

- Academic notebooks

- Dramatic enactments

Here, we explain each strategy and provide a number of technology tools that can enhance each.

Informal Outlines

In this strategy, students use indentation, numbering, bullets, or Roman numerals to organize information and display its relative importance. The main ideas are further to the left of the paper, with details listed beneath them. The following technology tools still require students to organize content but in a variety of creative ways not limited to a pencil-and-paper outline.

Students can use technology to record informal outlines in various ways. For instance, use audio recording software (such as Audacity) to capture oral student outlines. Students may also use speech-to-text apps to convert their oral outlines into text outlines. While planning a persuasive essay, for example, students can use Dragon Dictation to record ideas. The app instantly converts audio into text. Next, students can modify or add to their informal outlines.

Online word processing software such as Google Drive and note-taking apps like Evernote allow students to organize and record new knowledge in informal outlines. Alternatively, students can use mind-mapping apps like Mindjet to create diagrams connecting main ideas with supporting details. Because these informal outlines and diagrams are cloud based, students can access them on any device that has access to the Internet. Students then modify or elaborate on these informal outlines, saving multiple versions to record the progression of their learning.

Online publishing technology offers students the ability to collaborate on informal outlines. For example, groups of students might use Wikispaces to create and post informal outlines detailing main headings and supporting details about the causes of the women's suffrage movement in the United States. Students publish on classmates' wikis and create hyperlinks to form a network of student work. Because these wikis are cloud based, students can access and amend them using a variety of devices from any location.

Academic Notebooks

An academic notebook is an accumulation of notes, reactions, questions, and self-reflections that students update throughout the unit, term, or school year. As with informal outlines, academic notebooks are commonly thought of as hard-copy paper notebooks. However, updating, revising, and reflecting on content in an academic notebook can be made more efficient with technology.

Technology affords students the ability to record their notes, reactions, and questions in a variety of media formats. Digital notebooks can be easily recorded, archived, and retrieved from various devices. They can also allow students to represent their thoughts in ways that stimulate multiple senses. For example, students use audio recording software such as Audacity, text-to-speech apps such as Dragon Dictation, or video recording software on tablets, laptops, or smartphones to archive new knowledge in audio journals or video logs.

Dramatic Enactments

For this strategy, students act out scenes, events, processes, or concepts by role-playing characters or using movement to create gestures for different terms, such as *photosynthesis* or *fairy tale*. Technology allows these enactments to be revised and edited before being displayed to the class and to be stored in students' digital portfolios for parents to see. While dramatic enactments can be highly engaging for students, they can be superficial if handled incorrectly. Teachers must budget time in class for students to explain the explicit connections between their enactments and the content they represent.

Students use digital video tools (such as tablets or smartphones) to record, edit, and share dramatic representations of new content knowledge. Students might represent the greenhouse effect, for example, in the form of a choreographed dance that depicts the absorption and release of thermal radiation from a planetary surface. They first record the staged enactments using their smartphones and then play the videos via projector for the entire class.

Element 13: Helping Students Reflect on Their Learning

The final element in this design question involves reflecting on learning. Just as reflection is critical for teachers in developing their professional skills, reflection is also important to master a learning goal. Element 13 involves students reflecting on what they understand about new content or what they are still confused about. Strategies associated with this element include:

- Reflective journals

- Knowledge comparison

We elaborate on these strategies and detail technology tools that can be used to improve the effectiveness of each.

Reflective Journals

As previously mentioned, students continually refer to and revise academic notebooks throughout the unit, term, or school year. A portion of these notebooks is devoted to content-related reflection, in which students respond to questions such as:

- What predictions did you make about today's lesson? Which ones were correct? Which ones were incorrect?

- What parts of the lesson were easy for you to understand? What parts do you still have questions about?

- How does today's lesson relate to yesterday's lesson?

- What did you do well today? What could you improve on for tomorrow?

For example, rather than have students respond to every single question after each critical-input experience in element 6, we recommend that teachers select one question per critical-input experience to pose to students. Reflective journals are not intended to be complete, finished products; instead, they are living documents that give students the freedom to change, revise, and restructure their understanding. As such, reflective journals are well-suited to digital document formats.

As with academic notebooks, students use cloud-based software to create online reflective journals that can be accessed from a variety of devices at any location. Generate cloud-based online reflection templates on Google Drive for students to use before and after a lesson. For example, students create a reflective journal for each of their academic subjects by opening and saving a different Google Drive document for each content area. Students then regularly access and add to their journals via desktop computer, laptop, tablet, or smartphone.

Students can also use audio recording software (such as Audacity) or speech-to-text apps (such as Dragon Dictation) to record auditory reflective journals. Provide time at strategic points during the lesson to allow students to add entries to their journals using headphones with built-in microphones. Students can then access their stored journal entries to revise or restructure their understanding of new content knowledge.

Multimedia authoring tools enable students to capture learning reflections that incorporate different forms of media. Students use IWB software, presentation software (such as Prezi), or content-sharing sites (such as Pinterest) to create journals that incorporate text, images, sound, video, and hyperlinks. For example, students search the Internet for content-related media and then use different pinboards on Pinterest to create interactive reflection scrapbooks for each learning goal. Give students time at strategic points in the lesson to add or revise entries in their Pinterest scrapbooks.

Finally, blogs and wikis can enable students to collaborate on one collective journal per small group. For example, students can work in groups to respond to reflection prompt questions, such as, How does today's lesson relate to yesterday's lesson? Blogs and wikis allow students to pool their collective understanding, engage in cooperative reflection, and easily record ideas to share with the whole class.

Knowledge Comparison

Knowledge comparison involves students relating their current mastery of a learning goal to previous levels of mastery of that same learning goal. This comparison can include levels of knowledge on a topic or levels of competence with a procedure. Graphic organizers such as charts, graphs, tables, diagrams, and flowcharts work well for this strategy. A variety of software options are available for this purpose.

Students can use technology to compare representations of previously held and currently held conceptions about content. For instance, students use IWB software or online presentation software such as Prezi to diagram the connections between past learning and new learning. Online word processing or spreadsheet software such as Google Drive allows students to record reflections before and after learning new content. Students may also benefit from scaffolds to guide their comparisons. Create online templates that prompt students to show their knowledge through charts, tables, graphs, diagrams, or flowcharts.

Teaching With Technology

This chapter outlined strategies teachers can use to enhance students' interactions with new knowledge, including identifying critical information, previewing new content, chunking content into digestible bites, and reflecting on learning. The following vignette portrays a teacher using technology tools to supplement these strategies and others.

Mrs. Lederman teaches biology to tenth-grade students at a large high school in the Midwest. She is about to begin a lesson within a unit of study on natural selection. She knows from prior experience that understanding how species adapt and change over time is a cognitively challenging concept for many students. She has devised a variety of ways to use technology to help her students more effectively interact with this complex new knowledge.

Prior to class, Mrs. Lederman posted the learning goal and proficiency scale for the lesson on her class Edmodo page. She asked all of her students to write a comment beneath the post acknowledging that they read and understood the learning goal and the proficiency scale's evidence examples. Students know that they can also post questions they have about the learning goal and scale and that Mrs. Lederman, or one of their other classmates, will respond.

Mrs. Lederman knows that one of the first things she must do is draw out her students' various misconceptions about natural selection before starting the lesson. While teaching the unit over the past several years, she kept track of common misconceptions that students had about natural selection. Using these data as a framework, she devised a preassessment that she administers to her students prior to the start of the lesson on adaptation. This preassessment contains a series of questions she has designed to identify students' level of conceptual understanding about this key biological concept.

Mrs. Lederman administers the preassessment by providing a link to an online survey directly under her posting of the learning goal and proficiency scale on her class Edmodo page. Her students log into the online survey using their student ID numbers, which allows Mrs. Lederman to track their individual responses. By analyzing the results of the preassessment, she can discern which students struggle with the concept of adaptation and which specific tenets of natural selection were most challenging. Some of the questions ask students to consider how giraffes got such long necks. Others address the wing coloration variety of peppered moths, while still others address the occurrence of some of nature's oddities, such as the duck-billed platypus. The questions aren't designed to trick students but to draw out their current notions about biological adaptation.

A second post on Mrs. Lederman's Edmodo page asks students to share the strangest organisms they've ever seen and to consider how the unique traits of these organisms help or hinder their fitness for the habitat in which they live. Her students have always enjoyed this particular prelesson exercise and the exchange of friendly comments. As a result of these previewing efforts, Mrs. Lederman's students have already spent time thinking about the concept of natural selection before she formally introduces the concept in class.

In the classroom, Mrs. Lederman's laptop is connected to a projector in the front of the room. A row of computers lines the back of her classroom. She also has a cart with six tablets charging for her students to use in their groups. Numerous jars containing preserved animals are arranged in cabinets on one side of the classroom and an outdoor greenhouse abuts the windows on the other side.

She begins the lesson by using a random group generator on her laptop to organize students into six teams, as well as to assign roles within those teams. Using a countdown timer on her computer, Mrs. Lederman gives the students thirty seconds to rearrange themselves into their teams and take out their notebooks and devices to begin the lesson.

When the countdown timer reaches thirty seconds, students hear the sound of a duck quacking. Mrs. Lederman's students know that the sound of the quacking duck means that it's time to pay particular attention to new critical information. Mrs. Lederman begins a multimedia presentation on adaptation that she developed using Prezi. Her presentation incorporates numerous images, video clips, text, and sounds to introduce students to new knowledge and facilitate their interaction with that new knowledge.

The presentation is segmented into three key chunks of critical information. Mrs. Lederman has determined the size of each information chunk from her analysis of students' performance on the preassessment and from her previous experiences introducing the material. Mrs. Lederman presents each information chunk in a logical sequence so that the content builds in complexity. In other words, she knows that helping her students gain an understanding of the first chunk will in turn help them better understand the second chunk, and so on.

At the end of each presentation chunk, Mrs. Lederman asks her students a series of questions that reflect the conceptual questions in her adaptation preassessment. She uses polling software to have students respond to multiple-choice questions using their smartphones. Nearly all of her students have a cell phone that can send text messages. To equitably serve the students who do not, Mrs. Lederman has a set of previously owned smartphones (inexpensively purchased by her school from the community's local mobile provider). These devices are available to any student who needs them during the school year. Although the smartphones are not connected to a cellular phone network, they enable students to send messages over the school's wireless network.

In addition to collecting students' individual responses, Mrs. Lederman allows her students to discuss conceptual questions in their groups. When all of the students have responded to a question, she displays the poll results so every student can see how the class voted, but she doesn't show the correct answer yet. Mrs. Lederman uses a random number generator on her laptop to select students to describe the thinking that led to their answer, consider how a student might have come up with a different answer, or predict how that same person might respond to a different question addressing the same concept. By using polling results as prompts for individual and collective thinking, Mrs. Lederman helps her students understand how other members of the class responded to each question. This perspective informs students' own thinking about the concepts.

Upon completion of this exercise, Mrs. Lederman asks her students to continue their discussions and vote a second time. Once all of her students have voted twice, she shows them the correct answer to the question. She continuously refines and tests sequences of questions and follow-up questions to determine how well they guide student thinking toward an accurate representation of adaptation. She has found that this process helps clarify student misconceptions and elicits a clearer understanding of complex ideas.

Mrs. Lederman has become adept at using her students' own devices to help draw out their collective thinking. She displays the artifacts of their thinking using her computer and projector because the entire class benefits from each student's experiences and insights. She can also archive all of the student formative assessment data from her polling questions. She can retrieve the data at any point to analyze students' learning patterns and the changes in these patterns over the course of the lesson or unit of study.

At the end of her presentation on natural selection, Mrs. Lederman asks students to begin brainstorming in their groups and outline multimedia projects that will help them elaborate on and represent their new understanding of natural selection. For the project, each group selects an organism from the adaptation preassessment list and elaborates on how environmental or habitat changes might have contributed to its evolution.

The students use mind-mapping and note-taking apps on their tablets to organize their thinking and capture the collective ideas they generate about the project they will develop. Mrs. Lederman provides her students with online resources from the Linnaean Society of New York, the Smithsonian's National Museum of Natural History, the Natural History Museum in London, and the American Museum of Natural History. She encourages students to research other online resources that might be helpful.

Mrs. Lederman also shares links to interesting online articles, videos, animations, and simulations that she and previous students have discovered. She keeps a compendium of these sites and encourages students to explore them at their own pace. These online resources provide representations about how various species have actually changed over time. In addition, Mrs. Lederman asks her students to post comments on the class Edmodo page to discuss the resources found and to comment on the quality of each.

Mrs. Lederman's students have a range of technology tools they can use to create their projects. The students in one group have decided to create a blog that represents how their organism might have changed over time. Another group designs an interactive timeline in presentation software to represent a species' evolution, while still another uses screen capture software to record its representations of natural selection in action. Mrs. Lederman will share each of the products the groups produce on the class website and use ClustrMaps to track the number of hits each page receives.

All of Mrs. Lederman's students keep online reflective journals to record their reflections about what they've learned—new thoughts, ideas, diagrams, or other representations of their knowledge. Students use auditory dictation apps, note-taking tools, and flowchart apps to capture their reflections about their learning. Because their journals are cloud based, students can access them using tablets, smartphones, laptops, or the classroom computers.

As seen here, Mrs. Lederman uses several technology tools to enhance a variety of instructional strategies. For element 6, identifying critical information, she uses a consistent auditory prompt to establish that she is about to share critical new information with students. She then shares that new critical information using a multimedia presentation to engage students' senses as they are introduced to new knowledge.

Mrs. Lederman also uses technology tools and techniques to support element 7, organizing students to interact with new knowledge. As seen in the vignette, she uses a random group generator to divide students into work groups. She also uses a digital countdown timer to prompt students to quickly arrange themselves into new groups.

She effectively uses technology to enhance element 8, previewing new content, as well. Specifically, she administers a preassessment about adaptation in which her students relate their background experience or prior knowledge about the new content. She posts a request on her class Edmodo page asking students to reflect on and discuss the most unusual organism they have ever seen.

In order to enhance element 9, chunking content into digestible bites, Mrs. Lederman represents new content with a multimedia presentation. In order to determine the most appropriate size of each chunk of information, she analyzes the results of the adaptation preassessment.

Mrs. Lederman incorporates students' smartphones to enhance element 10, helping students process new information. After she presents each chunk of information, Mrs. Lederman uses a polling website to display the preassessment questions that correspond with each chunk. Students use their smartphones to respond to the questions a second time.

Mrs. Lederman also uses polling technology to enhance element 11, helping students elaborate on new information. As shown in the vignette, Mrs. Lederman displays the class polling results but conceals the correct answers. Rather, she uses a random name generator to call on students to defend their answers, describe the background knowledge that led to their answers, or infer how another student might have arrived at a different answer. She then allows the students to discuss these ideas and use their smartphones to respond to the question a second time. Finally, Mrs. Lederman shows the correct answer.

Mrs. Lederman also uses a variety of technology to enhance element 12, helping students record and represent knowledge. In particular, Mrs. Lederman's students use note-taking apps and mind-mapping apps on their tablets to capture their initial outlines for their presentations. She shares a list of online resources to support her students' project work. Finally, Mrs. Lederman's students use various technology tools including blogs, wikis, and presentation software to create their final projects.

Finally, Mrs. Lederman uses technology effectively to enhance element 13, helping students reflect on their learning. As shown, Mrs. Lederman's students record reflections about what they have learned in online journals. Her students use auditory dictation apps, note-taking tools, and flowchart apps to capture their reflections in a variety of ways.

Chapter 4: Comprehension Questions

1. Why might a teacher use IWB software to play a loud sound (such as a drumroll or a trumpet blast) in the middle of a lesson?

2. How can technology enhance the collection and use of preassessment data to determine the size of different learning chunks?

3. Describe technology tools that can be used to support each type of general inferential question.

4. How do you use technology to help students effectively interact with new knowledge in your classroom? Share your ideas by going to **marzanoresearch.com /classroomstrategies**, clicking on the *Enhancing the Art & Science of Teaching With Technology* link, and becoming a member of our virtual learning community.

Chapter 5

PRACTICING AND DEEPENING KNOWLEDGE

In order for students to use new knowledge on their own, they must practice and deepen their understanding of the content after it has been introduced. This design question—How can I use technology to help students practice and deepen their understanding of new knowledge?—falls under lesson segments addressing content and includes seven elements.

Element 14: Reviewing content

Element 15: Organizing students to practice and deepen knowledge

Element 16: Using homework

Element 17: Helping students examine similarities and differences

Element 18: Helping students examine errors in reasoning

Element 19: Helping students practice skills, strategies, and processes

Element 20: Helping students revise knowledge

When considering this design question, it is important to remember that there are two types of knowledge—procedural and declarative. As discussed previously, *procedural knowledge* includes skills, strategies, and processes that students must be able to perform. The skills, strategies, and processes associated with procedural knowledge must be practiced in order for students to perform them with speed and accuracy. *Declarative knowledge*, on the other hand, includes the content-related details, facts, and principles that students must understand. Rather than be practiced, declarative knowledge is deepened or expanded as students gain a better understanding of the content. The elements and corresponding technology strategies outlined in this chapter have been developed from research on practice (Kumar, 1991; Ross, 1998), revising and analyzing errors (Halpern, 1984; Hillocks, 1986; Rovee-Collier, 1995), examining similarities and differences (Halpern, Hansen, & Reifer, 1990; McDaniel & Donnelly, 1996), and homework (Cooper, Robinson, & Patall, 2006). The specific strategies and behaviors associated with each element, as well as the ways in which the elements can be enhanced with technology, are provided here.

Element 14: Reviewing Content

In order for students to gain a comprehensive understanding of new content, they must have a firm grasp on previous content from which to draw connections. To review content, the teacher briefly reiterates related information from an earlier learning goal or unit. Specific strategies associated with element 14 include:

- Cloze activities

- Summaries

- Demonstration

- Questioning

Each of these strategies can be adapted for use in the technology-enhanced classroom.

Cloze Activities

In a cloze activity, the teacher presents previously acquired content knowledge to students with specific words, phrases, or pieces missing. The teacher then asks students to complete the cloze by filling in the missing information.

Create interactive cloze activities that incorporate images and sentence stems using IWB software or online presentation software such as Prezi. Have students submit responses to complete the cloze using clickers with text input or mobile devices with polling software.

Summaries

To review previously learned content, the class can briefly discuss what information it remembers or found important using short summaries. Teachers can either create summaries for students to review or ask students to prepare their own summaries. The latter option requires teaching students how to create succinct, personalized records of the information they have learned from a new lesson. Summarizing is a complex skill and should be practiced frequently.

Technology can enhance how students summarize new knowledge by providing multiple ways for students to record and organize information. Give students multiple options for capturing summaries, including audio recording software like Audacity or speech-to-text apps such as Dragon Dictation.

Technology can also help students visualize the connections between prior knowledge and new knowledge. Use a timeline tool in IWB software or create a timeline template using online word processing software such as Google Drive. Display the learning goals from previous and upcoming units.

Demonstration

In a demonstration, the teacher engages students in a brief review by having them complete a task that requires previously acquired knowledge or a previously learned procedure to finish.

Students can use digital video recording software on tablets or smartphones to demonstrate their understanding of previously taught content. For instance, a group of students might collaborate to script a content review in the format of an evening newscast. Students then organize their tasks so that one student serves as the cameraperson, another as the sound technician, and the rest as newscasters.

The class can also use screen capture software (such as Jing, ScreenChomp, Educreations, or TouchCast) to create narrated tutorials of previously taught content. Students can demonstrate their understanding of a new mathematical process, such as prime number factoring, by teaching the process to other students, and they can even narrate their tutorials with explanations, analogies, and metaphors. Post your students' tutorials on a class website, and use ClustrMaps to track access to student tutorials.

Questioning

During questioning, the teacher asks specific types of questions that oblige students to remember, identify, or apply content from a previous class period. Teachers can also ask students to use prior knowledge from earlier lessons to make inferences about the new content.

Student response systems enhance questioning by enabling students to answer content review questions anonymously and at their own pace. Certain types of SRSs also record the amount of time it takes for students to answer each question. Analyze the SRS information to determine the types of questions students struggle with most. Use these data to provide students with targeted guidance, support, or additional resources.

Students can also self-assess their understanding of new knowledge. This provides useful data about students' perceptions of their understanding. While reviewing new content, students rate their understanding of content on a four-point scale (like the one on page 48) using clickers with text input or mobile devices with polling software.

Create online flashcards using websites like Quizlet to prompt students' practice of new knowledge or skills, or allow students to create their own flashcards. Students work in groups to consider important content and then generate review questions in Quizlet for the benefit of the class.

Students can deepen their understanding and fluency of new knowledge and skills by creating content-related questions. Use IWB or presentation software such as Prezi to cache the content review questions. Students might also post their review questions on the class website.

Element 15: Organizing Students to Practice and Deepen Knowledge

Element 15 involves the teacher organizing students into groups to review content knowledge or practice procedural skills. Organizing students into groups for collaborative practice is one way to bridge the gap in the learning process from whole-class guided practice to individual independent practice. Strategies associated with this element include:

- Cooperative learning

- Cooperative comparisons

- Performances and peer critiques

We briefly explain each of these strategies before describing various educational technology tools that can be used to enhance its use.

Cooperative Learning

In cooperative learning, students individually complete practice tasks, problems, or activities and then meet in small groups to discuss their answers. This strategy exposes students to diverse perspectives about content, reveals new ways to solve problems, and allows students to deepen their own knowledge by explaining their thought processes to classmates.

Use online software like Team Maker to randomly sort students into groups to practice and deepen knowledge. When organizing students into cooperative learning groups, simply enter each student's name into Team Maker, and click a button to randomly divide the students into equal teams. Team Maker can also be used to randomly assign jobs—such as recorder, facilitator, or presenter—within each student group. When students are randomly organized into equal groups, Team Maker will automatically assign one person to be the group's recorder, another to be the facilitator, a third to be the presenter, and so on.

Students use tablets or laptops to take notes or create audio or video recordings of their group's discussion. Have students use word processing software, note-taking apps such as Evernote, mind-mapping apps such as Mindjet, video recording tools, or Google Drive to capture their collaborative efforts to practice and deepen knowledge. For example, have students take turns solving math problems while the other students in the group record the problem-solving strategies used.

Students can also use technology to generate, capture, and pose practice questions to other students. Organize students in groups to craft a variety of questions. When students present the questions they have created, the class responds using clickers with text input or mobile devices with polling software.

Cooperative Comparisons

In this strategy, students collaborate in small groups to answer comparison questions. These questions can be self-reflective assessments about the group's performance (for example, How do our current multiplication skills compare to the skills we had when we first started learning how to multiply?) or comparisons designed to help others understand (for example, What metaphors or analogies could we use to teach younger students about the Boston Tea Party?).

Use technology to enhance students' creation of metaphors or analogies. Students can use IWB software, presentation software (such as Prezi), or screencast tools (such as Jing, ScreenChomp, Educreations, or TouchCast) to respond to cooperative comparison questions. For example, students work in cooperative groups to design metaphors or analogies that illustrate reasons why different groups of Americans fought in the Civil War.

Performances and Peer Critiques

To incorporate performance and peer critiques after teaching procedural knowledge, the teacher assigns students a culminating demonstration or performance of their newly acquired skills. If students learned how to conduct a research project, the teacher might assign a formal research paper. If students learned to complete a geometric proof, the teacher might assign an annotated poster of a famous mathematical proof. The teacher can incorporate peer review activities for the finished products, allowing students to practice giving and receiving constructive criticism.

Use technology to augment the process of creating, capturing, sharing, and critiquing a culminating demonstration or performance. Students can use screencasting software (such as Jing, ScreenChomp, Educreations, or TouchCast) to create screencasts that show their understanding of new knowledge or skills. Then, students post links of their screencasts on the class website. Students review and critique their classmates' culminating demonstrations using an agreed-upon rubric or scale. Finally, they post their constructive critiques online to stimulate whole-class reflection and discussion.

Students can also recreate a dramatic scene from a historic work of literature, such as Charles Dickens's *Great Expectations*, and situate it in a contemporary context using modern language, settings, and costumes. Students then record dramatic representations of these modernized scenes using the video recording tools on tablets or smartphones. They can edit their recordings using movie editing software such as iMovie to enhance the transitions, lighting, sound quality, and overall representation of the scene.

Technology also works well for creating nonlinguistic representations of content. Students can use IWB software, presentation software like Prezi, online word processing tools such as Google Drive, or mind-mapping apps like Mindjet to create images, flowcharts, diagrams, or advanced organizers to represent thinking and understanding. For example, students might represent their understanding of the human immune system's response to pathogen invasion by creating a graphic novella analogy of aliens invading a planet. The aliens represent pathogens; the planet's response to the invasion represents the human immune system. Such analogies can then be posted on the class website to encourage constructive criticism and discussion.

Engage students in academic projects online or create your own class project using collaborative project groups such as iEARN (International Education and Resource Network). For example, students demonstrate their understanding of poetry by contributing original poems to iEARN's poetry newsletter, a publication that is shared by students and teachers across the world.

Element 16: Using Homework

When used appropriately rather than regularly, homework can be a very useful tool for practicing procedural skills or for deepening understanding of new content. This element involves teachers using homework for independent practice or to prompt students to elaborate on information. Strategies associated with element 16 include:

- Preview homework

- Homework to deepen knowledge

- Homework to practice a process or skill

We first review these strategies and then provide examples of technology tools to enhance them.

Preview Homework

Before introducing a new concept in class, the teacher can assign students texts, media pieces, or creative projects that will briefly acquaint them with the material. The teacher might require students to record their reflections, observations, or questions about the preview homework to discuss in class the next day.

To take advantage of technology, create multimedia screencasts of new content that students can view before the start of a lesson. Use screencasting software (such as Jing, ScreenChomp, Educreations, or TouchCast) to create mini-tutorials that allow students to preview new material. A tutorial on the Spanish-American War, for example, might explain the main elements that led Americans into conflict with colonial Spain. Use images, text, and sound to introduce background information, important people, and key events that led to the conflict in order to engage students and activate related prior knowledge.

Enhance preview homework by using multimedia recording tools to engage students' senses. Use digital video tools on tablets, smartphones, or document cameras to create video tutorials that allow students to preview new content or skills. For example, record and narrate the problem-solving process for a new type of math problem. Post the problem-solving video to your class website. Then, add a caption asking students to review the video and comment on it. This will allow students to view the video as many times as needed, pause or repeat any sequence that is challenging to them, and retrieve the video file at any point in the future.

Many websites provide prerecorded video lessons that can enhance student engagement in preview homework. Assign students videos from content websites (such as Khan Academy). Be sure to preview the content first to ensure its alignment with your learning goals. Next, post a comment on your class website stating that the video is preview homework. Students then post comments about the video to show their understanding and encourage whole-class discussion.

Teachers can also leverage the vast array of content on the Internet to enhance preview homework for students. Ask students to review content-related primary-source material on websites such as the Smithsonian Institution, the National Archives, the Library of Congress, or PBS. Prior to a lesson on the Dust Bowl, for example, students find and classify specific images, audio files, newspaper headings, or other primary-source materials that directly relate to the learning goal. Students then post hyperlinks to the primary-source materials they find on the class website, and their classmates comment on each resource.

Homework to Deepen Knowledge

Homework designed to deepen knowledge pushes students to use higher-order thinking skills to develop their understanding of the content. Such cognitive skills include comparing and contrasting, classifying, creating analogies, and evaluating the content. Teachers should confirm that students are well-versed in the content before assigning homework to deepen knowledge.

Assign online scavenger hunts that prompt students to explore, compare and contrast, classify, or evaluate content-related videos, images, or tutorials. Sites like TED (www.ted.com) work well for these types of knowledge-deepening activities. For example, middle school students who are well-versed in the process of paragraph writing can compare and contrast videos about paragraph structure from content websites (such as Khan Academy) to critique the quality and helpfulness of each video. They then create a rubric or scale for evaluating the resources they find and consider ways in which they might be improved.

Students can also utilize multimedia tools to gather nonlinguistic representations of knowledge and create visual analogies. For example, students use cameras on tablets, or smartphones to create collages that relate to the instructional content. Students can use content-sharing websites (such as Pinterest) to categorize the images. Next, students generate visual analogies or metaphors using the images they have compiled. Encourage students to post hyperlinks to their visual collages on the class website. Finally, students post constructive comments in response to their classmates' visual analogies.

Homework to Practice a Process or Skill

Once students have demonstrated that they can independently use procedural knowledge to carry out a process in class, the teacher can assign practice tasks for that skill to be completed out of class. Practicing a series of steps outside of class increases students' speed, fluency, and accuracy in performing processes and skills.

Students can use technology to enhance their fluency with a new process or skill by recording themselves practicing it. For example, students might use digital video tools on their smartphones to film themselves practicing and narrating how to solve a quadratic equation. Alternatively, students can use screencasting software (such as Jing, ScreenChomp, Educreations, or TouchCast) to create screencasts that explain how they solve these problems. Next, they upload their videos and screencasts to video storage sites such as Vimeo or YouTube and post hyperlinks to them on the class website. Students comment on their own recordings and the recordings of others.

Element 17: Helping Students Examine Similarities and Differences

Element 17 involves engaging students in comparing, classifying, and creating metaphors and analogies. *Comparing* is the process of pointing out similarities and differences between concepts. *Classifying* is the process of sorting similar things, concepts, or ideas into categories. At the simplest level, students classify items into teacher-created categories. At more complex levels, students create their own categories in which to classify items. *Creating metaphors* is the process of perceiving a pattern that symbolically connects information. For instance, *life is a river* is a metaphoric statement because while life and rivers may not literally have much in common, they are figuratively related: both are filled with unexpected twists and turns, and both have multiple paths from which a traveler must choose. Finally, *creating analogies* is the process of figuring out how two items are related. Analogies usually take the form "A is to B as C is to D," such as *leaves are to trees as toes are to feet*. Specific strategies associated with element 17 include:

- Sentence stem comparisons

- Venn diagrams

- Comparison matrix

- Sentence stem analogies

- Visual analogies

Here, we clarify each strategy and explain how it can be improved with technology.

Sentence Stem Comparisons

When introducing students to the concept of comparisons, Robert Marzano and Debra Pickering (2005) suggested that teachers use the following sentence stems:

- _____ and _____ are similar because they both _____.

- _____ and _____ are different because _____ is _____, but _____ is _____.

Once students have used sentence stems to make comparisons, they can practice using metaphors to make comparisons. A chart like the one presented in table 5.1 (page 74) can guide students through the process of making abstract connections between people, places, concepts, or processes that, on the surface, seem to have little in common. In table 5.1, Frederick Douglass and Helen Keller are shown to share common abstract characteristics, despite their surface-level differences.

Table 5.1: Metaphor Generation Chart Example

Element 1	Common Abstract Characteristics	Element 2
Frederick Douglass		*Helen Keller*
Was a slave as a young boy	Had a rough beginning	Got sick as a baby, which left her deaf and blind
Learned to read and write anyway	Achieved goals even when difficult	Learned how to read Braille and write; also went to college
Wrote books and gave speeches against slavery	Worked to help other people who suffered like him or her	Inspired others to overcome their disabilities through her speech tours and writing

Source: Marzano & Pickering, 2005, p. 52.

Once students have practiced making comparisons, a wide array of technology tools is available to graphically represent similarities and differences between items.

Use connector tools in IWB software to create interactive mind maps that show similarities and differences. During a world history lesson, for instance, students might create interactive mind maps that compare and contrast Indian Prime Ministers Jawaharlal Nehru and Indira Gandhi. Students might describe the prime ministers' similar attributes using connector tools that link to text with a blue background and then describe their differences using connecter tools that link to text with a green background.

Alternatively, use IWB software, online presentation software such as Prezi, or online word processing software such as Google Drive to project side-by-side images of two different representations, ideas, concepts, people, places, or text. Students can then highlight the similarities and differences using clickers with text input or mobile devices with polling software.

Another way to examine similarities and differences is to create word clouds that represent weighted patterns of text usage. Students use two passages of text to create two different word clouds that compare and contrast texts by analyzing patterns of repeated words. In a civics class, for example, students might copy and paste two different speeches given by the same person—such as a presidential campaign speech and a State of the Union address—into Wordle and create a word cloud for each. Next, students analyze the two word clouds to identify similarities and differences between the two speeches.

The interactive and multimedia attributes of technology can also enhance the ways in which students classify or categorize items. Have students use IWB software or online presentation tools like Prezi to organize pictures, images, and text into teacher-created categories. For a more challenging activity, students could construct their own categories. For example, display various images of different types of organisms and have students groups those organisms based the levels of the Linnaean classification system (kingdom, phylum, class, group, order, family, genus, and species). To switch it up, students create their own categories and classify organisms based on this system (such as animals with four legs, plants that have flowers, and so on).

Venn Diagrams

A Venn diagram is a graphic organizer used for comparison in which two or three circles partially overlap. Students can use Venn diagrams to compare and contrast two or three different people, places, events, ideas, items, or processes. In the areas where the circles overlap, students write similarities between the items. In the areas that do not overlap, students write attributes unique to the individual items. In figure 5.1, for example, a second grader has identified similarities and differences between animals based on number of legs and ability to fly.

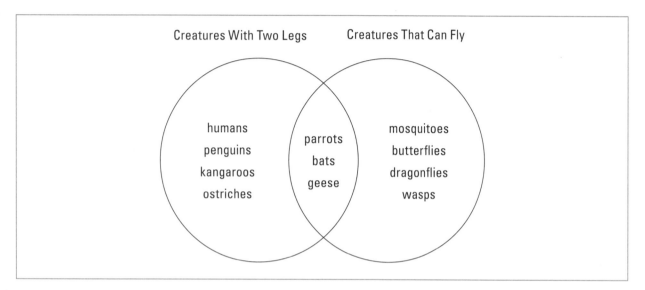

Figure 5.1: Venn diagram comparing creatures with two legs to creatures that can fly.

The left circle includes creatures with two legs; the right circle includes creatures that can fly. In the area of the left circle that does not overlap, the student has identified humans, penguins, kangaroos, and ostriches as animals that have two legs but cannot fly. In the area of the right circle that does not overlap, the student has identified mosquitoes, butterflies, dragonflies, and wasps as animals that can fly but have more than two legs. In the overlapping area in the center of the circle, the student has identified parrots, bats, and geese as creatures that have two legs *and* can fly. Because these three creatures embody both traits, they are visually included in both circles.

Technology tools can make Venn diagrams easier to create and more engaging to use. Use IWB software to design interactive Venn diagrams. Students can use a Venn diagram to arrange blocks of text, images, or sounds into categories based on their attributes. During a music lesson on orchestral instruments, for example, students click on an audio file that plays the sound of a woodwind instrument and one that plays the sound of a stringed instrument. Students can then organize the audio files using the title of the Venn diagram (for instance, "instruments that require air" versus "instruments that require a bow").

Comparison Matrix

In a comparison matrix, a student or teacher chooses items to be compared and writes them at the head of each column in a table. Next, the student or teacher identifies general characteristics to be compared among the items and writes them at the beginning of each row in the table. Finally, students use the general characteristics to guide them in identifying similarities and differences between the items. They record these similarities and differences in each cell. For example, in the comparison matrix shown in table 5.2, the student is comparing *monarchy, dictatorship,* and *democracy* and has recorded them in the column headers of the table. The student has also identified three characteristics of all governments—*how the leaders come to power, the reaction from the people,* and *the role of the people*—and recorded these in the row headers in the table. In the cells, the student has recorded how each characteristic of government is different or similar for each type of government.

Table 5.2: Example of a Comparison Matrix

	Monarchy	Dictatorship	Democracy
How the leaders come to power	King or queen gains throne out of heritage. Sometimes a monarch takes over country by force. Often is a leader for life.	The dictator usually takes power through coercion or force. Often is a leader for life.	Leaders are elected by the people; sometimes influenced by others. The leader doesn't have total power and may be voted out of office.
The reaction from the people	Throughout history are examples of monarchs loved by the people, but some were hated by certain persecuted groups.	Often in history, the dictator is hated or feared by most people.	People are often split on their reactions but accept the elected leader, knowing that they can try to elect a new one before too long.
The role of the people	People are generally expected to obey the rule of the monarch. The monarch holds power and can change laws but can also become like a dictator.	People must obey the dictator. Often there are serious consequences for being disloyal.	Generally, the people are seen to have power through their votes. If they don't like what's happening, they can elect new leaders.

Source: Adapted from Marzano & Pickering, 2005, p. 45.

Teachers can use technology tools like IWB software to increase the interactivity of comparison matrices, like the one shown in table 5.2. They can also use other technology tools to create a variety of graphic organizers to practice comparing and contrasting.

Teachers can use technology to create comparison matrices that enable an entire class to contribute ideas. Use IWB software to create interactive comparison matrices. Work as a whole class to fill in each cell by using clickers with text input or mobile devices with polling software. For example, create a comparison matrix for an art history lesson that displays similarities and differences between different styles of painting (such as cubism, expressionism, impressionism, surrealism, and so on). Students then use clickers or mobile devices to send text responses that complete the matrix. Use students' contributions to prompt whole-class discussion on the attributes of each response.

Use technology tools to enhance collaboration during comparison matrix activities. Use a random group generator like Team Maker to organize students into groups. Each group uses online word processing software such as Google Drive to create a document that presents similarities and differences side-by-side. For example, students might create a comparison matrix to record the similarities and differences of characters in a work of literature, including the personality traits displayed by each character, the psychological makeup of each character, and the degree of transformation that each character exhibits over time.

Sentence Stem Analogies

Creating and completing analogies is an advanced and complex task that can be cognitively difficult for students, especially for those who have never used them before. One way to guide students through the creation or completion of analogies is to use sentence stem analogies with missing elements. At the simplest level, students can complete analogies with one missing element, such as:

- Lungs are to mammals as gills are to _____.

- Lee Harvey Oswald is to John F. Kennedy as John Wilkes Booth is to _____.

At a more complex level, students can complete analogies with two missing elements, such as:

- *The Catcher in the Rye* is to teenage rebellion as _____ is to _____.

- César Chávez is to farm laborers as _____ is to _____.

You can use technology tools to engage a whole class in interactive analogy activities. Expand the use of sentence stem analogies in the classroom using polling technology. Create a sentence stem analogy, and display it in IWB or presentation software. Students complete the sentence stem analogy using clickers with text input or mobile devices with polling software. Challenge the class by creating sentence stem analogies with two missing elements, or have students create their own sentence stem analogies to share.

Visual Analogies

David Hyerle (1996) suggested that teachers use graphic organizers to prompt students to clearly express the relationship between items in an analogy. In a visual analogy, students articulate the relationship that connects two sets of items. In figure 5.2, for example, a student has deconstructed the analogy *blue is to orange as violet is to yellow* by writing the sets of items on opposite sides of the word *as*, which is positioned at the peak in the center of the image.

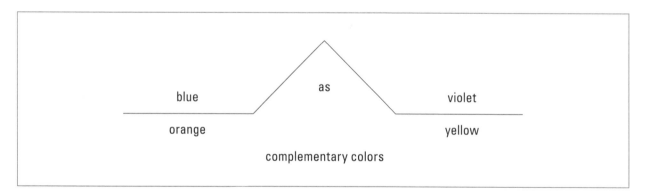

Figure 5.2: Visual analogy expressing the relationship between complementary colors.
Source: Marzano, 2012, p. 127.

As shown in the figure, the student has identified that the color *blue* is complementary to the color *orange*, and the color *violet* is complementary to the color *yellow*. Therefore, the student writes that the sets of items are related in that both are *complementary colors*.

Teachers can use multimedia software to enhance the application of visual analogies by adding images, sound, and interactivity to visual analogy activities. For example, in a biology class, insert pictures of a cell and a plant into a visual analogy diagram (like the one in figure 5.2, page 77) instead of words.

Create an interactive graphic organizer for visual analogies that includes images or sound, and display it in IWB or presentation software. Students collaborate in small groups to complete the organizer and submit responses using clickers with text input or mobile devices with polling software. Teachers could also use a random name generator to organize students into pairs to create their own visual analogies using photos taken via smartphone or tablet.

Element 18: Helping Students Examine Errors in Reasoning

Whether students are practicing argumentation skills or deepening their understanding of a content-related topic, they must be able to identify errors in reasoning. Element 18 involves the teacher asking students to examine errors in reasoning such as faulty logic, attack, weak reference, or misinformation. Strategies associated with this element include:

- Identifying errors of faulty logic, attack, weak reference, or misinformation

- Finding errors in the media

Here, we explain how each strategy for the element can be enhanced with technology.

Identifying Errors of Faulty Logic, Attack, Weak Reference, or Misinformation

Students must be explicitly taught how to identify and resolve errors in reasoning. Robert Marzano and John Brown (2009) identified four common categories of such errors. Table 5.3 lists these categories and their descriptions.

Teachers can use technology tools to present various errors in reasoning to students and help them analyze the misconceptions or faulty reasoning in each one.

Use interactive presentation software to introduce students to the concept of errors in reasoning. Create a presentation introducing the errors in reasoning using IWB software or online presentation software such as Prezi. Provide examples of each reasoning error by including hyperlinks to examples of the error in practice. Have students use clickers with text input or mobile devices with polling software to share further examples of reasoning errors. Use these responses to initiate a whole-group discussion about the accuracy of student contributions. Alternatively, students can use fill tools in IWB software to evaluate textual passages and highlight lines that contain errors in reasoning.

Archive and share examples of reasoning errors in online texts by using social bookmarking resources. Students use social bookmarking tools such as Diigo or Delicious to catalog and annotate the errors they find on the Internet. For example, in a journalism class, have students search the Internet for examples of different journalistic genres (such as broadcast, opinion, investigative, narrative, watchdog, and gonzo). Students analyze each genre for errors in reasoning, annotating the segment of text that the error is apparent in and bookmarking each error in Diigo. Encourage students to follow their classmates' social bookmarks in order to comment on the annotated errors in reasoning. Use trends in reasoning errors among genres to spark whole-class discussions about the ethical principles of journalism.

Table 5.3: Four Categories of Errors in Reasoning

Type of Error	How the Error Can Occur
Faulty Logic	**Contradiction:** Presenting conflicting information
	Accident: Failing to recognize that an argument is based on an exception to a rule
	False cause: Confusing a temporal (time) order of events with causality or oversimplifying the reasons behind an occurrence
	Begging the question: Making a claim and then arguing for the claim by using statements that are simply the equivalent of the original claim
	Evading the issue: Changing the topic to avoid addressing the issue
	Arguing from ignorance: Arguing that a claim is justified simply because its opposite has not been proven true
	Composition: Asserting something about a whole that is really only true of its parts
	Division: Asserting something about all of the parts that is generally, but not always, true of the whole
Attack	**Poisoning the well:** Being so completely committed to a position that you explain away absolutely everything that is offered in opposition to your position
	Arguing against the person: Rejecting a claim using derogatory facts (real or alleged) about the person who is making the claim
	Appealing to force: Using threats to establish the validity of a claim
Weak reference	**Sources that reflect biases:** Consistently accepting information that supports what you already believe to be true or consistently rejecting information that goes against what you believe to be true
	Sources that lack credibility: Using a source that is not reputable for a given topic
	Appealing to authority: Invoking authority as the last word on an issue
	Appealing to the people: Attempting to justify a claim based on its popularity
	Appealing to emotion: Using a sob story as proof for a claim
Misinformation	**Confusing the facts:** Using information that seems to be factual but that has been changed in such a way that it is no longer accurate
	Misapplying a concept or generalization: Misunderstanding or wrongly applying a concept or generalization to support a claim

Source: Adapted from Marzano, 2007, pp. 78–79.

Students can also catalog the errors in reasoning they find using audio recording software like Audacity to record their analyses of each error in reasoning. For example, when students notice an error in reasoning in some online text format, they bookmark the source and then use Audacity to record their thoughts. Students can then post these audio files to a shared online repository, such as Dropbox, in order to share their examples with the entire class. Alternatively, pairs of students record their video analysis of errors in reasoning using a talk show format. For example, one student plays the role of the host while another student can play the role of the guest or contestant. The host asks probing questions while the contestant shares examples of reasoning errors that he or she has discovered. Students then share their videos using online video sharing resources such as Vimeo or YouTube.

Post hyperlinks to textual, audio, or video resources that exemplify reasoning errors on the class website. Students view the links and post comments discussing the nature of the error. Open forums also allow teachers to post probing questions to refine students' reasoning about the errors.

Online collaboration tools can also enhance how student groups find, catalog, and analyze errors in reasoning from a variety of media sources. Use a random group generator like Team Maker to organize students into work groups. Groups can then use online word processing software such as Google Drive to create a compendium of errors in reasoning based on Internet searches. Have each team create its own Google Group to organize its discussions and collaborative documents. Encourage students to share their work with the class and comment on each other's posts and contributions.

Finally, use polling data to augment whole-group discussions of reasoning errors. Display selected text passages, or play videos that contain reasoning errors using IWB software or online presentation software like Prezi. Students use clickers or mobile devices to vote on the type of reasoning error they think is exemplified by the passage or video.

Finding Errors in the Media

To give students real-world practice with examining errors in reasoning, teachers can show students clips of audiovisual media and ask them to identify errors in reasoning. Clips might include footage of political debates, televised interviews, or commercials. Teachers can also distribute or direct students to print and online media, such as advertisements, newspaper articles, and blog posts. Students can examine the content for errors in reasoning on their own or in small groups.

Interactive technology can simplify the process of classifying and cataloging errors found in the media. Use IWB software to create and display a color-coded identification chart for errors in reasoning. For example, the color green represents errors that invoke faulty logic, red represents errors that reflect attack, yellow represents errors of misinformation, and blue represents errors of weak reference. Students then use the different colors to highlight or fill text passages—such as text from news blogs or political speeches—that correspond with the defined errors.

Students can also use online collaboration centers (such as iEARN) to create or engage in projects that involve students outside their classrooms. For example, students could participate in an error rewrite project in which students around the world identify errors in reasoning in the media (such as those found in news stories or blogs) and rewrite the pieces with the errors removed. Students could then share their rewrites for consideration and discussion among a global student network.

Element 19: Helping Students Practice Skills, Strategies, and Processes

While the preceding elements in this chapter have been geared toward declarative knowledge, element 19 addresses the need for teachers to provide students with opportunities to practice procedural knowledge: skills, strategies, and processes. This element involves the use of both massed and distributed practice. Strategies associated with this element include:

- Close monitoring

- Frequent structured practice

- Varied practice

- Fluency practice

We briefly elaborate on each strategy before identifying the technology tools that can be used to support it.

Close Monitoring

Close monitoring occurs directly after the teacher presents new content to the class. When students are just beginning to develop a new skill or procedure, the teacher creates a highly structured environment and provides scaffolding for more complex material. In the close monitoring stage, the teacher judiciously observes and corrects erroneous actions of students before they become ingrained.

Incorporate multisensory scaffolds into presentations of content to guide students as they practice new skills or procedures. Use IWB or presentation software to display problems in the main slides, but offer hints and cues to students in the presentation notes. Students can view the notes when they need assistance and hide them when they do not. For example, when teaching the process for solving polynomial equations, create an IWB presentation to support students as they practice the procedure. Include tips, guides, hints, or examples in the notes feature to give students guidance when it is needed. Keep track of which students refer to the notes—and how often they do so—in order to monitor their learning.

Embed audio guidance for students to use as needed in a variety of software tools, such as word processing, spreadsheet, and presentation software. If a student is practicing the process of balancing chemical equations, for instance, you might create and share a practice guide in word processing software or spreadsheet software. Embed audio clips of yourself explaining the process to students. Allow access to these audio scaffolds or guides as needed, and monitor the extent to which students use them.

Finally, use screen recording tools to enhance close monitoring. Students use the screen recording tools in IWB software or use screencast software—such as Jing, ScreenChomp, Educreations, or TouchCast—to record their practice with a new strategy, skill, or process. These tools also allow students to explain their thought processes as they apply the new skill or procedure as well as provide teachers with insight about student understanding. Teachers can more readily administer interventions before incorrect thinking becomes ingrained.

Frequent Structured Practice

In frequent structured practice, students are given multiple chances to solve problems for which they have a high probability of success. During this phase, the teacher may choose to divide a process into discrete parts for students to practice. Students may also practice the process in its entirety. Before the teacher transitions to the next type of practice, students should experience success several times during frequent structured practice.

Enhance structured practice with audio recording software like Audacity or the audio recording tools in IWB, presentation, or word processing software. Highlight and embed important problem-solving steps, clues, or guidance that can be accessed multiple times to provide help to students who need it. Students can access these files on a variety of devices—such as desktop computers, laptops, or tablets—to guide their structured practice of new processes, strategies, or skills.

Varied Practice

During varied practice, the teacher gives students less structured, more complex situations in which to use their newly acquired skills or learned processes. While students still experience success, they must work harder to attain it because they are challenged by fresh manifestations of the material. At this point, the teacher prompts students to monitor their own progress and evaluate their own strengths and weaknesses pertaining to the content.

Encourage students to use screen capture tools (such as Jing, ScreenChomp, Educreations, or TouchCast) or the audio or video recording features of laptops, tablets, or smartphones to describe the important steps in a procedure, such as the process of expository writing, in their own words. Students then listen to their own screencasts or recordings to self-assess their performance. Encourage students to use these multimedia descriptions to support their own practice or share them with other students by posting their files on a class website.

Fluency Practice

Fluency practice, often called independent practice, should only begin once students have experienced success in a range of simple to complex situations. When students are comfortable with the material, they can focus on performing the skill quickly, accurately, and automatically. To incentivize students to become faster and more accurate, the teacher can use a tracking chart like the one displayed in table 5.4 and celebrate when students have met their growth goals.

Table 5.4: Example of Student Progress Tracking Chart

Progress Measurement	Practice Session				
	1	*2*	*3*	*4*	*5*
Number of items in my practice set	5	5	5	10	10
Number of items performed correctly	2	3	4	7	9
Number of minutes to complete the items	3	3	2	5	4

Source: Marzano, 2007, p. 82.

Fluency practice can be assigned as homework, but students should still be encouraged to self-monitor their progress.

Students can use the multimedia tools in interactive software to enhance their fluency practice with new knowledge. For instance, students use the screen recording tools in IWB software or screencast software—such as Jing, ScreenChomp, Educreations, or TouchCast—to record multimedia representations of their own problem-solving practice. They narrate how they gained fluency with a skill, strategy, or process. Encourage students to share their breakthrough moments when creating these recordings and to generate analogies or metaphors to help enrich their explanations. Students then post these files on the class website. Encourage students to review and comment on the extent to which other students' fluency practice aided or enhanced their own.

Element 20: Helping Students Revise Knowledge

Element 20 pertains to the revision of knowledge, which involves asking students to revise entries in notebooks to clarify and add to previous information. During the revision process, students should be periodically asked to assess their own performance by articulating their own strengths, weaknesses, and areas of improvement in their academic notebooks. For this reason, academic notebooks can be powerful tools for students to develop self-reflective evaluation and progress-monitoring skills. Strategies associated with this element include:

- Academic notebook entries

- Academic notebook review

- Peer feedback

- Assignment revision

Here, we explain each strategy and highlight the technology tools teachers can use to enhance it.

Academic Notebook Entries

Students can periodically complete entries in their academic notebooks to be examined later in the lesson or during subsequent units. These entries can occur regularly—during the same lesson segment every day—or periodically—after a critical-input experience or while correcting homework.

Use cloud-based software to enhance student use of academic notebooks. For instance, students use online word processing tools (such as Google Drive or Evernote) to create learning journals in which they extend and revise their knowledge. Cloud-based tools allow students to create and access academic notebook entries from a range of devices, including desktop computers, laptops, tablets, and smartphones. Student entries can be textual, nonlinguistic, or visual and may include audio files or hyperlinks to previously recorded screencasts of practice sessions. Students' academic notebook entries may also include links to external resources, information that they can use for help or guidance, or supporting evidence for their ideas.

Academic Notebook Review

Students can use the key vocabulary terms, main ideas, steps in important procedures, and conceptual understandings they record in academic notebooks to prepare for tests, quizzes, and assessments.

One option is for students to use cloud-based academic notebook entries that contain text entries, audio recordings, and screen captures they created during previous lessons to support their reflection and knowledge revision and to review for assessment activities. As previously mentioned, the availability of cloud-based notebooks allows students to access their entries from a variety of devices. Include students' academic notebooks as part of their assessment "process-folios" to help students and parents track academic growth throughout a unit of study.

Teachers can also use technology to enhance how students reflect on their knowledge revision. Use word processing software or online word processing tools such as Google Drive to create sentence stem knowledge revision templates. Fill in certain elements to guide a student's reflection and growth. For example, the template might include a sentence stem, such as "I used to think that _____ was like _____. But now that I learned _____, I think _____ is more like _____." Create a different tab for each individual student within a classwide file on Google Drive or simply assign a different sentence stem to each student within a single tab.

Peer Feedback

In this strategy, students swap academic notebooks and write responses to their classmate's entries. To structure this process, teachers can generate a list of questions to guide students in the process of giving feedback. Strong feedback-inducing questions include the following:

- How did my classmate display information in a clear and useful way (for example, graphic organizers, images, or flowcharts)?

- What did my classmate record in his or her academic notebook that I did not record in mine?

- What is one thing my classmate could improve on the next time he or she uses this academic notebook?

Technology can help students give feedback to each other and create and save multiple drafts of their work. For instance, use cloud-based tools to enhance whole-class sharing, evaluating, and contributing to one another's content knowledge. In addition to sharing their academic notebooks with classmates, students save multiple versions of their own work to show revisions, progress, and feedback. For example, students can give different file names—such as V1 (version 1), V2, V3, and so on—to the same project when saving. This convention makes it easy for students to evaluate their own responses to feedback and monitor their progress throughout a lesson or unit.

Assignment Revision

When using assignment revision, teachers provide constructive feedback on student assignments but do not record the student's grade on the assignment (they only record the grade in the gradebook). Students have the option to use the teacher's comments to revise the assignment and turn it in again for a chance at a higher score.

Teachers can use the editing features of word processing software to enhance students' assignment revision. Use a comments feature in word processing software or in online word processing tools like Google Drive to offer suggestions and embed revisions in student assignments. Encourage students to incorporate the suggestions made in comments and resubmit their revised documents as a completed assessment exercise.

Finally, use IWB features to augment the process of assignment revision for students. Use the notes feature to embed suggestions, ideas, analogies, and other considerations to help students revise multimedia products. Give students the opportunity to make revisions to their files and resubmit them. Students should include the reasoning for their revisions along with their resubmissions.

Teaching With Technology

This design question involves various elements to practice and deepen students' understanding of new knowledge, such as reviewing content, using homework, revising knowledge, and practicing skills, strategies, and processes. In the following vignette, Mrs. Lederman continues her lesson on natural selection by demonstrating different ways in which these elements and others can be improved with technology.

Several days later, Mrs. Lederman continues her lesson on adaptation. She begins by reviewing previous information on the concept of natural selection. She uses a variety of technology tools to elicit student responses during the content review. Mrs. Lederman then displays a synopsis of her multimedia presentation that includes still images from various portions. Using a random name generator, she selects students to answer questions she has prepared about the images on the screen. She does this frequently throughout the review, sometimes asking students to elaborate on or provide more nuanced information on other students' answers.

Part of the content review includes an interactive cloze activity in which students use their smartphones to submit text that completes a critical sentence or idea. Mrs. Lederman introduces another activity where randomly selected students rearrange images on her laptop, linking the images to the corresponding terms or concepts they represent. The remainder of the class uses smartphones to vote on the accuracy of the linking exercise.

The questions increase in complexity as the content review proceeds. Some of the final questions are more open ended or divergent. For example, one group of questions asks students to speculate on the adaptation of species that were not explicitly taught in class. Students must successfully apply their understanding of natural selection to answer these questions. Mrs. Lederman asks these more challenging questions to preview the next part of the lesson, in which students will complete projects that deepen their understanding of natural selection.

Mrs. Lederman's students sit in their randomly assigned groups to begin constructing the projects they had outlined in previous class periods. Some of her students have decided to extend this project into their long-term graduation requirement by generating and testing hypotheses about organism adaptations that result from global climate change. One group decides to speculate on the possible impact of global climate change on the life cycle of cicadas. The students envision creating a project where they interview natural history experts from the Smithsonian and the American Museum of Natural History. Another group uses iEARN to collaborate with students in other parts of the world. The students are contributing to the Millennium Seed Bank Project through the website of the Royal Botanical Gardens, Kew.

Mrs. Lederman displays a picture of French naturalist Jean-Baptiste Lamarck. She asks the class to use smartphones to text her a message that briefly explains his most important contribution to science. Drawing on previously learned content, nearly all of the students correctly identify Lamarck as a forerunner to Charles Darwin and the theory of biological evolution. Mrs. Lederman explains that, like Darwin, Lamarck used scientific observation and identification of the similarities and differences between living things to inform his theories. She goes on to explain how the students can deepen their understanding of this important biological concept through both identifying similarities and differences between the two scientists and understanding how the contributions of one led to breakthroughs for the other.

Using her laptop to connect to a projector, Mrs. Lederman displays an interactive Venn diagram she created using presentation software. The diagram consists of two overlapping circles, one labeled with the name of Charles Darwin and the other labeled with the name of Jean-Baptiste Lamarck. Using her laptop, Mrs. Lederman demonstrates how an organism would change over time according to the tenets of the different theories posited by these two scientists. She manipulates digital images, text, and sound to help her students notice the distinct patterns of each scientific theory.

She stops at strategic points to check for understanding, asking each student to answer questions using polling software on his or her smartphone. The class discusses the polling results from each question, and at times, Mrs. Lederman asks students to contribute text that demonstrates their understanding of the similarities and differences between these two evolutionary theories.

When all of her students have exhibited a sufficient level of understanding of the two scientists' theories, Mrs. Lederman asks them to work in their groups to apply their new knowledge. The groups create their own interactive Venn diagrams that demonstrate how various organisms might have adapted based on the two theories. Using the random name generator, she randomly assigns an unusual organism to each group. She gives the groups five minutes to create their Venn diagrams and post them to the class Edmodo page.

Prior to the lesson, Mrs. Lederman created a template to help students identify and understand the four major types of reasoning errors. She posted an update on her Edmodo page that lists common errors in reasoning and links to media examples to show students the errors in practice. Because her students are familiar with this template, they can apply it to the concept of natural selection. Mrs. Lederman now uses her IWB to display passages from the transcripts of the Scopes Monkey Trial. She asks students to identify errors in reasoning made by the lawyers arguing for and against the teaching of human evolution in public schools. Students use their smartphones to submit errors in reasoning and explain how they relate to the lesson.

Mrs. Lederman has also collected online articles, essays, and comments about evolution. She projects selected passages from her collection, highlights each passage's error, and asks students to identify which category of reasoning error it represents. After asking a few of these questions, she displays passages without highlighting the errors and asks students to both identify and classify the reasoning error in the passage.

As a challenge homework assignment, Mrs. Lederman asks students to identify reasoning errors in online discussions about natural selection. She asks her students to track these errors using social bookmarking resources so that she can see the evidence the students have compiled and provide comments on the nature of their reasoning. She has designed this exercise to give students practice with reasoning errors but also to strengthen students' own use of logic to substantiate their ideas about adaptation.

Because students are all using cloud-based computing tools, their group projects about the adaptations of unusual organisms are saved online. Mrs. Lederman's students can therefore access their projects files from any mobile device or computer. Some students visit the school library to access their online files from library tablets or computers. Others use computers at the public library to complete their homework projects.

In addition to their multimedia projects, Mrs. Lederman's students write narratives that tell the story of how their organisms adapted over time. Students can use these narratives to teach others about adaptation, which helps deepen their understanding of this complex concept. Mrs. Lederman also encourages her students to post links to various iterations of their homework projects on the class's Edmodo page. She encourages them to preview, provide feedback, and contribute ideas in response to these iterations. Providing feedback on each other's projects helps her students develop communication skills as they apply their understanding of the process of natural selection in contexts that were not explicitly taught.

Just prior to the end of this lesson, Mrs. Lederman asks students the same questions from the preassessment. After students complete this postassessment, she electronically sends both pre- and postassessment scores to each student. Using their online journals, Mrs. Lederman's students complete a knowledge revision template based on the data from their pre- and post-assessments. The template prompts students to reflect on their initial understanding of natural selection and how it may have changed as a result of the lesson.

Students post their completed templates on the class's Edmodo page and post comments describing their understanding of the concept in their own words. Every student's unique insights on natural selection can be collected, archived, and shared. Such activities help Mrs. Lederman develop a contributive classroom culture that serves the present learning needs of her students and prepares them to resolve future learning problems.

Mrs. Lederman uses a variety of technology tools to enhance her instruction. For element 14, reviewing content, she presents a truncated version of the multimedia presentation she shares with her students and uses a random name generator to choose students to answer review questions about it. She also displays an interactive cloze activity, which all of her students complete using the text input features of their mobile devices. She then asks a series of increasingly complex follow-up questions to enrich the knowledge review process for her students.

For element 15, organizing students to practice and deepen knowledge, Mrs. Lederman uses a random group generator to organize students into work groups.

To incorporate technology into element 16, using homework, students search the Internet to identify errors in reasoning in online discussions about natural selection. Using the reasoning errors template Mrs. Lederman created as a guide, her students catalog and comment on the reasoning errors they found with social bookmarking tools. She also uses a social networking tool to allow her students to share and comment on the reasoning errors their classmates discover.

To enhance her application of element 17, helping students examine similarities and differences, Mrs. Lederman creates an interactive Venn diagram using presentation software. This visual representation helps her students identify the similarities and differences between two scientists' explanations of natural selection. Her students use their mobile devices to contribute elements to the Venn diagram, which Mrs. Lederman uses to prompt whole-class discussion. Students then use presentation software to create their own Venn diagrams, applying their understanding of evolution according to the two different scientific theories.

To enhance element 18, helping students examine errors in reasoning, Mrs. Lederman shares a reasoning errors template in her classroom social media group. She then uses her presentation software to display textual passages from the Scopes Monkey Trial—which contain highlighted errors in reasoning—and asks students to submit their perceptions via smartphone. Mrs. Lederman then displays passages without highlighting any errors and asks students to locate the reasoning errors and submit their answers via smartphone.

Mrs. Lederman also uses technology in element 19, helping students practice skills, strategies, and processes. Specifically, Mrs. Lederman's students work in groups and use presentation software to create interactive Venn diagrams. The diagrams exhibit students' understanding of adaptation according to the two different scientific theories they have learned. Her students also post their completed Venn diagrams to the class social media site for peer and teacher review. They then comment on their classmates' diagrams. In addition, students engage in projects to practice and demonstrate their understanding of natural selection.

Finally, Mrs. Lederman employs the use of technology for element 20, helping students revise knowledge. As illustrated by the vignette, Mrs. Lederman's students use their mobile devices to respond to the same questions as they did in the adaptation preassessment. She then sends both pre-and post-assessment scores to each student to help him or her reflect on the knowledge revision. She also asks students to add entries to their online academic journals and complete a knowledge revision template she has created. This template is designed to help students identify the changes in their understanding of natural selection.

Chapter 5: Comprehension Questions

1. What are the similarities and differences between using technology for homework to practice a process or skill and using technology for homework to deepen knowledge?

2. How can technology support the use of Venn diagrams to examine similarities and differences?

3. List three ways in which technology can be used to infuse collaboration into the examination of errors in reasoning.

4. How do you use technology to help students practice and deepen new knowledge in your classroom? Share your ideas by going to **marzanoresearch.com/classroom strategies**, clicking on the *Enhancing the Art & Science of Teaching With Technology* link, and becoming a member of our virtual learning community.

Chapter 6

GENERATING AND TESTING HYPOTHESES

Chapters 4 and 5 outlined steps, strategies, and educational technology tools that teachers can use to build a solid foundation of declarative and procedural knowledge for their students. The design question addressed in this chapter, which falls under lesson segments addressing content, is, How can I use technology to help students generate and test hypotheses about new knowledge? This chapter focuses on challenging students to experiment with their newly acquired knowledge. Three elements are important to this design question.

Element 21: Organizing students for cognitively complex tasks

Element 22: Engaging students in cognitively complex tasks involving hypothesis generation and testing

Element 23: Providing resources and guidance

The strategies and behaviors outlined in this chapter are influenced by the research on problem-based learning (Gijbels, Dochy, Van den Bossche, & Segers, 2005) and hypothesis generation and testing (Hattie et al., 1996; Ross, 1988). Technology can be used to enhance and support each strategy.

Element 21: Organizing Students for Cognitively Complex Tasks

Element 21 involves the teacher splitting students into small groups to facilitate their work on problem-solving, decision-making, experimental-inquiry, and investigation tasks. Strategies associated with this element include:

- Student-designed tasks

- Cooperative learning

- Think logs

- Journals

- Peer tutoring

In addition to explaining each strategy, we describe how each strategy can be enhanced with technology.

Student-Designed Tasks

An effective way to prepare students to generate and test hypotheses is for the teacher to ask them questions, such as What predictions or questions do you have about this content or information? Students can use their answers to design cognitively complex tasks related to the class learning goal or a personal learning goal. Once students have identified a question or prediction that interests them, they can develop their task by selecting one or two options from the following list.

Relative to my questions and predictions, is there an important:

- Hypothesis I want to test?

- Problem I want to study?

- Decision I want to examine?

- Concept I want to examine?

- Event I want to study?

- Hypothetical or future event I want to examine?

Technology can also be used to inspire questioning among students. Use IWB software to help students generate and test hypotheses. Students create interactive problem-solving or decision-making templates that can scaffold or guide the process they use to solve problems, make decisions, examine concepts, or generate and test hypotheses. For example, students interested in meteorology might further examine the phenomenon of global warming and create an interactive template to organize their thinking. They can download and store online resources—such as articles, images, scientific claims, and so on—into the template to guide their thinking and share their research with others.

Cooperative Learning

Through cooperative learning, teachers can implement structures for group and individual accountability, offer continuous coaching of group relational skills, and assign and periodically rotate roles and responsibilities for each group member.

Use random team generators (such as Team Maker) to organize students into groups. Students can then complete cognitively complex tasks. Moreover, use random number generators to assign students to various roles within the group.

Think Logs

Think logs are journals that allow students to reflect on their development of cognitive skills (for example, classification, drawing inferences, creative thinking, self-regulation, and decision making) during cognitively complex tasks. Teachers can use prompts to help students reflect on cognitive skills and write journal entries in their think logs. Sample prompts include:

- How might you explain *creative thinking* to a friend?

- What parts of classification do you understand the most? What parts do you understand the least?

- Describe an inference you made during today's lesson.

Technology can enhance the reflection process, especially by offering alternatives to writing for students who prefer to express themselves orally or visually.

First, students can use audio recording software (such as Audacity) to create audio think logs to capture their thoughts or ideas. Alternatively, students can use speech-to-text apps such as Dragon Dictation to capture rough ideas or thoughts to be converted to text, modified, augmented, and extended. For students who are intimidated by a blank page, thinking aloud using Dragon Dictation might allow for easier expression of ideas. Students further refine their thoughts once the audio file is converted to text. Second, students can use digital video recording tools on tablets or smartphones to create think log entries in the form of short films. Provide plenty of time in class for students to record their observations, reflections, and speculations using digital video recording tools.

Students and groups can also leverage the collaborative capacity of cloud-based software to enhance their individual or collective think logs. For instance, students use Google Drive to create and keep individual or collaborative online thinking journals. Groups of students can access shared think logs using a number of different devices from any location with Internet access.

Journals

Journals are similar to think logs because they capture student reflection; however, they differ in that they focus on the cognitively complex task itself rather than on the cognitive skills the student has developed. Students can devote a section of their academic notebooks to be used as journals, and teachers can prompt students with questions such as the following:

- What is the purpose of the task you are working on?

- How will your cognitively complex task boost your success with the learning goals?

- What problems did you encounter while working on your cognitively complex task today?

Use word processing software or online word processing software such as Google Drive to create templates that scaffold students' reflections on declarative tasks. For example, students can use the following sentence stem to express a reflection of declarative knowledge: "I previously thought _____, but because I now understand _____, I now think _____."

Similarly, students can use online software to enhance reflections on procedural knowledge in learning journals. With an online template that scaffolds reflections of procedural tasks, students can use a sentence stem like the following: "I previously thought the process was _____, but now that I understand _____, I think the process is _____."

Students can also use multimedia tools to enhance their learning journals. Use IWB software or Google Drive to create an interactive W-N-H chart to scaffold students' reflections about cognitive tasks. For example, students respond to questions like What did I think before?, Now what do I think?, and How are these thoughts different? to guide their reflection on cognitive tasks.

Peer Tutoring

Students who have reached the advanced level for a learning goal can volunteer to assist students who need extra help to get to the next level. This situation benefits students who need help while allowing advanced students to deepen their own skills by explaining complex processes to others. However, teachers should avoid pairing tutors with severely struggling students. Those students will benefit most from teacher instruction.

Both tutors and students who need help can use technology to enhance peer tutoring. For instance, students can create multimedia problem-solving tutorials that demonstrate complex cognitive tasks with the screen capture tools in IWB software or screencasting software, such as Jing, ScreenChomp, Educreations, or TouchCast. While a tutor works with a struggling student on a math problem, encourage the tutor to elicit responses from the struggling student, while capturing both the discussion and the problem-solving steps. This screen capture allows struggling students to see and hear their own thinking as well as the strategies used to solve the problem. It also highlights any misconceptions or faulty reasoning that may be impeding progress. Store these files in the cloud to allow struggling students to refer to them as needed.

Element 22: Engaging Students in Cognitively Complex Tasks Involving Hypothesis Generation and Testing

In element 22, the teacher engages students in cognitively complex tasks that involve hypothesis generation and testing. There are four specific types of cognitively complex tasks:

- Experimental-inquiry tasks

- Problem-solving tasks

- Decision-making tasks

- Investigation tasks

We explain each of these tasks along with ways that technology can enhance its use and execution.

Experimental-Inquiry Tasks

Experimental-inquiry tasks teach students to make a prediction based on observations, design an experiment to test that prediction, and then examine the results in light of the initial prediction. Teachers can guide students through experimental-inquiry tasks with the following questions:

- What is my prediction?

- How will I test my prediction?

- What do I expect to observe if my prediction is correct?

- Did my prediction come true?

- What have I learned?

Use IWB software or online word processing software such as Google Drive to create interactive experimental-inquiry templates for students. Post hyperlinks to these templates on a class website for students to access and retrieve. Archive completed experimental-inquiry templates from previous years to use as exemplars. These can help scaffold student thinking and understanding about experimental-inquiry tasks.

Students use online search tools to enhance the experimental-inquiry process. Online resources can help students by presenting hypotheses, results, relevant information, and evidence gathered by others. Students search the Internet for evidence that supports their predictions. Next, they catalog and annotate the evidence that they have found using social bookmarking tools (such as Diigo or Delicious). Finally, they share their findings with their classmates by posting updates on the class website.

Online survey tools (such as SurveyMonkey) or social media tools (such as Twitter, Edmodo, Blendspace, or Facebook) can help students gather data from peers or other Internet users. For example, if a student wishes to test a hypothesis about gender-based income disparity, he or she may create an online survey using SurveyMonkey. The student can then post a link to the survey via Twitter using a popular hashtag—such as #PayEquity—to increase the number of survey responses.

Students can also use digital audio software like Audacity or the video recording capacity of tablets or smartphones to provide multimedia representations of their predictions and supporting evidence. Alternatively, students use online word processing tools (such as Google Drive) to capture their thoughts about predictions.

Leverage the wide distribution of social media to enhance experimental-inquiry tasks. Have students work individually or collaboratively to build websites using online tools such as Weebly to present predictions and collect data using hyperlinks to surveys. Next, students analyze the data to determine whether they supported their predictions. Finally, students post their findings and conclusions. Use ClustrMaps to track global access to students' work on experimental-inquiry tasks.

Problem-Solving Tasks

Problem-solving tasks teach students to use knowledge in situations that are restricted by obstacles or constraints. Teachers can guide students through problem-solving tasks with the following questions:

- What is the goal?

- What obstacles will make it challenging to accomplish this goal?

- How might I overcome these obstacles?

- What solution do I predict will work best? Why?

- What actually happened?

- Was my original prediction right? If not, how should I change my thinking about this problem?

Students search the Internet for background information about problems they wish to study and solve. If a student is interested in resolving community water pollution issues, for example, he or she begins by framing critical elements of the problem. Next, the student brainstorms ways to come up with solutions for the problem. The student might research other communities with similar water pollution problems and assess how those people solved the problem. The student then uses a class website to share progress or uses social bookmarking tools like Diigo or Delicious to catalog and annotate online resources.

Decision-Making Tasks

Decision-making tasks teach students how to choose between a number of options that seem equally valid. Students establish a set of criteria to evaluate the options before actually making a decision. To simplify these tasks for beginners, teachers can provide a premade list of criteria for decision making. Students can use a decision matrix to systematically assess the criteria for each alternative. In table 6.1 (page 96), for example, the student uses a decision matrix to determine which of the alternatives (literary works, in this case) are considered classics, based on teacher-provided criteria.

Table 6.1: Decision Matrix for Identifying Classic Literary Works

Criteria	Alternatives					
	Romeo and Juliet	*One Flew Over the Cuckoo's Nest*	*To Kill a Mockingbird*	*Fail-Safe*	"The Most Dangerous Game"	*2001: A Space Odyssey*
Is recognized by literary scholars as an exemplary work	X	X	X	0	?	X
Is typically required reading in schools	X	0	X	?	X	0
Has a storyline that is applicable over the decades	X	0	X	0	0	X
Totals	3	1	3	0	1	2

Source: Adapted from Marzano, 2007.

As shown in table 6.1, students have used the criteria to classify *Romeo and Juliet* and *To Kill a Mockingbird* as literary classics. Decision-making tasks can serve as a springboard for whole-class discussions. A teacher might first provide students with a set of criteria, give students time to use the criteria to evaluate the alternatives, and finally, initiate a class discussion in which students share their decisions and explain their thinking. Decision-making tasks can also allow students to question the criteria used for decisions.

Technology can enhance decision-making tasks in several ways. For instance, create interactive decision matrices using IWB software or word processing software. First, fill in the critical elements of the matrices—include the items to be considered and the criteria by which to evaluate them. Next, have students discuss the extent to which each item meets each criterion. Be sure to demonstrate the process of completing a decision matrix yourself to show students how it is done, and then allow students to create matrices of their own.

Harness the potential of polling technology to increase the efficiency of decision-making tasks. Students can use clickers or polling software on their mobile devices to contribute to class decision matrices. For example, display an incomplete decision matrix—similar to that in table 6.1—using an IWB, projector, or document camera. Then, have students use polling technology to submit ideas for different elements of the matrix.

Investigation Tasks

Investigation tasks teach students to test hypotheses about past, present, or future events. Marzano (1992) outlines three types of investigations: (1) historical, (2) definitional, and (3) projective. *Historical* investigation involves responding to questions about what happened during a given historical period or event and why those events occurred. *Definitional* investigation involves identifying the defining characteristics of a person, place, event, thing, principle, or concept. *Projective* investigation involves answering hypothetical questions about future events.

Use online search tools to enhance students' investigation tasks. Have students search the Internet for resources or background information about issues they wish to study. For instance, they might search the archives of institutions such as the Smithsonian, the National Archives, the Library of Congress, or the American Museum of Natural History. Alternatively, students can search their local town, community, county, or state archives—such as those in libraries or state museums—to uncover evidence about events or people.

Use online bookmarking tools to enhance students' collections of evidence during the investigation tasks. Students can use social bookmarking tools like Diigo or Delicious to catalog and comment on online resources that support their investigations. Next, students organize the resources based on relevance and usefulness. Finally, students share their social bookmarks with classmates, prompting whole-group discussion and contribution to each other's investigation tasks.

Element 23: Providing Resources and Guidance

The focus of element 23 is providing resources specific to cognitively complex tasks and helping students execute such tasks. Strategies that accompany this element include:

- Providing support for claims

- Examining claims for errors

- Scoring scales

- Feedback

We briefly explain each strategy before offering ways to modify it with technology tools.

Providing Support for Claims

Teachers prompt students to provide grounds, backing, and qualifiers when they make claims or draw conclusions. *Grounds* are the initial evidence for the claim. They answer the question, Why do you think your claim is true? *Backing* is more specific, in-depth information about grounds that helps establish their legitimacy, such as research-based data. *Qualifiers* are exceptions to claims. The more qualifiers a claim requires, the less evidentially sound the claim is.

Have students use Internet search tools to locate reputable online resources to back their claims. They catalog, comment on, and annotate sources of evidence using social bookmarking tools like Diigo or Delicious. Next, students share the sources with their classmates to determine the legitimacy of the evidence, the extent to which it is weakened by erroneous reasoning, or to provide ideas or additional resources for further consideration. Encourage students to add comments by annotating sources of information directly in the social bookmarking site.

Students can also use web-based publishing tools to provide support for claims. They can create a wiki or blog that cites online resources supporting their claims. Encourage students to comment on each source to determine the initial grounds for the claims, the legitimacy of the backing, and any qualifiers that might weaken the original claim, as well as any qualifiers to the evidence. Other students in class then comment on the strength of claims and evidence.

Examining Claims for Errors

Students must be taught to evaluate their claims for errors in reasoning, which include errors of faulty logic, attack, weak reference, and misinformation (see table 5.3, page 79). In addition, a number of errors commonly arise when statistics are involved. Table 6.2 displays the errors, or limitations, commonly found among statistical information.

Table 6.2: Five Types of Statistical Limitations

Category	Description
Analyzing regression toward the mean	Being aware that an extreme score on a measure is most commonly followed by a more moderate score that is closer to the mean
Evaluating errors of conjunction	Being aware that it is less likely that two or more independent events will occur simultaneously than it is that they will occur in isolation
Keeping aware of base rates	Using the general or typical pattern of occurrences in a category of events as the basis on which to predict what will happen in a specific situation
Understanding the limits of extrapolation	Realizing that using trends to make predictions (that is, extrapolating) is a useful practice as long as the prediction does not extend beyond the data for which trends have been observed
Adjusting estimates of risk to account for the cumulative nature of probabilistic events	Realizing that even though the probability of a risky event might be highly unlikely, the probability of the event occurring increases with time and the number of events

Source: Adapted from Marzano & Brown, 2009, pp. 127–128.

Students can also use technology to examine claims for errors. For instance, apply the interactive capabilities of polling technology and IWB software to enhance the process of examining claims for errors in reasoning. Display a set of criteria on IWB software to help students analyze online resources for accuracy, reliability, and usefulness. Students can then use clickers or mobile devices to submit self-assessments of their understanding of each type of error. Use the results of the polling data to prompt whole-class discussion.

Teachers and students can also take advantage of social media tools to increase collaboration in the process of examining claims for errors. Students could catalog and annotate online resources using social bookmarking tools, such as Diigo or Delicious, and then share the resources they find with their classmates, who add annotations that locate reasoning errors in the text, provide links to other online resources that contain similar errors, rewrite the same claim with grounds that do not contain errors, or uncover patterns of reasoning errors in a particular resource.

Scoring Scales

Students can use teacher-created scales to self-monitor their progress and track their improvement during cognitively complex tasks. Scales should include the target learning goal (3.0), a simpler learning goal (2.0), and a complex learning goal (4.0). Technology can enhance the creation and use of these scales.

Use interactive technology to enhance the use of scoring scales when students are engaged in cognitively complex tasks. In IWB software, build interactive W-N-H charts (What did I think before? Now what do I think? How are these thoughts different?) for students to complete during cognitively complex tasks. Students then add to their W-N-H charts upon encountering new knowledge, useful information, or ideas that challenge their current way of thinking about the task.

Teachers can also use polling technology to improve the use of scoring scales. For instance, use IWB or presentation software to display a scoring scale like the one in table 6.3.

Table 6.3: Cognitive Task Scoring Scale

4.0	I understand the simple and complex elements of this task. I can generate insights or inferences about this task as it relates to different contexts beyond the learning goal.
3.0	I understand the simple and complex elements of this task as they relate to the learning goal.
2.0	I understand the simple elements of the task but need more help to understand the complex elements as they relate to the learning goal.
1.0	I need more help to understand both the simple elements and the complex elements of this task as they relate to the learning goal.

Students then share their level of understanding at strategic points during a cognitively complex task. Use this feedback to monitor and adjust the support you provide. Finally, use polling data to promote whole-class discussion and organize students for cooperative learning groups based on the results.

Feedback

Effective feedback often includes discussion about correct versus incorrect answers, tasks performed well, tasks that could be improved, and observable improvement shown. While teachers make comments and offer constructive criticism to students about their work, technology tools can also help students offer feedback to one another.

Use cloud-based word processing tools to enhance the use of feedback during cognitively complex tasks (such as generating and testing hypotheses). For example, students can use Google Drive or Evernote to keep a log or learning journal. This journal can help you identify the level of guidance each student needs. Students can also share selected journal entries with their classmates to elicit feedback or other forms of contribution to their learning. Finally, students post constructive comments that reflect their insights, interests, or background knowledge.

Technology also provides a way to comment on students' digital products. Use the comments feature in word processing software to guide student writing activities and projects. You can even embed hyperlinks within comments to external resources, information, or exemplary writing samples from past students.

Students can also use multimedia tools to share feedback with teachers. For instance, students using screen capture software (such as Jing, ScreenChomp, Educreations, or TouchCast) can narrate questions or problems they encounter with the learning goal. Students then share these screencasts with the teacher and include specific examples of the challenges they are experiencing. Respond to these student screencasts with screencasts of your own to provide targeted feedback.

Finally, students can elicit help and support from teachers via a variety of communication tools. They can email, text message, or use Facebook, Edmodo, or Blendspace to ask questions or request guidance from their teachers. Compile the most common questions from students into an archive for easy retrieval by future classes. Use Google Drive to build a searchable online list of frequently asked questions (FAQs) about specific content (for example, How do I simplify an equation that contains multiple operations?) or about the class in general (for example, Why do I need to learn algebra if I do not plan to be a mathematician?). Teachers can enlist the help of students in the creation of the FAQ list. Advanced students can also create interactive FAQ support resources to correspond with the questions.

Teaching With Technology

In this chapter, we have elaborated on the elements of generating and testing hypotheses about new knowledge, including organizing students for cognitively complex tasks, engaging students in hypothesis generation and testing, and providing resources and guidance. The following vignette illustrates ways in which these elements and others can be enhanced with technology.

Mr. Becker teaches ninth-grade ELA in a rural New England high school. His classroom walls are artfully decorated with posters of famous authors, literary characters, and book covers to stimulate students' interest in the art of storytelling. A charging cart containing six tablets sits on one side of the room. Mr. Becker has also arranged a number of computer kiosks around his classroom where students can explore digital stories and character analyses that previous students have crafted.

Prior to the start of class, Mr. Becker posted the learning goal for the lesson, the proficiency scale, and evidence of proficiency on his class Edmodo page. He asked students to read the learning goal and proficiency scale and post comments indicating that they understand both. He also asked that students post any questions they have—and encouraged them to respond to one another—about the learning goals during the lesson's group activities.

Using a tablet connected to his projector, Mr. Becker activates a random group generator to organize his students into teams. He does this on a regular basis, so his students are familiar with rearranging their desks and chairs based on the groupings. He uses a countdown timer to give them thirty seconds to move before continuing on with the lesson.

Mr. Becker's class is reading Harper Lee's novel *To Kill a Mockingbird*, and today's lesson involves making connections between the characters' traits and critical events in the plot. Throughout the lesson, students will generate hypotheses about the relationships between characters' traits and major events in the story. They will test these hypotheses by seeking textual evidence from the novel to support them.

Before class, Mr. Becker used a mindmapping app on his tablet to create a character trait index to prompt group thinking and discussion. The students download the template onto their tablets from a link on Mr. Becker's Edmodo page. Mr. Becker asks his students to evaluate each character based on his or her actions, decisions, and speech throughout the novel. Then, students use a four-point scale (0–3, with a zero denoting no representation of a particular trait and 3 denoting a high representation) to rate the extent to which characters exhibit each trait (table 6.4). For example, students have given Bob Ewell a low kindness rating because he spits in Atticus's face on p. 290 and a low courage rating because he needs liquor to feel brave enough to attack Scout and Jem in chapter 28.

Table 6.4: Student Character Trait Index

Character	Character Trait			Textual Evidence
	Kindness	Courage	Generosity	
Atticus Finch	3	3	3	"[Real courage] is when you know you're licked before you begin but you begin anyway and you see it through, no matter what" (Lee, 1960, p. 149). "Scout, I couldn't go to church and worship God if I didn't try to help that man" (Lee, 1960, p. 139).
Boo	3	2	3	"I never heard tell that it's against the law for a citizen to do his utmost to prevent a crime from being committed, which is exactly what he did" (Lee, 1960, p. 369). "To my way of thinkin', Mr. Finch, taking the one man who's done you and this town a great service an' draggin' him with his shy ways into the limelight—to me, that's a sin" (Lee, 1960, p. 370).
Scout	2	2	1	"'[Calpurnia] likes Jem better'n she likes me, anyway,' I concluded, and suggested that Atticus lose no time in packing her off" (Lee, 1960, p. 33). "Atticus was right. One time he said you never really know a man until you stand in his shoes and walk around in them. Just standing on the Radley porch was enough" (Lee, 1960, p. 374).
Bob Ewell	0	0	1	"Mr. Bob Ewell stopped Atticus on the post office corner, spat in his face, and told him he'd get him if it took the rest of his life" (Lee, 1960, p. 290). "Low-down skunk with enough liquor in him to make him brave enough to kill children" (Lee, 1960, p. 360).

The template shown in table 6.4 includes the character traits of kindness, courage, and generosity. Other templates might include selfishness, empathy, friendliness, trustworthiness, intelligence, and so on. The template also includes space for students to write supporting evidence found in the book. Mr. Becker asks the students to draw at least one example from the novel that supports the personality traits they have decided each character possesses. He sets a countdown timer on his tablet to give the students twenty minutes for this exercise. As he walks around the room interacting with groups, Mr. Becker reiterates that the point of the activity is to think deeply about the characters in the novel and how various scenes, dialogue, and events in the story support the traits they have ascribed to each character. He makes it clear that while there are no right or wrong answers for this activity, students must support their claims with evidence from the text.

When the countdown timer goes off, Mr. Becker asks the students to link their character trait indexes to the class Edmodo page so he can immediately share each group's work with the whole class. He uses a random name generator to call on students to describe their character trait indexes, provide evidence from the text, or give their opinions on other students' character trait indexes.

In the second part of the lesson, Mr. Becker builds on his students' character analyses by asking them to complete a more challenging task. He asks them to determine how the traits they've attributed to the characters might have affected critical events in the story. The students must generate hypotheses about causal relationships between a character's inferred psychological makeup and critical story events and find evidence from the book that supports their hypotheses.

As an example, Mr. Becker uses the character Atticus Finch, who scored high on all of the character traits in most students' indexes. He hypothesizes that Atticus's sense of empathy for others underpinned his decision to represent the wrongly accused Tom Robinson—even when that action was extremely unpopular with the townsfolk of Maycomb, Alabama. He provides evidence from the third chapter of *To Kill a Mockingbird*, in which Atticus teaches his daughter, Scout, about the importance of empathy. Atticus says, "You never really understand a person until you consider things from his point of view . . . until you climb into his skin and walk around in it" (Lee, 1960, p. 39). Mr. Becker says this quote supports his hypothesis because Atticus takes the time to teach his young daughter the importance of empathy. He points out that Atticus also demonstrates empathy for Tom Robinson when he defends him in court.

Mr. Becker gives the groups a few minutes to discuss this example to frame their understanding of the task. Then, using a random number generator, Mr. Becker assigns a character to each group. He asks the students to collaborate to find examples in which their character's personality traits affect one or more critical events in the novel. The students in each group begin reviewing the plot events in their online journals and consider how their character's traits—evidenced by actions, decisions, or speech—might have influenced a particular event. By asking his students to generate and test hypotheses about the characters in the novel, as well as cite supporting evidence from the text itself, Mr. Becker prompts them to think more deeply about storytelling.

The groups engage in spirited discussions about the novel, while Mr. Becker walks around the room observing the discussions and providing guidance as needed. At times, he stops to ask questions. His students use mind-mapping apps on their tablets to capture their discussions and elaborate on their ideas.

On his Edmodo page, Mr. Becker provides supporting resources, including links to scholarly discussions, articles, and essays about *To Kill a Mockingbird*. He also asks his students to use social bookmarking tools to capture and share the evidence they find. Students can annotate their findings, highlight key sections, and describe how particular passages support their hypotheses. They can also use apps to make digital audio recordings on their tablets and represent their hypotheses in a multimedia format.

Some students find it helpful to use audio recording apps on their tablets to record their thinking and orally express how they came up with their hypotheses. Other students use speech-to-text apps to convert their oral expressions into text that they can incorporate into a word processing document. Still others use avatar software to create virtual representations of their characters using the traits they identified in their character trait indexes. Students record the thinking they used to create the avatars, including the events they believe each character influenced and evidence to support their hypotheses.

When their projects are completed, Mr. Becker's students post them on the class's Edmodo page to share them with classmates and family, as well as with students who are reading the same novel in other parts of the world. The class tracks access to its projects using ClustrMaps. Thus, Mr. Becker's students create and publish resources that contribute to their own learning and the learning of others.

In this example, Mr. Becker has used a number of technology tools to enhance his instructional strategies for a variety of elements. For element 21, organizing students for cognitively complex tasks, Mr. Becker uses a random group generator to divide his students into work groups.

Mr. Becker also effectively uses technology for element 22, engaging students in cognitively complex tasks involving hypothesis generation and testing. Specifically, he uses a mind-mapping app on his tablet to create a character trait index that students can download. He also uses a countdown timer to monitor the time given to complete the task. In addition, his students use a mind-mapping app on their tablets to generate hypotheses about how character traits impact plot events.

Finally, Mr. Becker uses a variety of technologies for element 23, providing resources and guidance. As shown in the vignette, Mr. Becker provides a wealth of online resources on the class Edmodo page to help students with their cognitively complex tasks. His students use social bookmarking tools to collect, annotate, and share online resources, and Mr. Becker uses the same tools to provide feedback to students. Students also use audio recording apps and avatar animation apps to represent their hypotheses in a multimedia format.

Chapter 6: Comprehension Questions

1. Describe a win-win peer tutoring situation that incorporates technology.

2. How can technology enhance cooperative learning?

3. Effective teachers regularly provide feedback and constructive criticism to students about their work. However, teachers who offer frequent feedback can sometimes find themselves repeating the same comments and answering the same questions over and over. How can technology mitigate this issue and make feedback efficient for teachers and accessible to students?

4. How do you use technology to help students generate and test hypotheses about new knowledge? Share your ideas by going to **marzanoresearch.com /classroomstrategies**, clicking on the *Enhancing the Art & Science of Teaching With Technology* link, and becoming a member of our virtual learning community.

Chapter 7

ENGAGING STUDENTS

This design question, which falls under lesson segments enacted on the spot, is, How can I use technology to engage students? Chapter 7 highlights the significance of student engagement in promoting a lively, enthusiastic, and social classroom environment. Nine elements are important to this design question.

Element 24: Noticing when students are not engaged

Element 25: Using academic games

Element 26: Managing response rates

Element 27: Using physical movement

Element 28: Maintaining a lively pace

Element 29: Demonstrating intensity and enthusiasm

Element 30: Using friendly controversy

Element 31: Providing opportunities for students to talk about themselves

Element 32: Presenting unusual or intriguing information

The strategies and behaviors presented in this chapter draw on research on student attention (Connell, Spencer, & Aber, 1994; Connell & Wellborn, 1991; Reeve, 2006). Some argue that engaging students has gradually become more challenging with the rise of fast-paced Internet connections and other media outlets. According to a 2012 Pew Research survey, 87 percent of Advanced Placement (AP) and National Writing Project (NWP) teachers believed that digital technologies are producing "an easily distracted generation with short attention spans," and 64 percent believed that digital technologies "do more to distract students than to help them academically" (Purcell et al., 2012, p. 2). When carried out properly, however, best practices for instructional engagement are still effective in the classroom. Furthermore, teachers can harness the engaging potential of technology for instructional purposes. Each of the aforementioned elements can be supported by specific strategies from *The Art and Science of Teaching* (Marzano, 2007), and each strategy can be supported by specific technology tools.

Element 24: Noticing When Students Are Not Engaged

To use element 24, scan the classroom to monitor students' level of engagement, and react accordingly if you notice that students are not engaged. Strategies associated with this element include:

- Monitoring levels of attention

- Measuring engagement

Several technology tools can be used to enhance each strategy's effectiveness.

Monitoring Levels of Attention

When you detect a student or group of students who appear to be disengaged, re-engage the whole class with an activity. Teachers can also use proximity, questioning, gestures, or eye contact to subtly re-engage individuals or groups of students.

Polling technology can enhance the process of re-engaging students because it allows teachers to spontaneously involve a disengaged class in a questioning task. Pose content-related questions, and ask students to respond using clickers with text input or mobile devices with polling software. Be sure to ask relatively easy questions that all students should be able to answer; the percentage of students who answer the question correctly and the time it takes them to respond will be your indicators of students' levels of attention.

You could also organize students into small groups and give each group its own nickname. List the groups' nicknames on an IWB page, and when a particular group appears to be disengaged, post a symbol (for example, a ringing alarm clock) beside that group's name, indicating that the students in that group should attempt to re-engage.

Measuring Engagement

When measuring engagement, the teacher periodically asks students to signal their levels of engagement. The teacher uses this information to determine when and how to re-engage students.

Have students periodically report their current level of engagement using clickers or polling software on their mobile devices. Students might use the following scale for these reports: (0) not engaged at all, (1) hardly engaged, (2) moderately engaged, (3) engaged, or (4) highly engaged. If students report low levels of engagement, they also submit suggestions via text message about what might improve them.

Element 25: Using Academic Games

For element 25, the teacher can adapt popular games or use inconsequential competition to re-engage students and focus their attention on academic content. This element works well for re-engaging students whose attention is beginning to slip or to proactively maintain students' attention. There are four strategies associated with this element:

- What Is the Question?

- Classroom Feud

- Inconsequential competition

- Vocabulary review games

Here, we address each strategy and how it can be improved with technology tools.

What Is the Question?

In this *Jeopardy!*-inspired game, the teacher prepares a matrix with content-related categories at the head of each column (for example, Angles, the Coordinate Plane, Polygons and Area, Triangle Relationships, and Quadrilaterals) and numbered point values at the beginning of each row (typically, 100, 200, 300, 400, and 500). Next, the teacher puts a clue in every cell in the matrix, with higher point values corresponding to more challenging clues, and hides each one from view. Students can play individually or in teams. A student or team chooses a cell by calling for a category and point value. The teacher reveals the clue inside that cell, and the student or team responds with a question for which the clue would be the answer. For example, one clue might include an image of two angles, with one labeled as 50° and the other labeled as 40° (see figure 7.1).

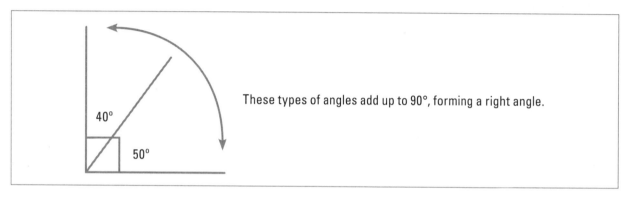

Figure 7.1: Clue for What Is the Question?

Beside the image, the clue also includes an answer: *These types of angles add up to 90°, forming a right angle.* The correct student response, phrased as a question, is, What are complementary angles? With a correct answer, the student or team earns the corresponding points and gets to select another cell. If the answer is incorrect, a different student or team can steal the points by answering the same question. If someone answers correctly, the student or team gets the points for the cell and the opportunity to pick the next cell. If no one gets the answer right, no one earns points, and the original student or team gets to pick a new question.

This strategy can be easily enhanced with technology; the interactivity of multimedia tools makes them a perfect fit for academic games. Create a series of questions and answers and embed them into IWB or presentation software such as Prezi to prepare a game of What Is the Question? for a content review. Split the class into teams with a random group generator like Team Maker, and use a random name generator to select students to respond to clues.

Classroom Feud

In this *Family Feud*-inspired game, the teacher generates a list of content-related questions—with at least one question for every student in the class—and divides the class into two teams. Each team selects an initial spokesperson. Every time the teacher asks a new question, the role of the spokesperson rotates to a different group member. The teacher reads a question to team 1, and the spokesperson for team 1 has fifteen seconds to discuss the answer with his or her teammates before responding on behalf of the team. If team 1 answers correctly, it earns a point, and the teacher asks the students another question. If the students answer incorrectly, team 2 has the opportunity to steal the point and answer the same question correctly. If team 2 answers correctly, it earns the point. If the students answer incorrectly, no points are awarded.

Polling technology is a good enhancement for academic games, because it facilitates whole-class contribution. For instance, play Classroom Feud using clickers with text input or polling software on students' mobile devices. Use a random group generator such as Team Maker to divide your classroom into two or more teams. Teams submit their answers using polling devices, and whoever answers the fastest earns points for his or her team. Alternatively, students can use polling technology to contribute questions for use in the game.

Inconsequential Competition

Inconsequential competition can be used for virtually any activity, but it is especially easy to incorporate in a content review (for example, vocabulary terms, spelling words, literary elements, or historical facts).

Interactive multimedia tools can enhance inconsequential competition. For instance, facilitate inconsequential competition using the container feature of IWB software. When students move an answer into the correct container, a reward sound plays. Answers placed into incorrect containers, on the other hand, snap back to their original positions. Label a series of containers with vocabulary terms, for example, and arrange them on the right side of a page in IWB software. Arrange a series of definitions on the left. Students come up to the IWB to match each vocabulary term to its definition.

Numerous academic game websites can also provide inconsequential competition. For example, students could use desktop computers, laptops, tablets, or IWBs to play educational games at PBS KIDS. Younger students can even play games as their favorite PBS characters while learning.

Polling technology can facilitate a wide variety of academic games as well. For example, elementary students can play rhyming games by using clickers or mobile devices to submit words that rhyme with a given word or phrase. Alternatively, have students play the same game using homonyms. Students can also use polling devices to submit captions for political cartoons or guesses about drawings in Pictionary-based games. Combine polling technology with random number generators to conduct inconsequential competitions in math, or play math memory games focusing on addition, subtraction, multiplication, and division facts. To play a review game for multiplication, use a random number generator to select two numbers, which students multiply together. Students can use clickers or polling software on their mobile devices to submit their answers.

Vocabulary Review Games

To help students practice vocabulary terms, teachers can use various other games and competitions. *Vocabulary Games for the Classroom* (Carleton & Marzano, 2010) describes many engaging and easy-to-prepare games designed to advance the vocabulary skills of students (as shown in table 7.1).

Table 7.1: Vocabulary Review Games From *Vocabulary Games for the Classroom*

Game	Description
Word Harvest	A relay game for lower elementary grade levels in which students race to "harvest" and categorize vocabulary terms from a word wall
Name It!	A relay game for lower elementary grade levels in which students choose pictures from a bucket and try to describe them in one word
Puzzle Stories	A game for upper elementary grade levels in which students rush to assemble puzzles and write narratives based on the revealed image

Game	Description
Two of a Kind	A Memory-inspired game for lower and upper elementary grade levels in which students match homophones (for example, *flour* and *flower*) or homonyms (for example, *left* and *left*) together
Opposites Attract	A Memory-inspired game for lower and upper elementary grade levels in which students match antonyms (for example, *multiply* and *divide*) together
Magic Letter, Magic Word	A game for lower and upper elementary grade levels in which students complete a fill-in-the-blank clue using the first letter of the word as a hint
Definition, Shmefinition	A Balderdash-inspired game for upper elementary through high school grade levels in which students create dictionary definitions for unknown terms and guess which definition is correct
Which One Doesn't Belong?	A *Sesame Street*–inspired game for lower elementary through high school grade levels in which students select the outlier from a group of items
Who Am I?	A twenty-questions game for upper elementary through high school grade levels in which students are assigned identities of famous people (for example, historical figures, authors, scientists, and so on) and need to ask yes-or-no questions of classmates to guess who they are
Where Am I?	A game for lower and upper elementary grade levels in which students use step-by-step verbal instructions to direct one another from point A to point B on a map
Create a Category	A classification game for upper elementary through high school grade levels in which students categorize three or more terms in as many ways as they can think of

Source: Adapted from Carleton & Marzano, 2010.

Open-ended software and online tools can supplement any of these games or your existing repertoire of vocabulary games. For instance, create vocabulary flashcards using Quizlet and play a What's That Term? game by displaying a card, word-side up, in IWB or presentation software. Then, students submit definitions using clickers with text input or mobile devices with polling software. Alternatively, use a random group generator to divide your class into equal teams. Award points to the team whose member is the first to submit the correct definition via clicker or mobile device.

Element 26: Managing Response Rates

Element 26 involves using strategies such as response cards or voting technologies to allow multiple students to respond to questions. Strategies associated with this element include:

- Random names
- Paired response
- Elaborative interrogation
- Multiple types of questions

We describe each strategy in detail and then incorporate technology tools.

Random Names

The traditional way to select students at random is to write students' names on Popsicle sticks and pull them from a paper cup, empty soup can, glass jar, or hat before asking a question. The student whose name is drawn is asked to answer the question, and the teacher picks a new Popsicle stick for the next question.

Technology can eliminate the prep time necessary for this strategy as well as demonstrate to students that the selection process is completely random. Instead of drawing Popsicle sticks, use random name or number generators (such as Team Maker) to call on individual students to answer questions or defend an answer.

Paired Response

In this strategy, students convene in pairs or small groups to respond to a question or prompt. When the teacher calls on a pair for the answer, one student can act as the spokesperson or both students can verbalize the answer together.

To incorporate technology, display a content-related question using IWB or presentation software such as Prezi. Use a random group generator like Team Maker to randomly organize students into pairs or groups who then work together to determine the correct answer. Next, the pairs or groups submit an answer using clickers or polling software on their mobile devices. Use the results of the polling data to generate new questions or initiate whole-class discussions.

Elaborative Interrogation

During elaborative interrogation, teachers can engage students by asking follow-up questions, prompting students to elaborate on or provide evidence for their answers.

Polling technology is highly conducive to elaborative interrogation activities, because it allows students to analyze and elaborate on the responses of the whole class. First, organize students into groups using a random group generator such as Team Maker. Next, pose a question using IWB or presentation software. Students then respond to the question using clickers or polling software on their mobile devices. Display the results of student polls, but do not reveal the correct answer yet. Be sure to provide students with plenty of time to analyze the class's responses in their groups. Offer probing questions, such as How do you know that's true? and Why is that so? After students have discussed the data in their groups, give them a chance to respond a second time. This time, they may change their original answers if they wish. Show the correct answer only after all students have voted a second time.

Multiple Types of Questions

Teachers can pull from various types of questions when trying to gauge or enhance student understanding of the content. Categories of questions include the following:

- Retrieval questions require students to recognize, recall, and execute knowledge that was directly taught.

- Analytical questions require students to take information apart and determine how the parts relate to the whole.

- Predictive questions require students to form conjectures and hypotheses about what will happen next in a narrative or sequence of information or actions.

- Interpretive questions require students to make and defend inferences about the intentions of an author.

- Evaluative questions require students to use criteria to make judgments and assessments of something.

Technology, especially clickers, can enhance students' responses to multiple types of questions. For instance, use the interactive features of IWB software to pose questions and a random name generator such as Team Maker to select students to answer these questions. Be sure to provide the student with ample think time. The student then answers, comes to the IWB, and erases a top layer image, revealing the correct response. If the student answers incorrectly, he or she clicks the undo button in the IWB software to reset the questions. Encourage the student to answer a different question on the same topic.

Students can also submit predictions about the content using clickers with text input or mobile devices with polling software. Check for understanding after introducing new information by having students submit texts to share their level of understanding about the new information. Use the polling results to prompt a class discussion.

Element 27: Using Physical Movement

To maintain a moderate to high energy level among students, teachers can engage students in movement during lessons. Eric Jensen (2005) cites numerous studies that connect physical activity to increased energy (Dwyer, Blizzard, & Dean, 1996; Dwyer, Sallis, Blizzard, Lazarus, & Dean, 2001). Element 27 involves using strategies that require students to move physically. Strategies associated with this element include:

- Stand up and stretch

- Corners activities

We describe each strategy and provide technology tools that can be used to increase the effectiveness of each.

Stand Up and Stretch

Stand-up-and-stretch activities—also called brain breaks—give students a chance to take a mental break from the content and a physical break from sitting down in seats. The teacher can ask students to stand up and stretch intermittently throughout lessons or regularly during transitions. Teachers can also incorporate more physical movement than simple stretching in order to increase oxygen flow and pump more blood to the brain.

Make stand-up-and-stretch activities more fun and interactive using features of IWB software. For instance, use the countdown feature in IWB software to coordinate regular stand-up-and-stretch intervals during class time. Provide these regularly timed brain breaks during instruction so students know when to expect a chance to move, and use the sound of a countdown timer to signify that the break is over. Alternately, schedule brain breaks to occur just before introducing important content. You can also use an online timer or the timer feature in IWB software to coordinate these intervals.

An array of group physical fitness videos is available online. Search the Internet for videos of stretching movements to guide students through stopping and stretching during class time. Use a projector to show warm-up stretching exercises at the beginning of class to help students become relaxed and focused. When the class accomplishes a learning goal, play Nintendo Wii exercise games or follow along with silly 1980s aerobic videos as a class.

Video recording tools allow students to choreograph and practice a flash mob dance sequence about the learning content. Students record the dance sequences using video recording tools on laptops, tablets, or smartphones. In a biology class, for example, students might recreate the process of protein synthesis in the form of a dance that incorporates different colored clothing to represent different nucleotides.

Teachers can also incorporate the use of polling devices to enhance the use of physical movement in their classrooms. Play games in which pairs of students race to the front of the room to solve a learning problem on the IWB, or have students come to the front of the room to interact with the document camera. Alternatively, play Clicker in the Middle, a game in which two teams of students on opposite sides of the classroom have a member race to a set of two clickers in the middle of the room to answer questions.

Corners Activities

In this strategy, the teacher organizes the class into four groups. The groups rotate between four different corners of the room; in each, a different in-depth, content-related question is posted. Each group designates a student to be the recorder. This person jots down notes about the group's examination and discussion of the question. After several minutes, the groups rotate clockwise one corner and the process repeats.

Use a random group generator such as Team Maker to separate the class into four groups. Each group moves to one of the four corners of the room to engage in a collaborative task. When the activity ends, students share representations of their work on the class website.

Element 28: Maintaining a Lively Pace

Element 28 addresses the need to maintain a lively pace in the classroom. This element involves slowing and quickening the pace of instruction to enhance the engagement of students. Strategies associated with this element include:

- Instructional segments

- Pace modulation

Here, we explain the strategies and establish ways in which they can be modified with educational technology tools.

Instructional Segments

To introduce the various instructional segments, the teacher briskly—though not hastily—guides the class through each part of the lesson, including presenting new content, practicing and deepening key knowledge and skills, getting students organized into groups, doing seat work, listening during transitions between activities, and distributing, scoring, and collecting assignments.

Use the visual components of presentation software to help maintain a lively pace during this strategy. The zoom tools in IWB software or online presentation software such as Prezi can focus on a single chunk within a learning progression and help students manage their own pace.

Pace Modulation

Effective teachers self-monitor the pace of their lessons and either speed up or slow down according to the engagement needs of their students. The technology tools outlined for this strategy allow the teacher to quickly and easily collect student feedback about the pace of instruction.

Determine the appropriateness of your instructional pace at any given time by asking students to rate it using clickers with text input or mobile devices with polling software. Use descriptors like "too fast," "too slow," or "just right." Use the data to consider the pace of your instruction, and modify it accordingly. For example, if the majority of students respond that the pace is too slow, consider cutting back on tangents and speaking more quickly. If the majority of students respond that the pace is too fast, consider slowing down and reviewing material you have already presented.

Element 29: Demonstrating Intensity and Enthusiasm

Element 29 involves the teacher using verbal and nonverbal cues to signal that he or she is enthusiastic about the content. Thomas Good and Jere Brophy (2003) stressed the importance of demonstrating enthusiasm. They also stressed the difference between enthusiasm, which consists of a teacher's own reasons for seeing a topic as interesting, and "unnecessary theatrics" (p. 238) that do little to highlight the value of the topic. They added that "teachers can use dramatics or forceful salesmanship if they are comfortable with these techniques, but if not, low-key but sincere statements of the value that they place on a topic or activity will be just as effective" (p. 238). Teachers should select techniques from the following list that suit their personalities and instructional styles. Strategies associated with this element include:

- Explicit connections

- Nonlinguistic representations

- Personal stories

- Humor

- Movies and film clips

Here, we describe each strategy and explain how to improve it with technology.

Explicit Connections

In this strategy, the teacher makes direct links between the content and local, national, or global events. Teachers can also explain connections between content and the personal interests, hobbies, or life experiences of students.

Use videoconferencing technologies to enhance explicit connections. The class can engage in academic videoconferences via Skype with similarly aged students in other parts of the world. During a Spanish language class, for example, students engage in an online discussion with students in a Spanish-speaking country.

Students can also use audio recording software such as Audacity to have students conduct and capture interviews with community members. For example, a class of elementary students might visit a local nursing home to interview senior citizens about their lives. Students ask questions about personal stories, accounts of historical events in American history, and the impact these events had on interviewees' lives. Alternatively, students might videoconference with experts from various institutions (such as NASA or the Library of Congress) that relate to the learning content.

Nonlinguistic Representations

The teacher exposes students to new methods of visualizing content by representing it in a variety of nonlinguistic ways, such as with graphic organizers, flowcharts, images, and infographics.

Various tools in IWB or presentation software allow you to create nonlinguistic representations of content. Incorporate pictures, images, sounds, animation, and videos to represent people, places, things, ideas, or concepts. For example, during a math lesson on triangulation, use images of navigational tools and maps that ancient mariners might have used to plot courses in open water. Show animation or movie clips of sailors using compasses to enhance students' understanding of how these triangulation tools aid navigation.

Present students with nonlinguistic representations of complex texts to help them ascertain new patterns of concepts or ideas. Create a word cloud using Wordle to compare and contrast different uses of rhetoric between writers. Search the Internet for digital transcripts of opposing presidential candidates' campaign speeches, for example, and use Wordle to create a word cloud of each speech. Display each word cloud side by side using presentation software, such as Prezi or Google Drive, or IWB software. Students can then analyze patterns of word usage and the implications of such patterns for each speech. For example, the phrase *geochemical exploration* sounds more romantic and less destructive than *drilling for oil*, even though both phrases essentially mean the same thing.

Personal Stories

When appropriate, teachers should share personal anecdotes related to the content. They might recall and retell their own reactions to the content when they first learned it or present unique facts about the content that are not in the textbook. Furthermore, teachers can encourage students to tell their own personal stories that connect to the content.

Use polling technology to enhance the impact of personal stories. Students respond to questions about personal stories using clickers with text input or mobile devices with polling software. For example, a teacher might tell a story about a time he or she was scared to try something new and then ask students to text in a one-sentence summary of a similar story. Teachers can also provide more close-ended prompts; for instance, How many siblings do you have? or Would you rather have the ability to fly or the ability to read minds? Then, students analyze the polling data to develop a different perspective of their classmates' interests and backgrounds.

Humor

Humor is a great way to show excitement about content and create an atmosphere of warmth and levity. Peter Jonas (2010) found that humor in the classroom was associated with a 40 percentile point gain in student achievement. He observed that "using humor to improve classroom instruction is not only supported by research, but it has proven to be successful" (p. 27). Depending on a teacher's personality and instructional style, he or she might show a funny political cartoon or video, direct jokes at him- or herself, use silly quotes or voices, or point out absurdities in a textbook, film, or article. To avoid unnecessary theatrics, always use humor appropriately, strategically, and in moderation.

Find humorous animations or videos online to share with your students. Present these using a projector or IWB, and prompt students to use polling technology to connect the video to the learning goal. Use the results of the polling data to hold classroom discussions about how the clip connects to the learning goal. Be sure to screen any clip before showing it in class to ensure its appropriateness.

Display single-panel cartoons with the captions removed or blocked from view on IWB or presentation software such as Prezi. Students can then contribute captions to the cartoons using clickers with text input or mobile devices with polling software. Alternatively, students can use polling technology to complete content-related sentence stems with jokes. For example, students learning about figurative language could complete simile sentence stems such as the following: "When he first saw her face, Romeo fell for Juliet like _____." Sample submissions include, "like my little brother falls on rollerblades" or "like a bird from a frayed electrical wire."

Movies and Film Clips

Teachers can use video clips of movies, documentaries, and news stories to connect content to real-world events and situations. Students can also make their own movies and broadcasts that connect the content to their lives. This strategy piques students' interest in the content.

Spark classroom creation of movie and film clips with video recording tools. Students use the video recording capabilities of laptops, tablets, or smartphones to create videos that demonstrate their understanding of new learning content. They can use movie editing software such as iMovie to add transitions, effects, and music. Post completed videos to a video sharing site like Vimeo or YouTube.

Screen capture software (such as Jing, ScreenChomp, Educreations, or TouchCast) can also enhance the use of movies in a learning activity. Students create multimedia tutorials that demonstrate their understanding of new learning content and post links to completed screencasts on a class website. Students can then promote the distribution of the projects using social media pages such as Twitter, Edmodo, or Facebook. Use ClustrMaps to track access to student-created screencast tutorials.

Element 30: Using Friendly Controversy

Element 30 involves techniques that require students to take and defend a position about content. In light of the focus on argumentation in the Common Core State Standards, using friendly controversy in the classroom serves as more than just an engagement strategy. When using friendly controversy, teachers should ensure that students adhere to a series of guidelines for respectful and productive discourse, including listening when others are talking, criticizing ideas rather than people, making an effort to understand the opinions of others, and providing reasons and evidence for all claims. Strategies associated with this element include:

- Class vote

- Expert opinions

- Diagramming perspectives

- Lincoln-Douglas debate

Here, we elaborate on each strategy and describe ways to enhance it with educational technology tools.

Class Vote

In a class vote, the teacher presents a controversial issue to the class and has students express their opinions through a vote. The teacher can have them vote before a whole-class discussion and then again afterward to see if any perspectives have changed. He or she can also incorporate physical movement by designating one side of the room as *pro*, the other as *con*, and the middle of the room as *undecided*. Students move to whatever area of the room corresponds with their opinion and discuss with their like-minded classmates. After each side has had a chance to state its case to the whole class, students have the opportunity to switch sides, and undecided students are asked to take a stance.

For obvious reasons, polling technology can enhance class voting. Use clickers with text input or polling software on students' mobile devices to submit anonymous votes on a controversial subject. Use the polling data to pair students with people who disagree with them. Provide guiding questions for the pairs to use in their discussions of their positions. At the end of the discussion, ask students to vote again. Analyze the pre- and postquestion data as a class to determine whether any students changed their minds.

Expert Opinions

In this strategy, students research the opinions of individuals who are experts on a particular issue. Students can determine whether someone is an expert by assessing that person's level of experience (a novice firefighter versus one who has worked for twenty-five years), skills (an undecorated novelist versus one who has earned the Pulitzer Prize), or credentials (a self-described anthropologist versus one who holds a doctorate in anthropology). To help students share the expert opinions they find, teachers can use a jigsaw strategy, assigning different opinions to small groups and having students report back to the class with the information found.

Search the Internet to find expert opinions when preparing for friendly controversy. Students can search online to locate resources and research various opinions on controversial issues, such as gun control or global warming. Next, they use social bookmarking tools such as Diigo or Delicious to catalog, annotate, and share their evidence with the class. Encourage students to determine the reliability of resources by examining the claims for errors in reasoning.

Diagramming Perspectives

Students can outline, compare, and contrast competing perspectives on an issue using a graphic organizer. Venn diagrams work well for diagramming perspectives because they clearly illustrate how two seemingly opposite opinions are similar as well as different.

Utilize multimedia recording tools to enhance activities involving diagramming perspectives. For instance, have students use audio recording software like Audacity or video recording software to record individual or group positions on a controversial subject. After the whole class views or listens to each recording, students individually compare the various perspectives using a Venn diagram. The Venn diagram in figure 7.2 depicts what a student might write after hearing classmates' digitally recorded arguments on the issue of school uniforms.

After students have individually recorded the opinions presented by the small groups, they can share their diagrams using a document camera. Complete an interactive Venn diagram as a class using IWB software. Prompt students to write a persuasive paragraph or essay expressing their own opinions on the topic.

Lincoln-Douglas Debate

Lincoln-Douglas debates allow students to practice verbally making assertions and articulating their evidential support. To begin, the teacher divides the class into small groups, organizes those groups into sets of two groups each, and assigns a controversial policy or issue to each set. One of the small groups

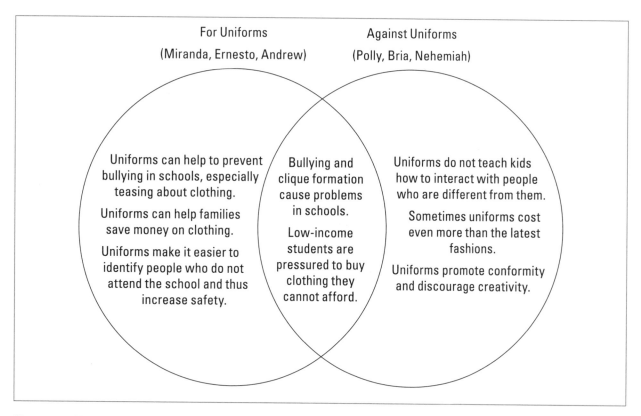

For Uniforms
(Miranda, Ernesto, Andrew)

Against Uniforms
(Polly, Bria, Nehemiah)

Uniforms can help to prevent bullying in schools, especially teasing about clothing.

Uniforms can help families save money on clothing.

Uniforms make it easier to identify people who do not attend the school and thus increase safety.

Bullying and clique formation cause problems in schools.

Low-income students are pressured to buy clothing they cannot afford.

Uniforms do not teach kids how to interact with people who are different from them.

Sometimes uniforms cost even more than the latest fashions.

Uniforms promote conformity and discourage creativity.

Figure 7.2: Venn diagram comparing diverse perspectives heard in classmates' digitally recorded statements.

in the set argues in favor of the issue, the other against it. Each side has an opportunity to present opening statements, cross-examine the opposing team, offer a rebuttal, and present closing statements. The whole class debriefs afterward to evaluate the performance of each team, and each student completes a self-evaluation.

Students can use videoconferencing tools such as Skype to engage in virtual debates with other classrooms. In a social studies class, for example, students learn about local government by participating in civil debates on local, state, or federal pieces of legislation. Students then engage in projects with students in other schools to research controversial bills or pending pieces of legislation and participate in a virtual debate via Skype. Alternatively, students can use Skype to engage in debates with state or federal representatives.

Element 31: Providing Opportunities for Students to Talk About Themselves

Rather than feel obligated to squelch all side conversations, teachers can take advantage of the social inclinations of their students by channeling them into content-related activities. Providing opportunities for students to talk about themselves involves using techniques that allow students to relate content to their personal lives and interests. Strategies associated with this element include:

- Student learning profiles
- Life connections

Here, we explain how to modify each of these strategies with educational technology tools.

Student Learning Profiles

Student learning profiles are surveys, inventories, or informal discussions that help teachers gather information from students. They can address the types of learning environments students like, their preferred forms of self-expression (for example, writing, oral communication, physical movement, artistic media, and so on), and what they feel is their personal learning style (for example, creative, analytical, practical, or mixed).

Online data-collection tools can be used to enhance student learning profiles. For example, use online survey tools such as SurveyMonkey to administer learning preference surveys to students. The survey might ask a question—for example, How do you learn best?—and provide the following multiple-choice options: (a) listening to lectures, (b) reading new information, (c) watching others, (d) doing projects, (e) talking things over, or (f) engaging multiple senses. Analyze the results of the survey to learn about students' preferences, and consider ways to improve your lessons.

Polling technology can also enhance student responses to student learning profiles. Create questions about students' preferred learning styles and the strategies students employ when tackling challenging content. Students respond using clickers with text input or mobile devices with polling software. Analyze the polling data to become better informed about the class and to prompt discussion about students' learning preferences and strategies.

Life Connections

Effective teachers intentionally plan breaks during instructional time for students to identify and discuss links between the content being studied and their own personal experiences, hobbies, and interests. Students can create analogies and nonlinguistic organizers to express the similarities and differences between the content and their own lives.

Encourage students to write and post entries on blogs, wikis, Facebook, Edmodo, or Blendspace that connect their life experiences to content. Students can also create and share multimedia screencasts about these connections with screencasting software, such as Jing, ScreenChomp, Educreations, or TouchCast. Alternatively, students could capture images representative of their interests with Instagram or Snapchat. They should also explain the connections between these images and learning content.

Students can use audio recording software such as Audacity to record their personal connections to content. Alternatively, students could record recited poetry, raps, or songs that express their thinking about the learning content with music recording software like GarageBand. Video recording tools on tablets or smartphones are also an option to help students record personal stories that relate to the content. They would then share these life connections on the class website.

Element 32: Presenting Unusual or Intriguing Information

Element 32 addresses the presentation of strange or fascinating information to spark student interest in the lesson. This element involves providing, or encouraging students to identify, intriguing information about the content. Strategies associated with this element include:

- Teacher-presented information

- Webquests

- History files

- Guest speakers and firsthand consultants

We briefly define each strategy and describe how to develop it with technology.

Teacher-Presented Information

In this strategy, the teacher presents strange or fascinating information to grab the attention of students. Obviously, content-related facts are ideal, but any piece of information that causes the class to listen a little more closely can be beneficial.

Before a lesson, post intriguing news stories and videos or unusual images, photos, and animation clips on the class website. Encourage students to post comments connecting the information to the learning content as preview homework. Alternatively, create multimedia screencasts of unusual or intriguing information and hyperlink them to the class social media page.

Search the Internet to find content-related information that is also unusual or intriguing. Image-based content-sharing websites such as Flickr, Instagram, or Pinterest are great places to start. Use an IWB or projector to display a content-related mystery image. Students then use polling technology to submit guesses about the nature of the image and about how it connects to the content.

Webquests

Using a teacher-designed learning path, students search the Internet to collect interesting details, theories, and facts that relate to the content.

After sending students on such a search, use student-found resources to elicit predictions and discussion. Use a random name generator each week to select a student to be the learning scout, who presents new, intriguing, or unusual information to the class. The class connects the learning scout's findings to the content, and students submit their connections using clickers or mobile devices with polling software.

History Files

In this strategy, teachers present different points of view and perspectives throughout history, or students research various perspectives and present their findings to the class. Facts about the way people thought or behaved in the past can provide an interesting contrast to students' thinking and behavior in the present.

Use technology tools to engage students in the presentation of history files. Share content-related primary sources (such as letters from soldiers, audio files, video files, images, or news headlines) from the online resources of the Smithsonian, the National Archives, PBS, or NPR. Embed these primary-source documents into IWB or presentation software such as Prezi. Alternatively, have your students search for primary-source documents.

Guest Speakers and Firsthand Consultants

Inviting guests to visit is automatically engaging due to the presence of someone new in the classroom. Teachers can draw from a wide range of expertise and careers to provide a real-world application of the content for students.

Increase the availability of guest speakers and firsthand consultants with videoconferencing tools. Consider using an online videoconferencing tool such as Skype to invite a guest speaker to present intriguing or unusual information to the class. Students should prepare questions for the speaker in advance. Be sure to request permission from the guest speaker to record the videoconference so you can share the discussion with absent class members or future students. Alternatively, use videoconferencing tools to invite a guest expert to pose a learning quest to the class—the guest could provide intriguing clues that students must use to solve a content-related riddle.

Teaching With Technology

This chapter has focused on the crucial task of engaging students, which includes using academic games and physical movement, maintaining a lively pace, demonstrating intensity and enthusiasm, and providing opportunities for students to talk about themselves, and more. This vignette illustrates technology-enhanced versions of these elements and others.

Mrs. Miller teaches mathematics to middle school students in an urban school district. She uses technology to sustain high levels of engagement in and out of the classroom. She regularly asks students questions—the answers to which all students should know—and uses their response times and the percentage of correct responses as indicators of students' current attention levels. Her students score themselves on their levels of engagement, and Mrs. Miller graphs the average levels of class engagement. Recently, she has also been using screencast lectures and social media tools to support students' interaction with new content outside of class. She guides and facilitates students' online discussions to help them think, communicate, and build background knowledge about the content before class. These tools have enabled her to spend less time delivering content knowledge during class and more time asking and answering questions to clarify students' understanding.

Mrs. Miller has found that her students often use social media to talk about themselves, as well. As they're familiar with social media interactions, her students comfortably use the class Edmodo site to post real-time status updates about their thoughts or feelings. She knows that it's important for her students to feel comfortable expressing themselves and contributing to the class's discussions, both face to face and online.

Mrs. Miller often uses her Edmodo page to post unusual or intriguing information to pique students' curiosity and stimulate their thinking. She posts compelling text files, images, audio files, and video files, as well as screencast tutorials created by past students. The information and links on the class Edmodo page can also stimulate friendly controversy, which helps students consider new content from different perspectives. Stimulating controversy in a moderated online forum also gives students safe opportunities to develop interpersonal skills in addition to cognitive ones. Because student responses can be archived and extended, they often generate new conversations based on the original controversy. Mrs. Miller's students love sharing their opinions, and she holds them accountable for posting respectfully based on the rules and procedures that they helped establish early in the year.

Prior to today's lesson, Mrs. Miller introduced the procedure for finding the slope of a line. She used the Educreations app on her tablet to create a screencast tutorial about the procedure and then posted it on the class Edmodo page for her class to watch as homework. Her students viewed the screencast the previous evening and engaged in an online discussion about the new content. Mrs. Miller reads and moderates her students' posts, regularly adding comments or questions. The Edmodo site maintains an archive of interactions, so Mrs. Miller can retrieve any of her students' posts to determine each student's level of engagement.

The screencast tutorial is simply a digital recording of Mrs. Miller's voice and handwriting as she introduces key concepts and narrates her process of finding slope. She includes several think-aloud examples, including a word problem in which she finds the slope of a skateboard ramp. As they watch the lesson, students can pause or replay various sections as needed. As a result of the time they've spent thinking, reflecting, and interacting about slope prior to class, students come better prepared to elaborate on, practice, and deepen their understanding.

Mrs. Miller's students sit in work group stations around the room. The classroom has an IWB in the front of the room, and each student has a tablet to work with. She begins the lesson by using her IWB to run a random name generator. The students pay attention in anticipation of having their name drawn. Mrs. Miller intensifies this anticipation by playing theme music from a familiar game show and modulating her voice to sound like a game show announcer. Finally, Susan's name appears on the IWB.

Susan approaches the IWB amid cheers from the teammates in her group. Mrs. Miller asks Susan if she has viewed the screen capture tutorial that was assigned for homework. Susan answers that she did and is ready to solve the problem. With that, Mrs. Miller uses the IWB to display a line on the coordinate plane for which Susan must find the slope. With a click, Mrs. Miller activates the screen capture function of the software to record Susan's interactions on the board as she solves the problem. When Susan completes the problem, Mrs. Miller asks her to gauge her confidence that the answer she came up with is the correct one. Susan responds that her level of confidence is a four out of five.

Mrs. Miller asks the class if it has any questions for Susan about how she found the slope of the line. Alan raises his hand. After being acknowledged by Mrs. Miller, Alan says that he understands the equation for finding slope—divide the rise by the run—but he is having trouble remembering which is which. He asks Susan how she tells them apart. Susan explains that she remembers that the rise is the difference in the y-axis by picturing a hot-air balloon rising vertically through the coordinate plane. She remembers the run is the difference in the x-axis by picturing a tiny person running horizontally across the plane. Alan thanks Susan and enters her analogy into his tablet so that he can remember it later.

At the end of this student exchange, Mrs. Miller asks the entire class to vote on whether or not Susan arrived at the correct answer. She sets up the polling event on her IWB, and students submit their answers using an app on their tablets. When all of the students have voted, Mrs. Miller displays the results of the poll. About 90 percent of the class has agreed that Susan's problem-solving process was accurate. Mrs. Miller then reveals the correct slope of the line, which confirms that Susan's work was accurate. The class cheers, and the process begins again as Mrs. Miller selects another student to work out a different problem.

Next, Mrs. Miller assigns students a more challenging set of problems to work on using their tablets. The students go to their work groups to practice and deepen their understanding of this new problem type. They record problem-solving tutorials using screen capture apps on their tablets and headsets with built-in microphones. Students invest a good deal of effort into these narrative tutorials because they know that they are meant to demonstrate their understanding of slope, as well as to teach other students what they now understand.

As the students work in their groups, Mrs. Miller walks around the room observing students' levels of interaction and engagement. When she notices a low level of engagement in any one of the groups, she casually approaches the group and asks questions in order to verify students' understanding of the content and to provide any needed interventions or explanations. Mrs. Miller can ascertain the level of students' engagement by observing their interactions in the classroom and by monitoring their online exchanges on the class Edmodo page.

Her students also use a cloud-based note-taking app to maintain their online journals, in which they record reflections on their learning and the projects they are developing. The online journals are cognitive construction sites for students: they can access the journals from various devices (such as smartphones, tablets, laptops, or desktop computers), capture their thoughts on the spot, and then expand on them at any time in the future.

Mrs. Miller changed the physical layout of her classroom to accommodate the use of physical movement because she knows that in order to keep her students cognitively engaged, she also has to keep their bodies occupied. After a period of time, Mrs. Miller uses a countdown timer on her IWB to give the students two minutes to finish and save their screencasts. Students hurriedly make final adjustments and save their work. At the end of the two-minute period, a song starts playing through the speakers on Mrs. Miller's IWB. On hearing this cue, the students stand up and follow Mrs. Miller's lead through a stretching routine that lasts about one minute. They stretch their arms, legs, backs, and necks and perform breathing exercises. At the end of the stand-up-and-stretch break, students leave their own tablets at their tables and carry their headsets to a different group's table. Sitting down at a classmate's tablet, each student plugs in his or her headset to view the screencast the classmate just created.

Students offer meaningful and valuable feedback on their peers' screencasts. The entire class becomes a beta test group for the tutorials and other products that the students develop prior to sharing them on their project blog site. The feedback that the classmates provide one another helps contribute to students' understanding of their own thinking and the thinking of their classmates.

Mrs. Miller maintains a lively pace during classroom instruction by constantly shifting the locus of learning from herself to the whole group, to small group, to the individual student, then back to the small group, to the whole group, and to herself. She knows that quickly switching the locus of student engagement helps sustain students' interest. Mrs. Miller also stops frequently to ask her students questions. Using polling apps on their tablets, every student responds to the questions, making their thinking visible to the entire class. Because she uses technology that allows every student to respond, Mrs. Miller can engage the entire class in thinking about the content.

Mrs. Miller often has students generate questions that are then posed to the entire class. She finds that in the process of generating good questions for their classmates, her students think deeply about their own experiences with the learning content. They come up with questions that reflect their unique backgrounds and learning experiences, and the variety of questions contributes to the group's understanding.

Mrs. Miller uses a number of technology tools to enhance her instruction. For element 24, noticing when students are not engaged, she regularly uses polling technology to monitor students' responses to relatively easy questions as an indicator of their levels of attention. She also tracks students' reported levels of engagement.

Mrs. Miller also effectively uses technology for element 25, using academic games. Specifically, Mrs. Miller uses a random name generator to select students. Students use the IWB to compete in a problem-solving game.

Mrs. Miller also manages response rates, element 26, with technology. Her students answer questions with a polling app on their tablets, and Mrs. Miller posts questions on her class social media page, prompting all students to respond via a random name generator and polling technology.

As illustrated in the vignette, Mrs. Miller uses technology for element 27, using physical movement. She randomly selects students to approach the IWB to solve problems. She also uses a countdown timer and a sound through the speakers in her IWB to guide students through a coordinated stretching routine.

Mrs. Miller maintains a lively pace, element 28, with technology as well. In the scenario, she uses IWB tools to keep up a tempo that preserves student engagement. In addition, her students use tablets for small-group work and to respond to questions.

For element 29, demonstrating intensity and enthusiasm, Mrs. Miller effectively uses screencast tools, social media, her IWB, and polling technology. Her students post comments on a social media site, engage in academic games on the IWB, and answer questions using their tablets.

To enhance element 30, using friendly controversy, Mrs. Miller posts hyperlinks on her Edmodo page to stimulate debates among her students. They respond to these posts by submitting comments and responding to one another. This level of online engagement carries over to the physical setting of the classroom.

Mrs. Miller also leverages the power of social media tools for element 31, providing opportunities for students to talk about themselves. She asks students to post comments on the class Edmodo page that reflect their unique backgrounds and interests. Students readily talk about themselves in this online format, which helps enhance their engagement in both online and face-to-face interactions.

Finally, Mrs. Miller uses technology for element 32, presenting unusual or intriguing information. In particular, she searches the Internet for strange and fascinating information, which she displays on her IWB or posts to the class Edmodo page.

Chapter 7: Comprehension Questions

1. Consider the academic games you use to keep students engaged in your own classroom. Brainstorm ways in which these games could be enhanced with technology.

2. How can teachers use technology to enhance students' life connections with learning content?

3. How can technology help teachers distinguish between showing enthusiasm (their own reasons for enjoying a topic) and engaging in the types of behavior that Good and Brophy (2003) refer to as unnecessary theatrics?

4. How do you use technology to engage students in your classroom? Share your ideas by going to **marzanoresearch.com/classroomstrategies**, clicking on the *Enhancing the Art & Science of Teaching With Technology* link, and becoming a member of our virtual learning community.

Chapter 8

RECOGNIZING LEVELS OF ADHERENCE TO RULES AND PROCEDURES

The design question presented in chapter 8 is, How can I use technology to recognize and acknowledge adherence or lack of adherence to rules and procedures? Throughout a lesson, teachers should exhibit strategies and actions that acknowledge students' behaviors. Three elements are important to this design question, which falls under lesson segments enacted on the spot.

Element 33: Demonstrating withitness

Element 34: Applying consequences for lack of adherence to rules and procedures

Element 35: Acknowledging adherence to rules and procedures

Each of these elements is supported by the general research on classroom management (Wang, Haertel, & Walberg, 1993) and discipline (Marzano, 2003). This chapter addresses specific strategies that support each element, as well as the technology tools that can be used to improve them.

Element 33: Demonstrating Withitness

If a teacher is demonstrating withitness, it means he or she is aware of variations in student behavior that might indicate potential disruptions and is attending to them immediately. Strategies associated with element 33 include:

- Being proactive

- Noticing potential problems

We outline each strategy and include technology tools that can be used to enhance it.

Being Proactive

Many behavior issues can be resolved with careful planning and being proactive. To prevent behavior issues, teachers can confer privately with potentially disruptive students to put them at ease and review classroom expectations. They can also create contingency plans for various behavior scenarios that might be likely to arise throughout the day.

Become more proactive by using video recording tools on a desktop computer, laptop, tablet, smartphone, or document camera to record a lesson. Analyze the video to determine your level of withitness in the classroom. For instance, if you wish to be more proactive about preventing emerging behavioral issues, set up a recording device to capture your interactions with students during class. Consider the methods you use to monitor classroom interactions and ways in which you might modify these methods.

Noticing Potential Problems

Effective teachers maintain alertness and vigilance during lessons, putting out behavioral fires before they spread. There may be trouble brewing if a teacher notices, for example, a group or pair of students crowded together and talking intensely, a student who has been unengaged for an extended period of time, multiple students glancing at one another and smiling at a certain location in the classroom, or students giggling or whispering when the teacher's back is turned.

Take advantage of polling technology to help you notice and respond to potential behavior issues. If you sense trouble brewing, defuse the situation by asking students to rate their feelings about adhering to classroom rules and procedures. Alternatively, ask students to rate the extent to which their behavior reflects adherence to the classroom rules and procedures. Use the results of the student poll to encourage a class discussion on the classroom constitution. Stress the importance of each student's contribution to classroom community.

Use technology tools to divert students' attention from potentially disruptive stimuli. If attention is waning, prompt students to log into their online reflective journals on Google Drive or Evernote to record their feelings and brainstorm alternatives to disruptive speech or behavior. Pause the activity, and ask students to write down the conditions or circumstances that may be causing them to act out, along with two or three favorable behaviors to enact instead.

Element 34: Applying Consequences for Lack of Adherence to Rules and Procedures

Element 34 addresses the tricky business of applying consequences for lack of adherence to classroom rules and procedures. The key to effectively using this element is to give consequences *consistently* and *fairly*. Strategies associated with this element include:

- Time-out

- Interdependent group contingency

- Home contingency

Here, we explain the strategies and how they can be supported with technology tools.

Time-Out

If a student is overcome with emotion, is losing control, or generally needs some space, a teacher can send the student to a designated area (either in or out of the classroom, as long as the student is supervised) to cool down. While the student is taking time out to refocus, he or she should complete a reflection activity and cultivate a written action plan that states what will be done differently upon returning to class. When the student has reflected, relaxed, and is ready to try again, he or she can resume regular classroom activities.

Use technology to help students refocus their emotions and behavior. Create reflective behavior templates using word processing tools such as Google Drive or cloud-based apps such as Evernote. Students complete these templates after exhibiting a lack of adherence to rules or procedures. For example, students might write about something that stimulated an undesirable emotion, reflect on the behavior they chose to display as a result, and list three appropriate choices they might have made instead.

Interdependent Group Contingency

In this strategy, if every student in the class is meeting a certain standard for behavior, the teacher rewards the whole class. Group contingency can prompt students to regulate behavior among themselves and hold one another accountable for the success of the group. Middle and high school teachers should proceed with caution, lest students perceive this form of sanction as "unfair." Combat this perception by preemptively explaining to students that during the learning process, a class succeeds and fails as a team.

Use a random group generator such as Team Maker to divide students into teams for group contingency. Track team points earned through engagement, citizenship, or contribution to the class using IWB software. Alternatively, use online behavioral management resources like ClassDojo to keep track of the points students earn for positive behavioral choices and strong contributions to the learning environment.

Utilize the community-building capability of social media to enhance group contingency. Post classroom rules, procedures, and consequences on a class website and encourage students to post comments and questions about them. Prompt student discussions by posting scenarios that reflect adherence and lack of adherence to rules and procedures. Students then comment in response to these scenarios, explaining whether the behavior is helpful or unhelpful to the learning environment.

Home Contingency

In this strategy, the teacher maintains regular communication with the families of individual students regarding their academic, personal, and behavioral success in school. Home-teacher communication takes many forms, including phone conversations, in-person conferences, and written communication. If students perceive a unity between adults at home and adults at school, all parties benefit: the student senses an expansion in his or her support network, the parents feel a sense of ownership regarding their child's education, and the teacher has an ally to provide support and implement consequences for students outside of school.

Behavior management websites can enhance home contingency in the classroom. ClassDojo, for example, allows you to set up a group for each of your classes. Students create accounts within the online community and generate digital avatars that represent their interests and backgrounds. You can then regularly attribute points to students who exhibit positive behaviors. Generate individual student behavior reports to send to parents while students set behavioral goals and track their progress. Digital communication tools can also make home contingency easier on teachers and parents. Communicate via texts or emails to inform parents of student contracts and behavior updates throughout the year.

Element 35: Acknowledging Adherence to Rules and Procedures

In addition to applying consequences, teachers should applaud positive behavior that occurs in their classrooms as often as possible. Element 35 addresses ways to acknowledge adherence to rules and procedures, which involves consistently and fairly recognizing students who are observing the rules and procedures. Strategies associated with this element include:

- Tangible recognition
- Phone calls, emails, and notes

Each strategy is explained here and supplemented with technology tips.

Tangible Recognition

Teachers can give students special privileges or activities to clearly emphasize and reward positive behavior. Effective tangible rewards include free time, field trips, classwide recognition, and individual recognition.

Use online word processing software such as Google Drive to create awards or certificates. These awards can include both behavioral and academic successes. Print and distribute these documents to students during classroom celebrations. Alternatively, convert the digital document into a PDF to be preserved and shared electronically with families.

Museums and other educational institutions can also enhance the use of tangible recognition in classrooms. Have students search the Internet to find ideas for digital field trips (such as a virtual tour of the Great Barrier Reef Aquarium or the Kew Gardens) that can serve as rewards for reaching a collective goal. Alternatively, organize classroom participation in a live videoconference using software such as Skype with a museum's subject area expert or with a partner class in another part of the world.

Use IWB software to create an interactive Student of the Week template that displays a student's photo and describes why he or she is receiving recognition. Display the form at the beginning of each day on the classroom IWB for a week. Alternatively, create a Student of the Week or Student of the Month page on the class website. Highlight examples of work by recognized students.

Phone Calls, Emails, and Notes

A positive phone call, email, or note home is an extremely effective way to reinforce adherence to rules and procedures. A good goal for a teacher might be to make one positive call every afternoon, not only because the affirmation can do wonders for the self-confidence and future behavior of students, but also because it can be very uplifting for a teacher to hear the sense of pride in a family member's voice. Particularly for students who have frequent behavior issues at school, a teacher or family member's acknowledgment of even one good day can make a huge impact.

Technology can allow teachers and parents to communicate about students more regularly. Communicate via text message or email to provide families with frequent academic and behavior updates. When communicating with families of students with a history of discipline issues, discuss instances of positive classroom behavior as soon as possible to establish high expectations. Catch students in the act of adhering to rules and procedures, and share these moments right away with parents via text or email. Use emoticons (such as ☺) and punctuation marks (such as !!!) to emphasize the positive nature of the message.

Teaching With Technology

This chapter addressed recognizing levels of adherence to rules and procedures, which includes demonstrating withitness, applying consequences for lack of adherence to rules and procedures, and acknowledging adherence to rules and procedures. The following vignette depicts a teacher who has enhanced her classroom management skills with technology.

As seen previously, Ms. Kushner has used technology tools to facilitate the process of planning and agreeing on classroom rules and procedures with her sixth-grade students. Her students have also contributed to the agreed-on consequences for adhering and failing to adhere to those rules and procedures. Ms. Kushner uses technology to acknowledge the varying behaviors of her students.

Ms. Kushner's students have signed contracts stating that they agree to adhere to the rules and procedures. As a result, they have established expectations for themselves and their classmates that result in a higher degree of ownership for individually and collectively upholding those expectations.

However, as often happens with young learners, disruptive circumstances inevitably arise. To avoid these circumstances, Ms. Kushner must maintain a keen awareness of potential sources of disruption. While she has done much to encourage students to act appropriately, over time she has come to recognize the patterns of student communication, body language, and behavior that are precursors to potential issues. She is quick to ascertain impending disturbances to her classroom's culture of contribution, and from this anticipatory vantage point, she can swiftly and judiciously handle such digressions. Over the years, Ms. Kushner has honed her ability to redirect students' attention. She can choreograph shifts from outward expressions of frustration to introspective reflection and consideration of behavioral alternatives.

Ms. Kushner's primary objective when applying consequences is to prompt students to think about their behaviors, to think about the consequences, and to take ownership for the decisions that led to the consequences. Whenever a student receives a consequence for not adhering to a classroom rule, the student also completes a behavior reflection template that becomes part of the student's archived behavior portfolio. Ms. Kushner strives to ensure that such data are captured as soon as possible after an infraction to give immediacy to the feedback and to help each student determine how well he or she is managing to address his or her behaviors.

Ms. Kushner uses technology resources to support and positively reinforce students' learning capacities. She uses an app to create an online behavior reflection template and asks students to complete it whenever they fail to adhere to any of the classroom rules or procedures. Because the template is cloud based, students and parents can access the data on multiple devices from any location, reinforcing the connection Ms. Kushner maintains with her students' parents. Classrooms are natural laboratories for students to apply their behavioral hypotheses in social contexts, continuously testing the boundaries of propriety by acting on the subconscious question, "If I do X, then Y will happen." The template is a thinking guide designed to help students work backward from their inappropriate behavior to the decision they made that led to that behavior. By thinking about behaviors impartially, Ms. Kushner's students can better identify and rectify their faulty behavioral hypotheses. This process helps students generate new behavioral hypotheses to determine the extent to which such premises help them better adhere to the classroom rules and procedures.

Ms. Kushner consistently provides positive affirmations for student behaviors that reflect adherence to classroom rules and procedures. Students are recognized for their contributions to the classroom community on a weekly, monthly, and yearly basis. She also provides multiple opportunities for students to give each other positive comments, which contributes to the classroom culture of mutual respect and support. Ms. Kushner constantly seeks ways to elicit positive reinforcement for students from all members of her classroom community—her teaching colleagues, the building administrator, her students' parents, and members of the community at large.

The class has previously agreed to a classroom token economy of accruing points as acknowledgment for adherence to rules and procedures. Ms. Kushner facilitates this system with ClassDojo. Her students create accounts and can earn points to exchange for privileges, activities, or items. Students can also offer points to one another for their contributions; Ms. Kushner facilitates this as well. The class has agreed that when it meets certain point thresholds, earned privileges should include class field trips, visits from special guests, and class parties. Her students work collectively to achieve each threshold, reminding each other of the class's collective goals and its progress toward them.

Ms. Kushner holds her class accountable for adhering to the rules and procedures that they created. She is committed to moving away from meting out punishments and moving toward developing a more positive management style. By giving students opportunities to self-monitor behavior and applaud the behavior of others, she has created a contributing classroom learning environment.

Ms. Kushner uses technology to enhance the effectiveness of a variety of elements. For element 33, demonstrating withitness, she uses technology tools to enhance her own withitness as well as the withitness of her students. Students contribute to the classroom rules and procedures via polling technology and sign printed contracts in which they agree to respect these rules.

For element 34, applying consequences for lack of adherence to rules and procedures, Ms. Kushner uses an app to create an online behavior reflection template. She asks students to complete this template whenever they do not adhere to rules and procedures. Students can access the behavior reflection template using desktop computers, laptops, or tablets to reflect on their behaviors and generate alternatives.

Finally, Ms. Kushner uses technology for element 35, acknowledging adherence to rules and procedures, by establishing a token economy in which students earn points for positive behavior. In particular, she uses the ClassDojo website to attribute points, track progress, and generate online behavior reports that she can share with her students' parents.

Chapter 8: Comprehension Questions

1. The best way to develop a sense of withitness is through self-reflection. How can technology facilitate the reflection process?

2. Explain the importance of home contingency, and list at least three technology tools that can be used to support it.

3. How might a teacher who is struggling with behavior issues use technology to revamp his or her classroom management plan?

4. How do you use technology to recognize levels of adherence to classroom rules and procedures? Share your ideas by going to **marzanoresearch.com/classroom strategies**, clicking on the *Enhancing the Art & Science of Teaching With Technology* link, and becoming a member of our virtual learning community.

Chapter 9

MAINTAINING EFFECTIVE RELATIONSHIPS WITH STUDENTS

Mutually respectful relationships between students and teachers are the foundation of an effective classroom. The design question for chapter 9 asks, How can I use technology to establish and maintain effective relationships with students? There are three elements associated with this design question, which falls under lesson segments enacted on the spot.

Element 36: Understanding students' interests and backgrounds

Element 37: Using verbal and nonverbal behaviors that indicate affection for students

Element 38: Displaying objectivity and control

The strategies and behaviors connected to building relationships are drawn from the research on striking a balance between student perceptions that the teacher is in control of the classroom and student perceptions that the teacher is their advocate (Brekelmans, Wubbels, & Creton, 1990; Wubbels, Brekelmans, den Brok, & van Tartwijk, 2006). Specific strategies support each of the three elements and specific technology tools, in turn, can be used to support each of these strategies.

Element 36: Understanding Students' Interests and Backgrounds

Element 36 involves seeking out knowledge about students and using that knowledge to engage in informal, friendly discussions with students. Strategies associated with this element include:

- Student background surveys
- Individual student learning goals
- Commenting on student achievements or areas of importance

We describe each strategy and explain how to improve it with technology.

Student Background Surveys

One of the easiest ways for teachers to learn about students' interests and backgrounds is through a survey distributed at the beginning of the year, term, or unit. The survey could include questions about students' academic interests (favorite and least favorite subject in school), personal interests (hobbies, sports, lessons, art, books, video games, movies, and television shows), dreams, fears, family members, and family activities (traditions, vacations, and gatherings). Teachers can also provide sentence stems for students, such as, "During my free time I like to _____" or "Someday I'd like to be _____."

Use clickers or polling software on student mobile devices to conduct a student interest survey. Based on the polling data from this survey, divide the class into small groups related to students' interests and backgrounds. Alternatively, create a student background survey using online survey tools such as SurveyMonkey. Students complete the survey questions and analyze responses to gain a richer understanding of students' unique backgrounds and interests.

Use a digital camera to take photos of each student in the class. Have each student digitally edit the image to add visual elements that reflect interests identified in his or her survey. The student then shares his or her digital image or avatar with the class.

Individual Student Learning Goals

Students connect teacher-identified learning goals to their own experiences and interests by creating personal learning goals during a unit. Individual student learning goals for declarative knowledge can take the format, "When this unit is completed, I will better understand _____." Individual student learning goals for procedural knowledge can take the format, "When this unit is completed, I will be able to _____."

Students can use technology to create reflective journals to establish and track their progress toward individual learning goals. Students can also write journal entries using word processing software such as Google Drive or Evernote, record them using audio recording software such as Audacity, or film them using video recording tools on laptops, tablets, or smartphones. Encourage students to comment on their learning preferences, new skills they are practicing, and the amount of effort they invested in building fluency with new content.

Commenting on Student Achievements or Areas of Importance

Once a teacher has some background knowledge about students' values and interests, he or she can notice and comment on individual accomplishments (achievements in clubs or athletics, academic recognitions, artistic and dramatic accomplishments, or assignments done well), important events (a wedding, vacation, or birthday), or changes in the student's family structure (a move, birth, death, marriage, divorce, or transition in employment).

Comment on student achievements or areas of importance using social media. Create an Edmodo page for the class in which students create accounts, and join the class group. Students can add comments to their own pages that reflect their interests, backgrounds, and life events. Be sure to comment on students' entries in a way that shows your interest in their lives. Encourage other students to post appropriate comments on classmates' Edmodo pages as well to foster a contributive classroom culture.

Element 37: Using Verbal and Nonverbal Behaviors That Indicate Affection for Students

Element 37, using verbal and nonverbal behaviors that indicate affection for students, involves the teacher using humor and friendly banter in an appropriate fashion with students. Strategies associated with this element include:

- Informal conferences

- Photo bulletin board

Here, we explain these strategies and provide ways in which technology tools can enhance them.

Informal Conferences

Teachers should find time to casually check in with students before class, in the hall, at lunch, during recess, or after school to give compliments, ask for their opinions, congratulate their successes, and deliver positive comments from other teachers. These informal conferences need not be long, and can be as quick as, "Kara, what did you think of that Broncos game last night?" or "Josh, I was so impressed by your performance in the school musical yesterday—you ought to be really proud of that!"

Create a class website, and encourage students to contribute by posting comments that reflect their interests, thoughts, and feelings. Respond with comments that indicate affection for students. Follow up with students after class or in the hallway to discuss recent posts or make informal comments about information they have added to their pages. Small gestures like these convey your interest in students' well-being and show them that they matter.

Send encouraging emails or texts to students and families in which you provide positive comments about students. Use emoticons, images, or statements that reflect your affection for students, including your genuine belief that all students can achieve their personal and academic goals. For example, use your smartphone to photograph a student engaged in positive classroom behavior. Send the image to the student's parents via text or email, and include a positive caption that shows your appreciation.

Photo Bulletin Board

In this strategy, the teacher designs a bulletin board that displays students' photos, personal goals, hobbies, interests, and other fun facts. The content of photo bulletin boards can change from time to time based on the unit or can highlight students who have performed well on assignments, shown dramatic improvement on a learning goal, or enacted classroom values outside of class.

Use a digital camera or the camera tools on a desktop computer, laptop, tablet, or smartphone to photograph each student at the beginning of the year. Use IWB or presentation software to copy and paste your students' pictures onto a background of a boat, spaceship, rocket, raft, or in another context that illustrates the importance of teamwork. Regularly refer to this image to reinforce the idea that all students are important to the classroom team. Use IWB tools or word processing software to include students' pictures in a digital seating chart to help you learn students' names. Additionally, continue to photograph your students throughout the year as they complete individual projects or collaborate in groups. Display these images in a slideshow as students enter the room to acknowledge adherence to classroom norms and reinforce positive interactions. Include music or sound effects that evoke shared memories from class. Alternatively, create a Student of the Month slideshow that incorporates images of an exemplary student, that student's favorite music, and quotes from the student.

Element 38: Displaying Objectivity and Control

Element 38 involves the teacher behaving in ways that indicate he or she does not take infractions personally. Maintaining this cool, consistent demeanor is essential to a functioning classroom management system. Strategies associated with this element include:

- Self-reflection

- Maintaining a cool exterior

Here, we detail each strategy and explain how it can be augmented with technology.

Self-Reflection

The teacher should reflect on his or her performance in the classroom on a daily basis. These reflections could include thoughts about consistency in applying consequences or acknowledging adherence to rules or procedures. During reflection, teachers should also ask themselves a series of questions such as:

- Did I accurately acknowledge students who followed the rules and procedures?

- Did I accurately apply consequences for students who did not follow rules and procedures?

- Did I respond to every opportunity to acknowledge adherence or lack of adherence to the rules and procedures?

- Did I strike a balance between "no-nonsense" and "nurturing" attitudes?

Technology tools can be used to facilitate the reflection process in a variety of ways. Use a digital video camera, a document camera, or the video recording tools in laptops or tablets to enhance your self-reflections. Record teaching strategies and classroom interactions with students. View, archive, and reflect on the effectiveness of the strategies for displaying objectivity and control. Consider any adjustments or improvements, and request suggestions from a colleague, mentor, or coach. Use these recordings to track progress toward professional growth goals.

Create a digital reflective journal using online word processing tools such as Google Drive or Evernote. Record reflections about strategies you have used to display objectivity and control, and use the reflective journal to self-assess strengths and weaknesses, establish goals, and reflect on progress. Because Google Drive and Evernote are cloud-based tools, teachers can access their reflective journals from almost any device, including desktop computers, laptops, tablets, and smartphones.

Maintaining a Cool Exterior

In this strategy, the teacher remains calm and collected when dealing with conflicts in the classroom. Maintaining a cool exterior includes using assertive body language, self-monitoring facial expressions, speaking in a calm and respectful tone of voice, actively listening to reasonable explanations, and avoiding engagement with students who argue, deny, or blame others for their conduct.

Craft carefully worded emails or text messages to students and parents that reflect your objectivity about behavioral indiscretions. When posting comments on students' websites, be sure to always display objectivity and control. Use these opportunities to demonstrate separation between students and their behaviors.

Random group generators, such as Team Maker, and polling technologies help create objectivity in the classrooms through anonymity. Use random group generators to break the whole class into small groups and to call on students. Students can use polling technologies to submit anonymous responses to questions.

Teaching With Technology

This chapter has delineated three elements involved with establishing and maintaining effective relationships with students: understanding students' interests and backgrounds, using verbal and nonverbal behaviors to indicate affection for students, and displaying objectivity and control. In this vignette, Mr. Flannery demonstrates a firm grasp of the design question, as well as ways in which technology can improve its elements and elements not specific to this design question.

Mr. Flannery teaches high school ELA to juniors and seniors. He's been teaching for over twenty-five years and has a very energetic teaching style, which he exudes through his love of literature and of helping students realize their potential as writers.

He is popular among the student body because of his ability to establish and maintain effective relationships with his students. He has often cited his knack for building positive rapport with students as the most important contributing factor to his effectiveness as a teacher. His colleagues see that he invests time and energy to sustain this rapport throughout the school year, often using technology tools to help him develop relationships with students and families.

Mr. Flannery uses social media to support interactive engagement among his classes. At the beginning of the school year, he posts questions that prompt students to share and discuss their backgrounds and interests. These surveys are informal but usually get a high number of student responses. Mr. Flannery posts positive comments on each of his students' social media pages and thanks students in advance for their contributions to the class.

Mr. Flannery's students also respond to each other's comments, and this dialogue helps establish a collective appreciation of unique experiences and interests. Using other forms of social media, Mr. Flannery posts questions that invite students to share information about themselves.

As students enter his classroom, they see a single laptop connected to a projector. It displays an image of the class on the deck of what appears to be an 18th century sailing vessel. Each student is represented by a cartoon avatar body adorned with different items—one student avatar is holding a guitar, another is dressed in ballet attire, and a third is wearing rollerblades.

During the first day of class, Mr. Flannery's students signed up for accounts on DoppelMe, an avatar-creation website, to create pictorial representations of their unique personalities, backgrounds, and interests. When all the students' avatars were completed, Mr. Flannery cut and pasted them onto the background of the wooden sailing ship and sent the image to each student and his or her parents via email.

The metaphor of the class as a learning crew on a journey of literary discovery is not lost on the students, who often refer to Mr. Flannery as "Captain Flannery," a jocular title to which he responds with good humor. Mr. Flannery has added a picture of his own avatar—complete with feathered cap, parchment, and quills—at the wheel of the ship. As all of these images are digital, they can be modified, updated, and shared. He has also put the image onto the class social media homepage. The students use the avatars they created to represent themselves when posting comments or discussing works of literature on the various social media and communication resources they use during class.

In his classroom, Mr. Flannery has established that students are allowed to use their smartphones but only under certain conditions that the students helped outline. For example, students are allowed to use their devices to answer questions via polling software. Active in local theater, Mr. Flannery has a flair for the dramatic and often uses voices, gestures, or other affectations while reciting passages from literary works. At times, he asks questions while in character, to which all students respond using their smartphones. He often pauses dramatically before displaying polling results, waiting until students are attentive and engaged. He then uses students' responses as prompts for in-depth discussions designed to increase their contribution to the collective understanding of the class.

In addition, Mr. Flannery understands the importance of contextualizing great works of literature within his students' cultural framework. He helps bring stories to life by asking his students to reinterpret literary passages or dialogue using contemporary vernacular. His students enjoy this and often use colorful and interesting analogies and metaphors from popular culture.

For example, many of his students enjoy books and movies featuring vampires. During one recent activity, students paraphrased characters' dialogue from the works they were studying, using vocabulary terms that incorporated their knowledge of vampire lore and behavior. Then, students used the video recording capabilities of their smartphones to stage and record vignettes of their reconstituted scenes and posted their recordings to the class social media page, which led to commentary from the class.

From the first day of school, Mr. Flannery has demonstrated that students are valued members of a contributive learning community. One thing he does on that first day is point to a scroll of parchment that adorns the front of his classroom. The parchment depicts his class motto in gothic script, which he recites: "No one knows so much that he or she can't learn something of value from everyone, and no one knows so little that he or she can't teach something of value to everyone." Mr. Flannery makes eye contact with each of his students during this recitation. He asks his students to reflect on the motto and share their interpretations of its meaning using polling software on their smartphones and then uses a random name generator to select students to elaborate on their answers. He uses this welcoming gesture to immediately demonstrate to students that they matter, what they know matters, what they think matters, and how they feel matters. His students, in turn, respond with desire to share their individual contributions to the entire class. Mr. Flannery's goal is for each student to fit into the class like a puzzle piece, contributing his or her individual perspective for the common good.

Students tend to respect Mr. Flannery as a leader in the classroom because he takes the time to get to know them at the start of the school year. He understands his students' past experiences and interests, which enables him to maintain an effective learning environment for the remainder of the year as students manage their own—and each other's—behavior in order to preserve the contributive classroom community.

In this vignette, Mr. Flannery uses technology to enhance a number of elements. For element 36, understanding students' interests and backgrounds, he uses social media tools to encourage students to share their unique backgrounds and interests. He also creates a student interest survey, to which students respond with answers that enrich his understanding of their lives.

Mr. Flannery also uses technology for element 37, using verbal and nonverbal behaviors that indicate affection for students. In addition to the positive comments he posts on his class Edmodo page, Mr. Flannery posts the students' avatars, which students create using online software, on an image of a sailing vessel in IWB software. This gesture demonstrates each student's unique importance to the classroom crew.

Finally, Mr. Flannery uses technology for element 38, displaying objectivity and control. As shown in the vignette, he uses a random name generator to select students to respond to questions via their smartphones. Mr. Flannery also uses dramatic pauses before displaying polling results to ensure that students are attentive and engaged.

Chapter 9: Comprehension Questions

1. Reflect on your own students' values and interests. Create five different comments you might post on a student's Edmodo page.

2. Explain at least two different functions of a photo bulletin board, and describe how each might be supported with technology.

3. How can teachers maintain a cool exterior when communicating sensitive issues (such as severe academic challenges or major behavioral indiscretions) to parents and families?

4. How do you use technology to establish and maintain effective relationships with your students? Share your ideas by going to **marzanoresearch.com/classroom strategies**, clicking on the *Enhancing the Art & Science of Teaching With Technology* link, and becoming a member of our virtual learning community.

Chapter 10

COMMUNICATING HIGH EXPECTATIONS

The design question for this chapter asks, How can I use technology to communicate high expectations for all students? The chapter emphasizes the need for teachers to clearly establish and consciously maintain high expectations for every single student, no matter what. Three elements are important to this final design question, which falls under lesson segments enacted on the spot.

Element 39: Demonstrating value and respect for low-expectancy students

Element 40: Asking questions of low-expectancy students

Element 41: Probing incorrect answers with low-expectancy students

Recognizing the importance of getting to know their students as soon as possible, teachers tend to evaluate and develop expectations for individual students very quickly. Sometimes, these expectations can cause teachers to treat high-expectancy students differently from low-expectancy students, often without realizing it. Students can be extremely perceptive and often notice subtle behavioral clues from teachers that indicate whether they are expected to do poorly or well academically. Furthermore, student behavior, self-image, and effort can actually change in response to teacher expectations (Brophy & Good, 1970; Ferguson, 1998; Jussim, Eccles, & Madon, 1996; Rist, 1970; Roscigno, 1998; Rosenthal & Jacobson, 1968). In this chapter, we outline specific strategies teachers can use to set everyone up for success by communicating high expectations for *all* students. Each one of these strategies can be modified with technology.

Element 39: Demonstrating Value and Respect for Low-Expectancy Students

Element 39 involves the teacher using the same positive tone with low-expectancy students as with high-expectancy students. One strategy associated with this element is:

- Nonverbal and verbal indicators of respect and value

This strategy can be enhanced with technology tools.

Nonverbal and Verbal Indicators of Respect and Value

The teacher should make a concerted effort to use eye contact, warm facial expressions, proximity, appropriate physical contact, and playful banter to show value and respect for every student. Teachers should also take care to self-reflect on their own communication of respect and value, purposefully showing these equally for both low- and high-expectancy students.

Use digital communication tools to share verbal and nonverbal indicators of respect and value for students. In addition, send positive texts or email messages to low-expectancy students. Positive emoticons—such as ☺—or images also demonstrate respect and value for students. Take photos of students with your smartphone, digital camera, or tablet, and send these images to students with encouraging captions and feedback. Additionally, send emails or texts to the parents of low-expectancy students to communicate that these students are valued, respected, and contributing members of your classroom community. Post encouraging comments on students' Edmodo or Facebook pages, and share hyperlinks to websites, images, sound files, or video files that you know certain students might be interested in. These gestures demonstrate that the unique backgrounds and interests of your students matter to you.

Element 40: Asking Questions of Low-Expectancy Students

Element 40 involves the teacher asking questions of low-expectancy students with the same frequency and level of difficulty as high-expectancy students. Strategies associated with this element include:

- Response opportunities

- Evidence and support for student answers

- Wait time

Here, we describe each strategy and address technology tools that can be used to improve it.

Response Opportunities

The teacher reinforces high expectations for all students by giving them equal opportunities to respond to teacher questions or prompts. In addition to the ideas listed here, also see the strategies for managing response rates on page 109.

Harness the potential of polling technology to enhance students' response opportunities. Clickers and mobile devices can increase response rates because they encourage all students to respond to questions. Use the resulting data to begin a discussion. Alternatively, enhance response opportunities by asking questions that specifically reflect students' unique interests and backgrounds. For example, a physics teacher might relate to a student's passion for basketball by creating a word problem in which students calculate the acceleration of LeBron James's jump shot.

Random group generators like Team Maker give every student—including low-expectancy students—an equal chance of being called on to answer a question. Students may feel more respected and valued when teachers use random selection methods that students perceive as fair, just, and equitable. While this process is impartial, it also encourages all students to maintain a state of readiness when a teacher asks a question.

Evidence and Support for Student Answers

In this strategy, the teacher uses probing follow-up questions to prompt students to elaborate on their own answers or the answers of others. Whenever a student makes a claim, the teacher asks that student to provide grounds or evidence for the claim, regardless of the student's expectation level. Whenever a student makes an inference, the teacher asks that student to explain the reasoning behind the inference, regardless of whether the student is considered high- or low-expectancy.

Use random name and number generators to probe for more evidence and support from all students. Random name generators allow you to randomly call on students to share their thinking and explain how they arrived at an answer. Alternatively, randomly ask students to practice empathy by considering how another student may have arrived at a different answer.

Wait Time

When providing wait time, the teacher pauses for several seconds between asking a question and requesting an answer to provide students with enough time to digest information and generate responses.

Certain polling technologies include a self-paced mode, which allows students to answer questions at their own speed. If students who respond at a slower pace use self-paced clickers, students who respond at a quicker pace are not overly encumbered. Track the time it takes for low-expectancy students to answer different types of questions. Use these data to measure their growth toward reasonable goals. Include nonlinguistic representations of the question's content to help students understand what the question is asking.

Element 41: Probing Incorrect Answers With Low-Expectancy Students

Element 41, the final element of the framework, involves teacher inquiry into incorrect answers with low-expectancy students with the same depth and rigor as with high-expectancy students. Strategies associated with this element include:

- Answer revision

- Think-pair-share

Here, we define each strategy and further identify how to improve it with technology.

Answer Revision

Teachers can use elaborative interrogation strategies to help a student critique his or her answer until that student realizes the answer is illogical or indefensible. Ultimately, teachers should give students a chance to revise their answers and applaud them for being critical and open-minded enough to reach a different conclusion.

If you are unsuccessful when probing an incorrect answer, give low-expectancy students the opportunity to respond to the question via email or text message to give them more time to think. Furthermore, provide low-expectancy students with different ways to respond to the questions, including audio recording or screencast software. These tools allow students to respond to the question using either verbal or nonlinguistic elements.

Think-Pair-Share

Think-pair-share (Lyman, 2006) is a conversation between two students in which both share their responses to a question posed by the teacher. After two to three minutes of paired discussion, the teacher randomly calls on a student. The student can report his or her own answer, a partner's answer, or some combination of both. One primary benefit of the think-pair-share strategy is that it gives students a chance to rehearse and reflect on their answers before sharing them with the whole class. Technology tools can also be used to yield these benefits.

Enhance the think-pair-share strategy by using the screen recording feature on an IWB or screen capture software (such as Jing, ScreenChomp, Educreations, or TouchCast). Pairs record and narrate their group problem-solving processes, and then archive and share these representations of their collaboration with the class. Students then post hyperlinks to the files on the class website. Classmates retrieve these files, pause them at any point, and review them as often as needed to learn through the contribution of their peers. Students can then post comments about the multimedia files and use these comments to prompt deeper thinking and reflection.

Teaching With Technology

This design question addresses the importance of communicating high expectations for every student. It incorporates three major elements, which include demonstrating value and respect for low-expectancy students, asking questions of low-expectancy students, and probing incorrect answers with low-expectancy students. The following vignette depicts how technology can enhance these elements and others.

> Mr. Rodas teaches science and mathematics at a high school for students at risk of not completing their graduation requirements. His classroom is filled with exemplars of science and math fair projects from past students. In the back of the room is a Wall of Fame where Mr. Rodas posts pictures of all of his previous students. He also has a laptop connected to an IWB and a tablet cart for his students.
>
> Teachers sometimes have low expectations for the students who attend this school due to academic or behavioral concerns. Mr. Rodas has taught in this learning environment for fifteen years and understands that these students have been treated differently from high-expectancy students in the past. He recognizes that students meet the level of expectation set by their teachers: if the teacher's expectancy level is high, students will rise to that level. He also understands that his thoughts, words, and actions communicate his expectations for students. Students pick up on and respond to tone of voice, body language, and other nonlinguistic cues that teachers consciously or unconsciously display and adjust their own personal expectations accordingly. Because of this, Mr. Rodas does his best to communicate the expectation that all of his students can attain high levels of achievement.
>
> An early adopter of learning technology, Mr. Rodas uses a suite of social media and communication technologies to communicate to students that he genuinely values and respects each of them. He imbues both the physical classroom and the online learning environment with his sincere belief that all students can attain their academic goals if they are willing to invest the necessary time and effort. He sends positive messages via email and text message to his students and their parents.

Mr. Rodas creates a social media page for his class during the first few days of school. He then asks each student to create an account in the system. During the first week of school, he engages the class in culture-building activities to help the students get to know each other. At the end of the week, he posts a positive comment about each of the students on his or her respective social media pages. Over the weekend, he assigns each student the task of reflecting on the week's activities and posting a positive comment on every classmate's social media page. By Monday, each student's page is filled with compliments and positive energy from the other members of the class. The students respond enthusiastically to this activity, sharing considerate and often insightful messages about one another. Mr. Rodas continues to use these types of affirmative exercises during the course of the school year to demonstrate his own respect and value for students, as well as to help students genuinely value and respect each other and themselves.

In order to increase the response rates in his classes, Mr. Rodas uses polling software to ask questions during class and have students respond with smartphones. He gives his students wait time to think through questions, walking around the classroom and providing additional support if students need it. He uses students' polling responses as prompts for further questions or classroom discussions about the thinking that led students to their answers.

Using a random name generator, Mr. Rodas selects students to answer a variety of questions. Because students are chosen at random over the course of the school year, everyone in the class is called on with equal frequency. Mr. Rodas strives to ask questions to draw out students' understanding or identify misconceptions they may have. He knows that it's important to scaffold these questioning sequences by varying the types of questions he asks; ultimately, he works to push all of his students to answer questions that challenge them. For example, he might pose a simpler question and then follow up with a more complex question, perhaps one that requires students to generate an analogy or a metaphor about the content.

Mr. Rodas also varies classroom seating assignments by using a random group generator to organize students into work groups. When students collaborate in groups, Mr. Rodas expects them to make sure that each group member understands how to solve the problem and can explain the problem-solving process to the rest of the class. This way, Mr. Rodas leverages the collective wisdom of the group for the benefit of each student and the entire class.

Often, Mr. Rodas asks groups to generate questions that can be posed to the entire class. His students create online flashcards using Quizlet to review key concepts or processes from the unit of study. He prompts students to generate complex questions that reflect their own learning challenges, as well as the strategies that they use to mitigate these challenges. This activity helps reinforce students' existing learning strategies while exposing them to new tips and tricks that their classmates use.

Before he probes incorrect answers with his students, Mr. Rodas prepares a series of questions to guide the learning progression of the lesson. This helps him break down questions that students answer incorrectly into simpler, more digestible chunks. When students answer incorrectly, he gives previously prepared hints and cues to individual students (via text or email) or to the whole class (via IWB) to help students revise their answers. Mr. Rodas has learned to redirect students' thinking by working backward from a point of understanding through a progression of questions. His students appreciate Mr. Rodas's questioning techniques, which are more useful than simply hearing that their answers are wrong.

> When working to investigate incorrect answers with students, Mr. Rodas asks his students to capture their problem-solving processes with the screen capture feature of IWB software or with screen capture software on their tablets. These tools allow the entire problem-solving interaction between Mr. Rodas and his students to be recorded as a video file so that their voices, annotations, and interactions can be saved and reviewed. He maintains a searchable cloud-based library containing hundreds of these video files from former classes. He shares these recordings with current students to help them glean problem-solving strategies from his past students. Mr. Rodas's students appreciate seeing that others have struggled through similar problems and benefit from the unique strategies these past students employed to solve them.
>
> Mr. Rodas uses technology tools to aggregate the collaborative potential of every student in his class, as well access the potential of former students. By valuing each individual's contribution, he cultivates the self-esteem of his students and fosters a sense of mutual respect in the classroom. Because Mr. Rodas takes care to communicate high expectations for all students, his classroom feels safe and supportive enough to allow everyone to contribute.

Mr. Rodas effectively uses technology to enhance a variety of elements. For element 39, demonstrating value and respect for low-expectancy students, he uses social media technologies to post positive, encouraging comments demonstrating his belief in his students' potential. He also uses digital communication tools such as emails and text messages to demonstrate high expectations for students.

Mr. Rodas enhances element 40, asking questions of low-expectancy students, by using his IWB and polling software to collect student responses to questions. He also uses a random group generator to organize his class into learning groups and to select students to respond to questions. In this way, Mr. Rodas can ask as many questions of low-expectancy students as of high-expectancy students. Students also generate questions that can be posed to the class using an online flashcard generator.

Finally, Mr. Rodas employs technology tools for element 41, probing incorrect answers with low-expectancy students. He prepares a series of questions related to the learning goal and uses IWB and polling technology to pose these questions to students. When a low-expectancy student offers an incorrect answer, Mr. Rodas is prepared to ask that student probing questions. He augments these questions with multimedia objects on his IWB. He also accommodates low-expectancy students by providing the option of responding to questions with screen capture software on their tablets. This software can help students process their thinking through speech and share their answers using nonlinguistic elements. Mr. Rodas also archives a library of problem-solving screencasts from former students, which he offers as an additional resource for low-expectancy students.

Chapter 10: Comprehension Questions

1. When a student seems to be having a tough day, how might a teacher use technology to privately communicate to the student that he or she is valued?

2. Why are think-pair-share exercises helpful for low-expectancy students, and how can they be enhanced with technology?

3. How can technology help teachers ask challenging questions of low-expectancy students as often as they would with high-expectancy students?

4. How do you use technology to communicate high expectations for all students in your classroom? Share your ideas by going to **marzanoresearch.com/classroom strategies**, clicking on the *Enhancing the Art & Science of Teaching With Technology* link, and becoming a member of our virtual learning community.

EPILOGUE

The basic premise of this book is that educational technology and effective instructional strategies, when used together, result in greater student achievement than when either is used alone. Technology tools have the power to enhance instructional strategies, increasing students' engagement, participation, and learning. In the text, we reviewed forty-one elements of effective teaching, outlined strategies for each one, and explained various ways that technology can enhance each strategy. As educational technology becomes increasingly ubiquitous in K–12 education, this text will help teachers use the available technology resources to enhance their foundation of effective teaching practices.

As teachers put the strategies and techniques from this text into practice in their classrooms, we recommend that they focus on using technology to enhance one element of effective teaching at a time. For example, a teacher might decide to use technology to enhance strategies for tracking student progress, such as using formative assessments and charting student progress. For formative assessment, she asks students to respond to a series of assessment questions (that correspond to the 2.0, 3.0, and 4.0 levels of her proficiency scale) using the set of clickers she has available in her classroom. Then, to chart students' progress, she imports the electronic results of the polling into spreadsheet software, which automatically creates a graph of the class's answers. She then uses the electronic results to update each student's individual electronic tracking chart and emails each student a copy. As seen here, technology can enhance effective classroom practice by making teacher and student activities faster, more efficient, and more easily accessible. By focusing on one element of effective teaching at a time, teachers can target their technology enhancements and monitor the results to ensure that students are achieving the desired outcomes.

APPENDIX A

ANSWERS TO COMPREHENSION QUESTIONS

Answers to Chapter 2: Comprehension Questions

1. *Why is it beneficial to use technology to expose students to a learning goal before beginning a lesson?*

   Class websites allow teachers to share a learning goal with students before a lesson begins. One benefit of presenting a clearly articulated learning goal in a blog entry or comment is that it gives students an opportunity to start making connections between learning goals, background knowledge, and personal experiences. Another reason to share a learning goal in advance of the lesson is that it prepares students to link their classroom activities, assignments, and discussions directly back to the content.

2. *Describe at least two benefits that come with using digital journals (as opposed to paper-and-pencil journals) to track student progress.*

   Unlike paper notebooks, cloud-based digital journals (in Google Drive or Evernote) cannot be misplaced or accidentally left at home, because they are accessible from a variety of electronic devices. For instance, if a student uses Google Drive to begin writing a journal entry at school, she does not have to remember to bring a notebook home in order to finish that entry for homework. Instead, she can access the same entry online from a home computer, a smartphone, a tablet, or a computer at the public library. Additionally, digital journals afford teachers the opportunity to type comments and feedback directly into their students' files. Finally, students can easily revise entries in a digital journal, as well as save multiple drafts to review their progress over time.

3. *In what ways do online publishing and social media tools have the potential to enhance the process of celebrating success?*

   Put simply, online publishing and social media tools broaden the number of people who can see and celebrate student progress. Use a class website to publish a list of the students who have made the greatest knowledge gains in a unit. Post digital photos of finished projects on the class website for all students to see and comment on. Encourage students to share these websites with their friends and family members, especially with those who live far away. Technology tools can allow a student in Brooklyn to share his research paper with anyone from a parent at home to a grandparent in Phoenix to another student living in Tokyo.

4. *How do you use technology to provide clear learning goals, track student progress, and celebrate success in your classroom?*

   Answers will vary from teacher to teacher. To see responses from other educators, visit **marzanoresearch.com/classroomstrategies**, click on the *Enhancing the Art & Science of Teaching With Technology* link, and become a member of our virtual learning community.

Answers to Chapter 3: Comprehension Questions

1. *Why is it important for students to create digital representations of classroom rules and procedures?*

   It is important for students to express rules and procedures in a way that makes sense to them. Such projects make it easier for students to remember the rules and understand why they are important. One reason that screen capture technology (such as Jing, ScreenChomp, Educreations, or TouchCast) is well-suited for this task is because it allows primary students to explain rules orally instead of writing them out. Furthermore, screen captures are a form of multimedia technology, which means that students engage multiple senses at once. This aspect of screen captures may make rules and procedures more accessible for kinesthetic, visual, and auditory learners.

2. *Describe how technology can be used to enhance vignettes and role playing.*

   Students use vignettes and role playing to act out scenarios in which rules and procedures are or are not followed. Video recording technology on tablets, digital cameras, or smartphones can enhance this process if students use editing software such as iMovie to polish their performances. Prerecording a performance also eliminates the need to physically perform it live in front of a group of classmates. This can allow for more elaborate scripts, and it alleviates some of the stress of students with stage fright.

3. *Provide two examples that demonstrate your own intentionality regarding the planning and organization of learning centers in your classroom.*

   Answers will vary from teacher to teacher. Ideally, learning centers will be organized in such a way as to promote easy movement around the classroom. Digital learning centers should be accessible but out of the way to prevent distractions among students working at different centers.

4. *How do you use technology to establish and maintain rules and procedures in your classroom?*

   Answers will vary from teacher to teacher. To see responses from other educators, visit **marzanoresearch.com/classroomstrategies**, click on the *Enhancing the Art & Science of Teaching With Technology* link, and become a member of our virtual learning community.

Answers to Chapter 4: Comprehension Questions

1. *Why might a teacher use IWB software to play a loud sound (such as a drumroll or a trumpet blast) in the middle of a lesson?*

   The teacher is using the sound as a signal to identify critical information for students. Multimedia cues (such as a musical sound or an animated image on an IWB) can catch the attention of students from a variety of learning styles because they activate several different senses at once. Establish a routine, and use it consistently to engage students whenever important information is on the horizon.

2. *How can technology enhance the collection and use of preassessment data to determine the size of different learning chunks?*

   Use technology to accelerate the process of chunking without allowing it to devolve into a guessing game. Polling technology (used with clickers or student mobile devices) collects large quantities of data from individual students in a short amount of time, making it a perfect tool for preassessment. With polling technology, teachers can carefully determine an appropriate size for each chunk, without taking the time to individually score and analyze a pile of preassessments. No need to rewrite a list of preassessment questions if you already have one that works—just copy and paste the list into an IWB. Students respond using clickers instead of pencils.

3. *Describe technology tools that can be used to support each type of general inferential question.*

   General inferential questions are designed to prompt students to make inferences, or educated guesses, about content. There are two types of general inferential questions: (1) default questions, which require students to use background knowledge to come up with the answer, and (2) reasoned inference questions, which require students to use their reasoning to draw conclusions about their observations. Polling technology tools—particularly clickers or mobile devices that have text input features—enhance default questions because they are efficient, but also because they allow every student to share his or her unique background knowledge with the class. Reasoned inference questions, on the other hand, can be tricky for teachers to generate because they must include evidence. Asking a question such as What is this image? makes a great reasoned inference prompt. In order to provide enough evidence for students to draw upon, all a teacher needs to do is display a distorted image. Use a document camera to take a content-related object and magnify it past the point of being recognizable.

4. *How do you use technology to help students effectively interact with new knowledge in your classroom?*

   Answers will vary from teacher to teacher. To see responses from other educators, visit **marzanoresearch.com/classroomstrategies**, click on the *Enhancing the Art & Science of Teaching With Technology* link, and become a member of our virtual learning community.

Answers to Chapter 5: Comprehension Questions

1. *What are the similarities and differences between using technology for homework to practice a process or skill and using technology for homework to deepen knowledge?*

   Assign homework that involves practicing a process or skill to increase students' fluency, accuracy, and automaticity with the procedure. There are a few different ways to enhance this practice with technology. For one, students use screencast software and video recording tools to film and narrate a process or skill. They can record themselves practicing the process of solving a math problem and talking the viewer through the steps, for instance. Additionally, students can use websites like Quizlet, which allow the user to create a set of digital flashcards and practice with them online. Homework to deepen knowledge, on the other hand, should push students to use higher-order cognitive skills—such as analyzing and utilizing information, addressing complex problems and issues, and creating patterns and mental models—to expand their knowledge of the content. Therefore, practice with flashcards will increase students' fluency with skills but will not deepen their knowledge of content. To deepen knowledge, assign online scavenger hunts in which students evaluate content-related videos or websites, such as videos of TED Talks, tutorials at Khan Academy, or *Radiolab* podcasts from NPR.

2. *How can technology support the use of Venn diagrams to examine similarities and differences?*

   As with many other strategies, technology can enhance the use of Venn diagrams by increasing their auditory, visual, and kinesthetic interactivity. With a traditional Venn diagram, a student would draw two overlapping circles with a pencil and then fill in the diagram by writing differences in each circle and similarities in the area of overlap. The student receives little output from the Venn diagram in response to his or her input. With a Venn diagram in IWB software, however, students can receive output in response to certain inputs. For instance, an elementary teacher might use an IWB to create a Venn diagram template to introduce the concept of carnivores, omnivores, and herbivores. He labels one circle as animals that eat meat and the other as animals that eat plants, and students come up to the IWB to drag and drop images of different animals into the three sections of the diagram. When students click on an image, the sound that animal makes plays through the IWB speakers. If a student incorrectly places an image in a section, the image bounces back out of the circle and into the image bank, prompting the student to try a different one.

3. *List three ways in which technology can be used to infuse collaboration into the examination of errors in reasoning.*

   First, students can search the Internet for errors in reasoning and use social bookmarking tools such as Diigo or Delicious to catalog the sites. Bookmarking tools facilitate collaboration because students can share their bookmarks with the class and annotate the findings of other students. Provide sentence stems for students to encourage respectful and constructive feedback, such as "I think this

article might actually exemplify a different error in reasoning because _____."
Second, divide students into small groups using Team Maker, a random group generator. Each group locates errors in the media based on guided Internet searches (provide students with a few reputable websites or databases to explore). Collective word processing software such as Google Drive allows students to perform individual searches on separate computers while creating a single catalog of errors in one shared document. Finally, students can create videos, audio recordings, or screencasts of discussions about errors and share these with the class. Videos can be shared via Vimeo or YouTube. Audio and screencast files can be exchanged via shared online repositories such as Dropbox.

4. *How do you use technology to help students practice and deepen new knowledge in your classroom?*

   Answers will vary from teacher to teacher. To see responses from other educators, visit **marzanoresearch.com/classroomstrategies**, click on the *Enhancing the Art & Science of Teaching With Technology* link, and become a member of our virtual learning community.

Enhancing the Art & Science of Teaching With Technology © 2014 Marzano Research • marzanoresearch.com
Visit **marzanoresearch.com/classroomstrategies** to download this page.

Answers to Chapter 6: Comprehension Questions

1. *Describe a win-win peer tutoring situation that incorporates technology.*

   In a win-win peer tutoring situation, a student who has surpassed the target level for a learning goal is paired with a student who is struggling to reach the target level. This situation is a win-win because the struggling student gets the help that he or she needs, and the advanced student deepens his or her own understanding in the process. Technology can aid in facilitating these win-win peer tutoring situations in a few different ways. Tutors can use screen capture tools to take a picture of a computer or tablet screen or use screencasting software (such as Jing, ScreenChomp, Educreations, or TouchCast) to create multimedia tutorials. Tutors can also record videos independently or during work with struggling students to preserve their questions, answers, and step-by-step breakdowns of problem-solving processes. Save these tutorials using a content-sharing service such as Dropbox or YouTube for future student use.

2. *How can technology enhance cooperative learning?*

   Technology can enhance cooperative learning groups in several ways. Use random group generators such as Team Maker to randomly organize students into work groups or teams, and use random number generators to assign students to various roles in the group, such as facilitator, summarizer, questioner, and so on. There are also a number of other useful apps for collaboration that students can use on tablets, smartphones, or laptops. Evernote, for example, allows students to take and share images and textual notes. Mindjet, a mind-mapping app, offers tools for planning, brainstorming, and task management during collaborative projects. Dropbox is an online repository for files of multiple formats and sizes, including documents, PowerPoint presentations, videos, audio files, and photos.

3. *Effective teachers regularly provide feedback and constructive criticism to students about their work. However, teachers who offer frequent feedback can sometimes find themselves repeating the same comments and answering the same questions over and over. How can technology mitigate this issue and make feedback efficient for teachers and accessible to students?*

   The simplest way to accelerate the process of giving feedback is to collect student work in electronic file formats instead of on paper. This gives teachers the opportunity to type out feedback using comment features in word processing software instead of writing it out in longhand on a student's hardcopy assignment. When multiple students require the same piece of feedback, copy and paste a comment from one file to the next, modifying it as necessary to suit the needs of each individual student. This saves you the time of rewriting a similar comment on numerous papers. Compile the most common feedback into an online archive in Google Drive for future classes to easily access. The same tool can also be used to create a searchable database of students' frequently asked questions. Update this archive from year to year to make it as thorough and useful as possible. Using the digital comments feature also allows you to include hyperlinks to additional resources, references, or exemplary writing samples.

4. *How do you use technology to help students generate and test hypotheses about new knowledge?*

Answers will vary from teacher to teacher. To see responses from other educators, visit **marzanoresearch.com/classroomstrategies**, click on the *Enhancing the Art & Science of Teaching With Technology* link, and become a member of our virtual learning community.

Answers to Chapter 7: Comprehension Questions

1. *Consider the academic games you use to keep students engaged in your own classroom. Brainstorm ways in which these games could be enhanced with technology.*

   Answers will vary because each classroom is unique. However, certain technology tools can be used to enhance a wide range of games. Use a random group generator to divide students into teams, or use a random name generator to select one student to answer a question for *Jeopardy!*-style games. If the game requires students to be organized in teams, use a random number generator to select a spokesperson or relay racer from each team. To illustrate, with groups of four, assign each student in the group a number from 1 through 4. Program the random number generator to only select numbers within the 1 through 4 range. If the generator selects the number 3, the three from each group must act as his or her team's spokesperson for that round, race to the board to answer the same question, or something similar, depending on the game. Additionally, use polling technology to turn almost any content review activity into a game.

2. *How can teachers use technology to enhance students' life connections with learning content?*

   Technology can help teachers connect students' interests with learning content in several ways. Students can create blogs, wikis, Facebook pages, Edmodo pages, or Blendspace pages to express their life connections to the content. They can use screencasting software (such as Jing, ScreenChomp, Educreations, or TouchCast) to create and share multimedia screencasts that express their connections to the content. Apps like Instagram or Snapchat can capture images that are representative of students' interests, accompanied by brief explanations that connect the image to the content. Students can also use audio recording software such as Audacity to record discussions of their perspectives on the content. To guide the discussion, they might reference a set of teacher-provided questions about how the content relates to students' life events, hobbies, or interests. Students can also use audio recording software like Audacity or GarageBand to record spoken-word poetry, raps, or songs that express their connections, or use video capture tools on tablets or smartphones to conduct and record personal stories or interviews of friends and family. Any of the aforementioned expressions can be shared on the class website.

3. *How can technology help teachers distinguish between showing enthusiasm (their own reasons for enjoying a topic) and engaging in the types of behavior that Good and Brophy (2003) refer to as unnecessary theatrics?*

   The most important way to show content-relevant enthusiasm is to demonstrate the activity's explicit connection to the learning goal. In a social studies class, host videoconferences with partner classes in other regions, and discuss current local and international events. Create nonlinguistic representations of content using images and sounds in IWB software, and help students connect the representations to the learning goal. When using humor to engage students, do so in a way that obviously relates to the content. Screen a film like *Monty Python and the Holy Grail* during a unit on medieval times, and compare and contrast Arthurian legend with the way it is parodied in the film. Use polling technology to collect student-created captions for political cartoons and connect the captions to the learning goal.

4. *How do you use technology to engage students in your classroom?*

   Answers will vary from teacher to teacher. To see responses from other educators, visit **marzanoresearch.com/classroomstrategies**, click on the *Enhancing the Art & Science of Teaching With Technology* link, and become a member of our virtual learning community.

Answers to Chapter 8: Comprehension Questions

1. *The best way to develop a sense of withitness is through self-reflection. How can technology facilitate the reflection process?*

   Withitness refers to an awareness of certain student behaviors that may eventually become disruptive and the ability to address these behaviors instantaneously. Because instances of withitness must be enacted on the spot, there is no way to plan them out in advance. Instead, you must use reflection to develop your ability to be proactive and notice potential problems. Record videos of lessons and watch them to evaluate your own level of withitness. Pay careful attention to changes in student behavior, and assess ways in which your teaching could be modified to prevent them in the future. For instance, if you notice that students begin to become chatty and unruly during distribution of handouts or between lesson segments, tighten up your transitions.

2. *Explain the importance of home contingency, and list at least three technology tools that can be used to support it.*

   Home contingency refers to regular communication between teachers and parents about students' academic and behavioral performance in school. Unity between parents and teachers is important because it shows students that they are valued in multiple arenas, involves parents in the education of their children, and gives teachers a supportive ally. Numerous technology tools support this type of communication, including behavior management websites such as ClassDojo, digital communication tools such as text messages or emails, and online videoconferencing tools such as Skype for parents who are unable to visit the school for a conference.

3. *How might a teacher who is struggling with behavior issues use technology to revamp his or her classroom management plan?*

   Establish a system in which students earn points for exhibiting positive behavior. Provide tangible recognition (such as special privileges or activities) to students who earn a certain number of points. Examples of tangible recognition include free time, field trips, special jobs, certificates, and classroom recognition. Technology tools like ClassDojo, an online behavioral management resource, can help you track points, monitor students' progress, and generate online student behavior reports to share with students' parents. Additionally, launch a reflective journal system for behavior. Pause class when it is getting out of control, and prompt students to write an entry in their digital reflective journals. If one or two students are primarily at fault for the disruption, send them to a designated area to take some independent time for reflective journaling. Give them a chance to vent about a tough day and come up with alternative behavior decisions. Prompt them with questions or sentence frames, if necessary.

4. *How do you use technology to recognize levels of adherence to classroom rules and procedures?*

   Answers will vary from teacher to teacher. To see responses from other educators, visit **marzanoresearch.com/classroomstrategies**, click on the *Enhancing the Art & Science of Teaching With Technology* link, and become a member of our virtual learning community.

Answers to Chapter 9: Comprehension Questions

1. *Reflect on your own students' values and interests. Create five different comments you might post on a student's Edmodo page.*

   Answers will vary, but effective comments are usually informed by a teacher's individual background knowledge about his or her students. Appropriate topics for comments include students' individual accomplishments (in school clubs, athletics, academics, and the arts) and important events in students' lives (such as weddings, vacations, or birthdays). Another way to demonstrate value for students is by checking in with them about major changes in their home lives (such as a big move, a divorce, or a death in the family). Use technology to check in with students, but do not post public comments about sensitive topics. Instead, offer your support through private emails, text messages, or Facebook messages.

2. *Explain at least two different functions of a photo bulletin board, and describe how each might be supported with technology.*

   A photo bulletin board can serve several different purposes in the classroom. For one, it can build and strengthen relationships among students by displaying photos and information about their personal goals, hobbies, and interests. Use a digital camera or the camera tools on a desktop computer, laptop, tablet, or smartphone to take pictures of each student at the beginning of the year. For another, a photo bulletin board can convey the message that learning requires teamwork. Use IWB or presentation software to copy and paste students' pictures onto an image of a soccer field, for example, to illustrate that the class is a team of people striving for the same goal. Finally, a photo bulletin board can demonstrate a teacher's value for students. Use PowerPoint or an IWB to create a slideshow that highlights a different student each week. Include photos of the week's student and ask him or her to provide three fun facts and a favorite song to be played during the slideshow.

3. *How can teachers maintain a cool exterior when communicating sensitive issues (such as severe academic challenges or major behavioral indiscretions) to parents and families?*

   If you are anticipating a delicate and potentially difficult conversation with a parent or guardian, send the information in a tactful, well-crafted email. Instead of calling home on a whim or sending a hastily scrawled note home with a student, take time to cool down and choose your words carefully. Do not send the message immediately after writing it. Save a draft, go for a walk, and then return to your desk to reread what you have written. Make changes if necessary before sending it to the student's family.

4. *How do you use technology to establish and maintain effective relationships with your students?*

   Answers will vary from teacher to teacher. To see responses from other educators, visit **marzanoresearch.com/classroomstrategies**, click on the *Enhancing the Art & Science of Teaching With Technology* link, and become a member of our virtual learning community.

Answers to Chapter 10: Comprehension Questions

1. *When a student seems to be having a tough day, how might a teacher use technology to privately communicate to the student that he or she is valued?*

   Teachers can always use eye contact, warm facial expressions, proximity, appropriate physical contact, and playful banter to show value and respect for students. However, these gestures are not always as subtle as a teacher might like, particularly if a student seems upset. Reach out in a text message, or send a positive email to the student to show that you care. Including emoticons in text messages can convey familiarity and ease tension (for example, "How is today going? I am always available to talk. ☺").

2. *Why are think-pair-share exercises helpful for low-expectancy students, and how can they be enhanced with technology?*

   A think-pair-share can be a great way to probe incorrect answers with low-expectancy students because it allows them to compose and practice their responses before sharing them in front of the class. Students can use the screen recording feature on IWB software or screen capture software (such as Jing, ScreenChomp, Educreations, or TouchCast) to narrate their problem-solving processes in think-pair-share groups. Students who have trouble speaking in front of large groups of people can prerecord their thoughts during a think-pair-share and play them for the class.

3. *How can technology help teachers ask challenging questions of low-expectancy students as often as they would with high-expectancy students?*

   Students can use clickers and polling technology to anonymously submit answers to difficult questions. Alternatively, use a random name generator to select students to answer questions. This ensures that low-expectancy students in the class are responding to questions with equal frequency as high-expectancy students.

4. *How do you use technology to communicate high expectations for all students in your classroom?*

   Answers will vary from teacher to teacher. To see responses from other educators, visit **marzanoresearch.com/classroomstrategies**, click on the *Enhancing the Art & Science of Teaching With Technology* link, and become a member of our virtual learning community.

APPENDIX B

GLOSSARY OF TECHNOLOGY TERMS

animations. Moving pictures that simulate movement by cycling through a series of still images.

annotations. Markups, notes, or comments that can be embedded in word processing documents. Annotations can be used in Google Drive.

app (short for *application*). Type of inexpensive software that can only be downloaded from the Internet. Apps are typically used on mobile devices, such as smartphones and tablets.

Audacity. Software for digitally recording and editing sound. Go to http://audacity.sourceforge.net for a free download.

avatar. An image or animation that users can customize to represent themselves on the Internet (such as in gaming, social media, or email services).

Blendspace. A website that allows teachers to create virtual lessons by compiling related digital media resources into a single landing page. For example, a Blendspace lesson on plate tectonics might include video footage of earthquakes, animated simulations of Pangaea's movement, diagrams of the San Andreas Fault, links to a geologist's blog post about plate tectonics, and other relevant media. Teachers can also use Blendspace to administer quizzes and track student progress. Go to www.blendspace.com to set up a free account.

blog (short for *web log*). A personal website made up of journal entries or opinion articles (called *posts*). The word *blog* can also be used as a verb that means *to write a blog post* (for example, "Last night, I blogged about my vacation").

Blogger. A Google-based website that hosts blogs. Its clean, user-friendly interface makes it a perfect website for beginning bloggers. Go to www.blogger.com to set up a free account.

ClassDojo. An online behavior management system that allows teachers to set up an account for each class, award points to students for positive behavior, send notifications to students' mobile devices, and generate behavior reports to share with parents. Go to www.classdojo.com to set up a free account.

class website. Any page on the Internet that is created and updated by a classroom of students and the teacher. A class website can be a blog, a wiki, or a social media page. For example, class websites may be hosted on Facebook, Edmodo, Blendspace, Blogger, WordPress, LiveJournal, Tumblr, or Weebly.

clickers (also called *polling devices* or *student response systems* [SRSs]). Devices that allow students to submit responses electronically when a teacher asks a question. There are several clicker brands on the market, and each brand has its own special features. For instance, clickers with text input allow students to type in and submit responses to open-ended questions, and clickers with self-paced mode allow students to respond to questions at their own speed.

cloud. A metaphor for the wireless network of computers connected through the Internet.

cloud-based file. A file stored online. Cloud-based files can include documents, photos, music, videos, or hard-drive backups and can be retrieved from any device with Internet access.

ClustrMaps. An online service that collects and displays demographic information about the visitors to a particular website. Users post a tracker—which looks like a tiny map of the world—on their own websites, and the tracker displays the site's visitors in real time as tiny red dots on the map. Go to www.clustrmaps.com to add a free tracker to a class website.

comments feature. A tool in word processing software that embeds notes and feedback into a document. Comments are formatted to look different from the original text of the document. Typically, comments that refer to specific words, lines, or passages are connected to them with a straight line or are highlighted in a matching color.

connector tool. A feature of IWB software that joins objects on a page together with a straight line. Once objects are connected, they can be moved around on the screen without being separated; the connector line expands or contracts depending on the space between the objects. Connector tools work well for creating nonlinguistic representations (such as diagrams, flowcharts, and brainstorming maps).

container tool. A feature of IWB software that creates a receptacle on a page (usually a box or other shape) to hold other objects on the page. Containers can be set up to accept or reject certain types of objects. For example, an ELA teacher might configure a container to accept only similes. A student could drag and drop "as quiet as a newborn lamb" into the container, but "an ocean of possibility" would bounce out because it is not a simile.

countdown tool. A feature of IWB software that displays the passage of time before a lesson segment begins or ends. Countdown tools can either count up from zero (like a stopwatch) or backward from a fixed amount of time (like a rocket launch or the ball drop on New Year's Eve). Depending on the software, teachers can choose from various appearances for countdown tools (such as a digital stopwatch, sand falling through an hourglass, or a candle burning lower and lower) and from various sounds made when time runs out (for example, a ringing alarm clock, a bomb going off, or a series of beeps). For teachers without IWB software, go to www.online-stopwatch.com to use a free countdown tool online.

Delicious. A social bookmarking website that allows users to save (or "bookmark") and organize links on the Internet for future reference. Its interface is attractive and very user-friendly; however, Delicious does not include some of the more advanced features found in other social bookmarking services (such as Diigo). Go to https://delicious.com to set up a free account.

dictation feature. Software that converts recorded speech to digital text.

digital camera. An electronic device that captures videos or photos for easy upload onto a computer. Mobile devices such as laptops, tablets, or smartphones often contain a built-in digital camera that can be used for videoconferencing, taking pictures, or recording short videos.

digital drawing program. Software that allows the user to create an image using computer-generated marks and lines.

digital journal. A cloud- or computer-based document in which students keep a daily or regular record of their reflections on learning and academic progress. Students can set up digital journals using blog websites or word processing software.

digital signature. An electronic, cloud-based marking of a person's name that is used to verify an identity. Go to www.echosign.adobe.com/en/home.html to set up a free account through Adobe EchoSign.

digital video tool. A type of software that records video and sound to be played back and viewed on a screen or monitor. Most mobile devices—such as laptops, smartphones, or tablets—contain built-in digital video tools.

Diigo. A social bookmarking website that allows users to save (or "bookmark"), annotate, organize, and share links on the Internet. It includes advanced bookmarking features such as sticky notes and highlighting for text on websites; however, beginning users may find that these extra tools make Diigo more complicated to use than Delicious. Go to www.diigo.com to set up a free educator account.

document camera. A device that uses a built-in digital camera to project a live, full-color image of an object on a large screen. Document cameras typically share many of the same features as digital cameras, such as the ability to take photos and the ability to zoom in on or magnify images.

DoppelMe. An avatar-creation website that allows users to design cartoon images of themselves to use in blogs and social media forums. The service is free and does not require registration; however, signing up does come with benefits (registered users can create multiple avatars, save and revise their designs, and choose from a wider variety of features when customizing their avatars). Go to www.doppelme.com to create an avatar or set up a free account.

Dragon Dictation. An app for Mac that records speech and converts it to digital text. Visit Apple's App Store online or in iTunes for a free download.

Dropbox. A cloud-based service for storing, editing, and sharing files with other users online. Dropbox provides two gigabytes of free storage, allowing users to store numerous files in one place and share large files (such as photo albums and videos) that would not fit in an email attachment. Go to www.dropbox.com for a free download.

Edmodo. A safe and secure social media website for educators, students, and parents that can only be accessed via personal invitation. Teachers create a different page for each class and use it to ask questions, conduct polls, post information about upcoming events (such as exams, field trips, or assignment deadlines), and communicate with students and parents. Go to www.edmodo.com to set up a free account. Visit Apple's App Store online or in iTunes for a free download.

Educreations. An app for iPad that allows users to create video tutorials by using a tablet like a recordable IWB. Users can record handwriting and speech, as well as import pictures. For example, tutorials might include labeling a diagram of the human body, completing an algebra problem, or annotating a poem. Visit Apple's App Store online or in iTunes for a free download.

email (short for *electronic mail*). A service that sends, sorts, and displays text-based messages via the Internet. Popular servers that provide email for free include Gmail, Outlook, and Yahoo! Mail.

emoticon. An electronic symbol that represents human emotions through keyboarded characters. Examples of emoticons include ;-) and >:-0, which represent a winking face and an angry face, respectively. Emoticons are most commonly found in social media websites, instant messaging services, and email servers, many of which automatically convert popular emoticons from combinations of characters into tiny pictorial images, such as ☺, which looks like :-) when originally typed.

eraser tool. A feature of IWB software that wipes out all traces of an object on a page. For instance, teachers might use an eraser tool to eliminate a top-layer image or clean away highlighter tool markings from a passage of text.

Evernote. A free online note-taking app that synchronizes digital notes across a variety of devices, such as desktop computers, laptops, tablets, and smartphones. Go to https://evernote.com for a free download.

Facebook. The most popular social media website in the world. Users can add friends, chat, upload photos, post comments, send private messages, join groups, create events, and browse a newsfeed of friends' posts. The Timeline layout also transforms the site into a virtual scrapbook, allowing users to navigate backward through all of the photos, status updates, and conversations (private and public) that they have ever posted. Go to www.facebook.com to set up a free account. Visit Apple's App Store online or in iTunes for a free download.

fill tool. A feature of IWB software that covers the background or foreground of a selected object with a color or pattern. Fill tools can be used to decorate pages, add color to shapes, or highlight important passages of text.

Flickr (pronounced *flicker*). A website that allows users to upload and share high-resolution digital photographs using any device with Internet access. Go to www.flickr.com to set up a free account. Visit Apple's App Store online or in iTunes for a free download.

GarageBand. Software for Mac that records, creates, edits, and mixes digital music or spoken word files. Visit Apple's App Store online or in iTunes to purchase a download.

Google Drive. A Google-based website that allows users to collaboratively create, edit, and share files—such as word-processed documents, spreadsheets, and presentations—using any device with Internet access. Go to https://drive.google.com to set up a free account.

Google Earth. A Google-based application that offers dynamic satellite images and aerial photographs of Earth. Users can enter any address, see it from space, and gradually zoom in on it all the way to the street level. Features include video flyovers and panoramic 360° views. Go to www.google.com /earth to use the service for free.

Google Groups. A Google-based website that allows users to create and participate in discussions with other online users. Go to https://groups.google.com to set up a free account.

Google Maps. A Google-based online navigation system that allows users to find local businesses, get driving directions, and view maps (including zoomed-in and zoomed-out satellite images). Go to https://maps.google.com to use the service for free. Visit Apple's App Store online or in iTunes for a free download.

hardware. A term for the physical parts of a computer. Keyboards, hard drives, and internal wiring are examples of hardware.

hashtag. The use of the # symbol in front of key words or phrases in a Twitter post (called a *tweet*). When clicked, a hashtag navigates the user to a list of all the tweets that contain that same hashtag. Because the popularity of certain keywords on Twitter is constantly changing, hashtag lists are excellent indicators of recent media trends or news stories. During the 2012 U.S. presidential election, for instance, common hashtags included #obama2012, #romney, and #teaparty.

highlighter tool. A feature of IWB software that emphasizes important pieces of text by marking them with a bright—yet transparent—color.

hosting software. Software that allows users to upload and share content (such as blog posts, photos, and videos) on the Internet.

hyperlink. A word or image that users can click to automatically navigate to a new page or to a different section of an existing page. Commonly referred to as *links*, hyperlinks are often used on websites to allow users to click from page to page without typing anything new into the address bar.

iEARN (International Education and Resource Network). A nonprofit organization in which educators and students from all over the world use the Internet to collaborate in academic and service-learning projects. Go to www.iearn.org to purchase a membership and search for a project that fits with a particular curriculum.

iMovie. Software for Mac that allows users to edit recorded video footage. Features of iMovie include titles, music, and basic effects and enhancements, such as color correction. Visit Apple's App Store online or in iTunes to purchase a download.

Instagram. An image-based social media website that enables users to take digital photographs through various filters, edit them, and share them with followers. Go to http://instagram.com to set up a free account. Visit Apple's App Store online or in iTunes for a free download.

interactive math tool. A feature in IWB software that functions as a digital math instrument or manipulative, providing hands-on instruction in abstract mathematical concepts or easy computation of equations. Interactive math tools include rulers, compasses, protractors, calculators, and so on.

IWB (interactive whiteboard). A large surface that displays the desktop of a computer. Users can write, select, or move objects on the screen using a fingertip or stylus.

Internet. A network that connects millions of devices (such as desktop computers, laptops, tablets, and smartphones) together from all over the world. When a device is connected to the Internet, that device is said to be *online*.

iPad Notes. Software for Mac that allows users to type, store, and edit written reminders, outlines, or memos. iPad Notes is exclusively a feature of Apple products—such as iPhone and iPad—and cannot be downloaded. However, visit Apple's App Store online or in iTunes for a free download of similar software, such as Evernote.

iPad. An Apple-brand tablet, a flat mobile computer about seven to ten inches in length that users control via touchscreen.

IWB software. The combination of computer programs that allows users to interact with an interactive whiteboard (IWB). This software includes all of the features that are included in or can be downloaded for use on an IWB—for example, countdown tools, highlighter tools, and eraser tools.

Jing. Software that records the user's voice and all of the activity in a given area of a computer screen to create a screencast tutorial. Screencasts can then be shared via social media websites and instant messaging services. Go to www.techsmith.com/jing.html for a free download.

Khan Academy. An academic website that contains thousands of tutorial videos, practice problems, and assessment tools for various content areas. Go to www.khanacademy.org to set up a free account.

laptop (sometimes called a *notebook*). A mobile computer that is smaller than a desktop computer and larger than a tablet. A laptop typically folds up into a hard external shell and is equipped with a display screen, a keyboard, speakers, and a touchpad—instead of a mouse—to move a cursor around on the display.

layer tool. Feature of IWB software that positions images or other objects in a page using different tiers of the background and foreground. For instance, a layer tool might be used to cover an image of a butterfly (in the background) with an image of a chrysalis (in the foreground). After asking students to predict the next stage in the chrysalis's metamorphosis, the teacher would move or erase the chrysalis in the first layer to reveal the butterfly in the second layer.

LiveJournal. A website that hosts blogs. It offers a community-focused blogging experience similar to that provided by social media websites like Facebook or Twitter. Go to www.blogger.com to set up a free account.

Mindjet. An app that allows users to create interactive diagrams and flowcharts to organize their thoughts. Mindjet works especially well for group work because of its tools for collaborative planning, brainstorming, and task management. Go to www.mindjet.com for a free thirty-day trial or to purchase a download.

mobile device. A small computing device, such as a smartphone or tablet. Mobile devices are typically handheld and operate through touch-screen displays.

multimedia. Tools that use two or more different communication forms (such as text, audio, video, photos, animation, and so on) in combination. For instance, a list of information displayed statically in a PowerPoint slide is not a multimedia product because it is using only one form of communication (text). However, if that same PowerPoint slide also contained pictures, sounds, and animations, it would be a multimedia product.

Nintendo Wii. A video game console that uses wireless, handheld controllers that operate in 3-D. Unlike most controllers, which operate only with buttons, users can shake, wave, tilt, or jab the Wii controller to interact with the game. For example, the controller can be swung like a racket to hit a ball in tennis video games or tilted back and forth to simulate a steering wheel in racing games.

notes feature. Part of IWB and presentation software (such as PowerPoint) that allows users to type in text notes to use for guidance as they present a flipchart or slideshow.

PBS KIDS. A website that offers educational games and videos for children. The website works best for elementary-aged students because it features characters from children's television shows on PBS, such as *Sesame Street, Arthur,* and *Clifford the Big Red Dog.* Go to http://pbskids.org to use the website or set up a free account.

Pinterest. A website that allows users to save—or "pin"—images, videos, and articles on online bulletin boards called *pinboards.* Users create a personal account and multiple pinboards, such as for recipes, fitness, or home décor, which they can share with friends. With an account, students can create a pinboard for each class project or preserve content they find online. Go to www.pinterest.com to set up a free account. Visit Apple's App Store online or in iTunes for a free download.

podcast. A spoken-word audio or video series of episodes that can be downloaded or streamed online. Podcasts can be spinoffs or recordings of popular radio broadcasts (such as NPR's *This American Life* and *Radiolab*), books (such as *Freakonomics Radio*), or other media (such as TED Talks).

Poll Everywhere. A website that functions as a student response system when paired with mobile devices. Teachers create polls or ask questions in open-ended and multiple-choice formats and students submit answers via desktop computer, laptop, tablet, or smartphone. A bar graph displays the results of the poll, tallying and presenting student responses in real time. Go to www.pollevery where.com to set up a poll for free.

polling software (also called a *student response system*). A type of computer program that automatically collects and analyzes users' responses to a question or poll. Users submit responses via clickers or polling software on mobile devices like smartphones, laptops, or tablets.

PowerPoint. A type of presentation software in which users add images, text, animation, and sound to individual pages to create a multimedia slideshow. Users can then save this slideshow on a computer and present it using a projector or IWB.

presentation software. A type of computer program in which users create and share multimedia demonstrations of content. Presentation software includes everything from traditional slideshows like PowerPoint to animated "zooming" presentations like Prezi and can incorporate images, text, music, sound, animation, or videos.

Prezi. A website that provides a type of presentation software known for its cloud-based storage and animated zooming visuals. In Prezi presentations, the content on the screen does not change from slide to slide as the user clicks forward. Rather, all of the content in the presentation is displayed in a single slide, and clicking forward causes the presentation to rotate and zoom in on different sections of the slide. This feature makes Prezi great for concept maps, storytelling, and group presentations. Prezi presentations can only run on an Internet connection, which allows users to embed online media—such as YouTube videos—directly into the presentation. Go to http://prezi.com to set up a free account.

projector. A device that uses light to electronically display slides or film on a large blank screen (often an IWB or pull-down screen). Classroom projectors typically connect to a computer.

publishing software. A type of computer program that creates documents with elements too complex for a word processor (such as web pages, newsletters, and magazines). Publishing software allows users to design layouts, create nonlinear passages of text, and edit photos. Popular brands of publishing software include PagePlus, Adobe InDesign, and Microsoft Publisher.

Quizlet. A website that generates sets of flashcards to use while studying and practicing with new content. Quizlet offers features that help users design their own flashcards for a variety of content areas. For example, art history students can add images of different paintings or sculptures, and foreign language students can include special characters (such as ü and ش) to practice vocabulary words. Go to http://quizlet.com to set up a free account.

random group generator. Software that randomly divides a large group of people into multiple small groups or teams.

random name generator. Software that randomly selects a name from a pre-entered list of names.

random number generator. Software that randomly selects a number from a pre-entered range of numbers.

reveal tool. A feature of IWB software that alternately hides and displays objects on a page, such as text or images. Reveal tools are good for building anticipation and excitement among students.

screen capture software. A type of computer program that takes a picture or records a video of the activity being displayed on the screen of a computer or tablet. Depending on the screen capture software, users can also add effects to the recording and share it with others.

screencasting. The process of using screen capture software to record the activity in a given area of a computer display. This creates a recording, or screencast, that can be played back and viewed.

ScreenChomp. An app that creates tutorials that can be shared via hyperlink. The app records the user's voice and features a touchscreen whiteboard, allowing the user to write on top of screenshots while explaining a concept. For instance, a student might bring up an image of a tree on his or her tablet and use ScreenChomp to label its component parts. Visit Apple's App Store online or in iTunes for a free download.

scrolling text function. A feature of IWB software that moves the viewer up and down through a passage of text to view its various sections.

self-paced mode. A setting on certain types of clickers that allows students to respond to questions at their own speed.

SketchUp. Software that creates 3-D models of architecture on a computer or tablet. Go to www.sketch up.com for a free download.

Skype. Online software that allows users to make international phone calls, send instant messages, or talk face-to-face (videoconference) with people in any location in the world. To videoconference via Skype, users also need a microphone and a built-in computer video camera or webcam, which is a small video camera that hooks up to a computer. Go to www.skype.com to set up a free account. Visit Apple's App Store online or in iTunes for a free download.

smartphone. A type of mobile phone that uses a computer operating system to connect the user to Wi-Fi networks or online data. Like most mobile phones, smartphones make wireless phone calls and send text messages; however, smartphones come with more advanced features than ordinary cell phones (such as Internet access, built-in digital cameras, video recording, and touchscreens).

Snapchat. An app that captures videos and photos (called *snaps*) and sends them to individuals or groups of people. Users can add text and doodles to photos and set a time limit on snaps, causing them to disappear from the recipient's phone in ten seconds or fewer. Go to www.snapchat.com or visit Apple's App Store for a free download.

social bookmarking tool. Online software that allows users to save or "bookmark," organize, and share links on the Internet.

social media website (also called a *social networking website*). Website that allows users to create personal profiles, which typically include photos and basic information about their beliefs and interests, and then cultivate an online community by accumulating "friends" (Facebook) or "followers" (Twitter). Users can use social media websites to create events, upload photos, and post hyperlinks and comments on friends' pages.

Socrative. A website that functions as a student response system (SRS) when paired with mobile devices. Teachers create questions in a variety of formats, including multiple choice, true or false, short answer, quick quiz, and exit ticket. Students then use a desktop computer, laptop, tablet, or smartphone to submit their answers. Additionally, Socrative automatically collects data on student responses and allows teachers to download and analyze reports using spreadsheet software such as Microsoft Excel. Socrative also offers games that track students' performance as they play. Go to www.socrative.com to set up a free account.

software. A term for all of the programs and information that a computer uses to run. Microsoft Windows, PowerPoint, and iTunes are examples of software.

spreadsheet software. A type of computer program that creates grid-like documents made up of cells, rows, and columns. Users can type data into the cells and program the document to automatically make calculations based on the entered numbers. Microsoft Excel is an example of spreadsheet software.

SRS (student response system). See entry for *polling software*.

SurveyMonkey. A website that allows users to create original surveys, to which participants respond using the Internet. Users can share hyperlinks to SurveyMonkey surveys via social media websites to broaden their pool of respondents. Go to www.surveymonkey.com to set up a free account.

survey tool. Software that allows users to create and publish original online surveys.

tablet. A type of mobile computer that is primarily controlled via touchscreen. Tablets are typically seven to ten inches long and can run—for the most part—the same software as a laptop or desktop computer.

Team Maker. An online random group generator that is used to divide a large group of people into small groups. Teachers input the names of all the students in a class, select a number of teams, click "Generate Teams!," and Team Maker takes care of the rest. Go to http://chir.ag/projects/team-maker to use the service for free.

TED (Technology, Entertainment, Design). An international series of conferences (TED Talks) that highlight innovators across an array of fields, from medicine to social justice to agriculture. Past TED speakers have included Bill Gates, Isabel Allende, Bono, Roger Ebert, Jane Goodall, and Stephen Hawking. Go to www.ted.com to stream and view TED Talks for free.

text message. A short note sent from one mobile phone to another. To send a text message (called *texting*), one user types into a phone by pressing keyboard buttons or tapping a touchscreen keyboard. When the user clicks *send*, the message appears on the recipient's phone screen.

timeline tool. A feature of IWB software that organizes drag-and-drop images—representing people, places, things, events, or ideas—according to a given chronology.

timer feature. See entry for *countdown tool.*

TodaysMeet. A website that functions as a student response system when paired with mobile devices. Teachers create an online chat room, which students can join and use to submit text messages of 140 characters or fewer. If displayed on an IWB or projector screen, teachers can share student messages with the whole class. TodaysMeet works well for lectures, open-ended discussions, or short-answer questions because students can submit questions or comments that a teacher can see in real time. Go to https://todaysmeet.com to set up a free "room" for your class.

TouchCast. An app for iPad that allows users to create their own videos. Its most unique feature is the ability for users to incorporate customizable vApps (short for video applications) into their videos. vApps include pop-up polls, pull quotes, lists, Twitter feeds, Google Maps, Flickr photos, and web pages, all of which a viewer can click, expand, and interact with while the video continues to play. Visit Apple's App Store online or in iTunes for a free download.

touchscreen. A type of computer display in which users control the device by physically tapping and dragging a finger around on the screen instead of using a mouse to click or a keyboard to type. Touchscreens are most commonly found on smartphones and tablets.

Tumblr (pronounced *tumbler*). A website that hosts blogs. It is among the most popular websites for blogging because it allows users to easily upload content, select other blogs to appear in their newsfeed, re-blog posts from other users, and choose from a variety of attractive templates or themes. Go to www.tumblr.com to set up a free account.

TweetDeck. An app that manages and organizes multiple social media accounts within a single interface. Instead of checking in with several different social media websites—such as Twitter, Facebook, Myspace, and LinkedIn—users can access and update all of their different accounts in one place. Go to www.tweetdeck.com for a free download.

Twitter. A social media website that allows users to post messages of 140 characters or fewer (called *tweets*) for their followers to read. Tweets often include hashtags and hyperlinks to other websites and can be directed to specific Twitter users by typing an @ symbol before a username (such as @justinbieber). Go to https://twitter.com to set up a free account.

username (also called a *screen name* or a *handle*). An online pseudonym that a person uses to identify him- or herself on the Internet. Users frequently go by their usernames when tweeting (on Twitter) or posting comments on blogs or articles. Usernames can also serve as part of a user's login information when accessing a computer, website, or network.

videoconferencing tool. Software that uses the Internet to allow two or more users to talk face-to-face via a computer, a camera, and a microphone.

video recording tool. Tool that creates a filmed copy of an event that can be played back and viewed on a computer, television, or mobile device.

Vimeo. A website that allows users to upload, store, and watch digital videos in high definition. Features of Vimeo include the ability to share videos, mark other peoples' videos as *liked*, follow friends' accounts, and save videos in an album to watch later. Relative to YouTube, Vimeo tends to be a more student-friendly and professional way to watch and share videos. Go to https://vimeo.com to watch videos for free or to set up a free account.

website. A collection of related Internet pages united under a single name or identity. Users can access websites by opening a web browser such as Google Chrome or Internet Explorer and typing in the website's address (called a *URL*) into the address bar. Examples of popular websites include Google, Amazon, Wikipedia, YouTube, eBay, and Craigslist.

Weebly. A website that allows users to create and publish their own websites. Weebly has a simple, clean interface that provides users with a variety of features, including various themes and layouts, video and photo uploading, blogging from multiple devices, and built-in tools that analyze the success of the website. Go to www.weebly.com to create a free website.

wiki. A type of website that is created, edited, and maintained by a community of users. Wiki pages are extremely easy to change and update, making it possible for many people to modify them. The most famous example of a wiki is Wikipedia, an online encyclopedia in which the entirety of the website's content is generated by its users.

Wikispaces. A website that allows users to create and edit their own wikis. Wikispaces works well to facilitate collaboration, project-based learning, and safe social networking among students. Go to www.wikispaces.com to set up a free educator account.

word cloud. A graphic made up of the most frequently occurring words in a text. The more often a word is used in a text, the larger it appears in the word cloud. In a word cloud based on L. Frank Baum's *The Wonderful Wizard of Oz*, for instance, the largest words are *Dorothy*, *Scarecrow*, *Woodman*, *Lion*, *Oz*, and *Witch*, because those words appear most frequently in the novel (word clouds typically exclude commonly used words such as *and*, *the*, and *is*).

WordPress. A website that hosts blogs. ELA teachers may especially appreciate WordPress's thriving online community of skilled writers, including an array of blog posts about creative writing. Go to http://wordpress.org to set up a free account.

word processing software. A type of computer program that allows users to create, edit, format, and save text-based documents. Microsoft Word is an example of word processing software.

Wordle. A website that automatically generates word clouds based on text provided by the user. Go to www.wordle.net to create word clouds for free.

YouTube. A Google-owned website that allows users to upload, store, and watch digital videos in high definition. Features of YouTube include the ability to search within the world's largest video database, subscribe to video channels, and build a list of favorite videos for future reference. YouTube gets significantly more traffic from viewers than Vimeo; however, this can make it impossible to regulate the appropriateness of content that appears on the website. Go to www.youtube.com to watch videos for free or to set up a free account.

zoom tool. A feature of IWB software that magnifies images and text on the screen.

REFERENCES AND RESOURCES

Alvermann, D. E., & Boothby, P. R. (1986). Children's transfer of graphic organizer instruction. *Reading Psychology, 7*(2), 87–100.

Anderson, L. M., Evertson, C. M., & Emmer, E. T. (1980). Dimensions in classroom management derived from recent research. *Journal of Curriculum Studies, 12*(4), 343–356.

Anderson, T. (2012). Networks, Web 2.0, and the connected learner. In R. A. Reiser & J. V. Dempsey (Eds.), *Trends and issues in instructional design and technology* (3rd ed., pp. 299–308). Boston: Pearson.

Anderson, V., & Hidi, S. (1988). Teaching students to summarize. *Educational Leadership, 46*, 26–28.

Aubusson, P., Foswill, S., Barr, R., & Perkovic, L. (1997). What happens when students do simulation-role-play in science? *Research in Science Education, 27*(4), 565–579.

Ausubel, D. P. (1968). *Educational psychology: A cognitive view.* New York: Holt, Rinehart & Winston.

Azevedo, R. (2005). Using hypermedia as a metacognitive tool for enhancing student learning? The role of self-regulated learning. *Educational Psychologist, 40*(4), 199–209.

Bangert-Drowns, R. L., Kulik, C.-L. C., Kulik, J. A., & Morgan, M. (1991). The instructional effects of feedback in test-like events. *Review of Educational Research, 61*(2), 213–238.

Barrow, L., Markman, L., & Rouse, C. E. (2008). *Technology's edge: The educational benefits of computer-aided instruction* (NBER Working Paper No. 14240). Cambridge, MA: National Bureau of Economic Research. Accessed at www.nber.org/papers/w14240 on June 4, 2013.

Bayraktar, S. (2000). *A meta-analysis on the effectiveness of computer-assisted instruction in science education.* Unpublished doctoral dissertation, Ohio University, Athens.

Beeland, W. D., Jr. (2002). *Student engagement, visual learning and technology: Can interactive whiteboards help?* Accessed at http://citeseerx.ist.psu.edu/viewdoc/download?doi=10.1.1.135.3542&rep=rep1&type=pdf on June 4, 2013.

Bergmann, J., & Sams, A. (2012). *Flip your classroom: Reach every student in every class every day.* Eugene, OR: International Society for Technology in Education.

Bernard, R. M., Abrami, P. C., Lou, Y., Borokhovski, E., Wade, A., Wozney, L., et al. (2004). How does distance education compare with classroom instruction? A meta-analysis of the empirical literature. *Review of Educational Research, 74*(3), 379–439.

Blachowicz, C. L. Z., Bates, A., Berne, J., Bridgman, T., Chaney, J., & Perney, J. (2009). Technology and at-risk young readers and their classrooms. *Reading Psychology, 30*(5), 387–411.

Blok, H., Oostdam, R., Otter, M. E., & Overmaat, M. (2002). Computer-assisted instruction in support of beginning reading instruction: A review. *Review of Educational Research, 72*(1), 101–130.

Blood, E., & Gulchak, D. (2013). Embedding "clickers" into classroom instruction: Benefits and strategies. *Intervention in School and Clinic, 48*(4), 246–253.

Bloom, B. S. (1976). *Human characteristics and school learning.* New York: McGraw-Hill.

Bojinova, E. D., & Oigara, J. N. (2011). Teaching and learning with clickers: Are clickers good for students? *Interdisciplinary Journal of E-Learning and Learning Objects, 7,* 169–183.

Branch, R. M., & Deissler, C. H. (2008). Processes. In A. Januszewski & M. Molenda (Eds.), *Educational technology: A definition with commentary* (pp. 195–211). New York: Erlbaum.

Brekelmans, M., Wubbels, T., & Creton, H. A. (1990). A study of student perceptions of physics teacher behavior. *Journal of Research in Science Teaching, 27*(4), 335–350.

Brophy, J. E., & Evertson, C. M. (1976). *Learning from teaching: A developmental perspective.* Boston: Allyn & Bacon.

Brophy, J. E., & Good, T. L. (1970). Teacher's communication of differential expectations for children's classroom performance: Some behavioral data. *Journal of Educational Psychology, 61*(5), 365–374.

Carleton, L., & Marzano, R. J. (2010). *Vocabulary games for the classroom.* Bloomington, IN: Marzano Research.

Cavanaugh, C., Gillan, K. J., Kromrey, J., Hess, M., & Blomeyer, R. (2004). *The effects of distance education on K–12 student outcomes: A meta-analysis.* Naperville, IL: Learning Point.

Chambers, B., Slavin, R. E., Madden, N. A., Abrami, P. C., Tucker, B. J., Cheung, A., et al. (2008). Technology infusion in Success for All: Reading outcomes for first graders. *The Elementary School Journal, 109*(1), 1–15.

Christensen, C., Horn, M., & Johnson, C. (2008). *Disrupting class: How disruptive innovation will change the way the world learns.* New York: McGraw-Hill.

Christmann, E. P., & Badgett, J. L. (1999). A comparative analysis of the effects of computer-assisted instruction on student achievement in differing science and demographical areas. *Journal of Computers in Mathematics and Science Teaching, 18*(2), 135–143.

Christmann, E. P., & Badgett, J. L. (2003). A meta-analytic comparison of the effects of computer-assisted instruction on elementary students' academic achievement. *Information Technology in Childhood Education Annual, 1,* 91–104.

Cohen, J. (1988). *Statistical power analysis for the behavioral sciences* (2nd ed.). Hillsdale, NJ: Erlbaum.

Cohen, P. A., & Dacanay, L. S. (1992). Computer-based instruction and health professions education: A meta-analysis of outcomes. *Evaluation and the Health Professions, 15*(3), 259–281.

Collins, A., & Halverson, R. (2009). *Rethinking education in the age of technology: The digital revolution and schooling in America.* New York: Teachers College Press.

Connell, J. P., Spencer, M. B., & Aber, J. L. (1994). Educational risk and resilience in African-American youth: Context, self, action, and outcomes in school. *Child Development, 65*(2), 493–506.

Connell, J. P., & Wellborn, J. G. (1991). Competence, autonomy, and relatedness: A motivational analysis of self-system processes. In M. Gunnar & L. A. Sroufe (Eds.), *Minnesota symposium on child psychology* (Vol. 23, pp. 21–56). Chicago: University of Chicago Press.

Cooper, H., Robinson, J. C., & Patall, E. A. (2006). Does homework improve academic achievement? A synthesis of research, 1987–2003. *Review of Educational Research, 76*(1), 1–62.

Cristia, J. P., Ibarrarán, P., Cueto, S., Santiago, A., & Severín, E. (2012). *Technology and child development: Evidence from the One Laptop per Child Program* (IDB Working Paper Series No. IDP-WP-304). Washington, DC: Inter-American Development Bank Department of Research and Chief Economist. Accessed at http://idbdocs.iadb.org/wsdocs/getdocument.aspx?docnum=36706954 on April 4, 2013.

Cross, K. P. (1998). Classroom research: Implementing the scholarship of teaching. In T. Angelo (Ed.), *Classroom assessment and research: An update on uses, approaches, and research findings* (pp. 5–12). San Francisco: Jossey-Bass.

Cuban, L., Kirkpatrick, H., & Peck, C. (2001). High access and low use of technologies in high school classrooms: Explaining an apparent paradox. *American Educational Research Journal, 38*(4), 813–834.

Culp, K. M., Honey, M., & Mandinach, E. (2005). A retrospective on twenty years of education technology policy. *Journal of Educational Computing Research, 32*(3), 279–307.

David, J. L. (2009). Teaching media literacy. *Educational Leadership, 66*(6), 84–86.

Deci, E. L., Ryan, R. M., & Koestner, R. (2001). The pervasive negative effects of rewards on intrinsic motivation: Response to Cameron (2001). *Review of Educational Research, 71*(1), 43–51.

Demetriadis, S., Barbas, A., Molohides, A., Palaigeorgiou, G., Psillos, D., Vlahavas, I., et al. (2003). "Cultures in negotiation": Teachers' acceptance/resistance attitudes considering the infusion of technology into schools. *Computers and Education, 41*(1), 19–37.

Dexter, S. L., Anderson, R. E., & Becker, H. J. (1999). Teachers' views of computers as catalysts for changes in their teaching practice. *Journal of Research on Computing in Education, 31*(3), 221–239.

Diamond, N. (1980). America. On *The Jazz Singer* [CD]. New York: Columbia Records.

Druyan, S. (1997). Effects of the kinesthetic conflict on promoting scientific reasoning. *Journal of Research in Science Teaching, 34*(10), 1083–1099.

Dwyer, T., Blizzard, L., & Dean, K. (1996). Physical activity and performance in children. *Nutrition Review, 54*(4), 27–31.

Dwyer, T., Sallis, J. F., Blizzard, L., Lazarus, R., & Dean, K. (2001). Relation of academic performance to physical activity and fitness in children. *Pediatric Exercise Science, 13*, 225–237.

Eisenhart, M. (1977, May). *Maintaining control: Teacher competence in the classroom.* Paper presented at the American Anthropological Association, Houston, TX.

Emmer, E. T., Evertson, C., & Anderson, L. (1980). Effective classroom management at the beginning of the school year. *Elementary School Journal, 80*(5), 219–231.

Federal Communications Commission. (2010). *FCC enables high-speed, affordable broadband for schools and libraries* [Press release]. Accessed at http://hraunfoss.fcc.gov/edocs_public/attachmatch /DOC-301649A1.pdf on May 31, 2013.

Ferguson, R. (1998). Teacher perceptions and expectations and the black-white test score gap. In C. Jencks & M. Phillips (Eds.), *The black-white test score gap* (pp. 273–317). Washington, DC: Brookings Institution Press.

Fishbein, H. D., Eckart, T., Lauver, E., Van Leeuwen, R., & Langmeyer, D. (1990). Learner's questions and comprehension in a tutoring setting. *Journal of Educational Psychology, 82*(1), 163–170.

Forstater, M., White, M. (Producers), Gilliam, T., & Jones, T. (Directors). (1975). *Monty Python and the holy grail* [Motion Picture]. United Kingdom: Python (Monty) Pictures.

Gallardo-Virgen, J. A., & DeVillar, R. A. (2011). Sharing, talking, and learning in the elementary school science classroom: Benefits of innovative design and collaborative learning in computer-integrated settings. *Computers in the Schools, 28*(4), 278–290.

Gee, J. P. (2011). The classroom of popular culture: What video games can teach us about making students want to learn. In N. Walser (Ed.), *Spotlight on technology in education* (pp. 47–54). Cambridge, MA: Harvard Education Press.

Gijbels, D., Dochy, F., Van den Bossche, P., & Segers, M. (2005). Effects of problem-based learning: A meta-analysis from the angle of assessment. *Review of Educational Research, 75*(1), 27–61.

Gillard, C. (2011). "Equity, access, and opportunity": Despite challenges, more districts adopt one-to-one laptop programs. In N. Walser (Ed.), *Spotlight on technology in education* (pp. 81–90). Cambridge, MA: Harvard Education Press.

Glassett, K., & Schrum, L. (2009). Teacher beliefs and student achievement in technology-rich classroom environments. *International Journal of Technology in Teaching and Learning, 5*(2), 138–153.

Good, T. L., & Brophy, J. E. (2003). *Looking in classrooms* (9th ed.). Boston: Allyn & Bacon.

Gray, L., Thomas, N., & Lewis, L. (2010). *Teachers' use of educational technology in U.S. public schools: 2009* (NCES 2010-040). Washington, DC: National Center for Education Statistics.

Grunwald Associates. (2013). *Living and learning with mobile devices: What parents think about mobile devices for early childhood and K–12 learning.* Accessed at www.grunwald.com/pdfs /Grunwald%20Mobile%20Study%20public%20report.pdf on June 4, 2013.

Haas, M. (2005). Teaching methods for secondary algebra: A meta-analysis of findings. *NASSP Bulletin, 89*(642), 24–46.

Halpern, D. F. (1984). *Thought and knowledge: An introduction to critical thinking.* Hillsdale, NJ: Erlbaum.

Halpern, D. F., Hansen, C., & Reifer, D. (1990). Analogies as an aid to understanding and memory. *Journal of Educational Psychology, 82*(2), 298–305.

Halpin, J., & Muth, M. (2012). *2012 yearbook: Technology innovation in education.* Folsom, CA: Center for Digital Education. Accessed at http://images.erepublic.com/documents/CDE12+YB+Draft.pdf on June 3, 2013.

Harris, J. (2005). Our agenda for technology integration: It's time to choose. *Contemporary Issues in Technology and Teacher Education, 5*(2), 116–122.

Hattie, J. (2009). *Visible learning: A synthesis of over 800 meta-analyses relating to achievement.* New York: Routledge.

Hattie, J., Biggs, J., & Purdie, N. (1996). Effects of learning skills interventions on student learning: A meta-analysis. *Review of Educational Research, 66*(2), 99–136.

Hattie, J., & Timperley, H. (2007). The power of feedback. *Review of Educational Research, 77*(1), 81–112.

Haystead, M. W., & Magaña, S. (2013). *Using technology to enhance the* art and science of teaching *framework: A descriptive case study.* Centennial, CO: Marzano Research. Accessed at www.marzanoresearch.com/research/reports/using-technology-to-enhance-asot on June 5, 2013.

Hidi, S., & Anderson, V. (1987). Producing written summaries: Task demands, cognitive operations, and implications for instruction. *Review of Educational Research, 56*(4), 473–493.

Hillocks, G., Jr. (1986). *Research on written composition: New directions for teaching.* Urbana, IL: ERIC Clearinghouse on Reading and Communication Skills and National Conference on Research in English.

House, D. J. (2002). Effects of classroom computer instruction on mathematics achievement of a national sample of tenth-grade students: Findings from the education longitudinal study of 2002 (ELS: 2002) assessment. *International Journal of Instructional Media, 38*(4), 391–399.

Hsu, Y.-C. (2003). *The effectiveness of computer-assisted instruction in statistics education: A meta-analysis.* Unpublished doctoral dissertation, University of Arizona, Tucson.

Huang, K. H., & Ke, C.-J. (2009). Integrating computer games with mathematics instruction in elementary school: An analysis of motivation, achievement, and pupil-teacher interactions. *World Academy of Science, Engineering and Technology, 60,* 261–263.

Hyerle, D. (1996). *Visual tools for constructing knowledge.* Alexandria, VA: Association for Supervision and Curriculum Development.

Inan, F. A., & Lowther, D. L. (2010). Laptops in the K–12 classrooms: Exploring factors impacting instructional use. *Computers and Education, 55*(3), 937–944.

Internet World Stats. (2013). *Internet usage statistics: The Internet big picture—World Internet usage and population stats.* Accessed at www.internetworldstats.com/stats.htm on June 3, 2013.

Jenks, M. S., & Springer, J. M. (2002). A view of the research on the efficacy of CAI. *Electronic Journal for the Integration of Technology in Education, 1*(2), 43–58.

Jensen, E. (2005). *Teaching with the brain in mind* (2nd ed.). Alexandria, VA: Association for Supervision and Curriculum Development.

Jonas, P. M. (2010). *Laughing and learning: An alternative to shut up and listen.* Lanham, MD: Rowman & Littlefield Education.

Jussim, L., Eccles, J., & Madon, S. (1996). Social perception, social stereotypes, and teacher expectations: Accuracy and the quest for the powerful self-fulfilling prophecy. In M. P. Zanna (Ed.), *Advances in experimental social psychology: Vol. 28* (pp. 281–388). San Diego, CA: Academic Press.

Knewton. (2013). *Adaptive learning: Build the search engine for education.* Accessed at https://coderwall .com/team/knewton on September 5, 2013.

Kuchler, J. M. (1998). *The effectiveness of using computers to teach secondary school (grades 6–12) mathematics: A meta-analysis.* Unpublished doctoral dissertation, University of Massachusetts, Lowell, MA.

Kumar, D. D. (1991). A meta-analysis of the relationship between science instruction and student engagement. *Education Review, 43*(1), 49–66.

Lankshear, C., & Knobel, M. (2006). *New literacies: Everyday practices and classroom learning* (2nd ed.). Maidenhead, England: Open University Press.

Latham, P. (2002). *Teaching and learning primary mathematics: The impact of interactive whiteboards.* London: BEAM Education.

Lee, H. (1960). *To kill a mockingbird* (50th anniversary ed.). New York: Grand Central.

Leu, D. J., Kinzer, C. K., Coiro, J. L., & Cammack, D. W. (2004). Toward a theory of new literacies emerging from the Internet and other information and communication technologies. In D. E. Alvermann, N. J. Unrau, & R. B. Ruddell (Eds.), *Theoretical models and processes of reading* (5th ed., pp. 1570–1613). Newark, DE: International Reading Association.

Leu, D. J., O'Byrne, W. I., Zawilinksi, L., McVerry, J. G., & Everett-Cacopardo, H. (2009). Comments on Greenhow, Robelia, and Hughes: Expanding the new literacies conversation. *Educational Researcher, 38*(4), 264–269.

Li, Q., & Ma, X. (2010). A meta-analysis of the effects of computer technology on school students' mathematics learning. *Educational Psychology Review, 22*(3), 215–243.

Linden, D. E., Bittner, R. A., Muckli, L., Waltz, J. A., Kriegeskorte, N., Goebel, R., et al. (2003). Cortical capacity constraints for visual working memory: Dissociation of fMRI load effects in a fronto-parietal network. *Neuroimage, 20*(3), 1518–1530.

Lipsey, M. W. (1990). *Design sensitivity: Statistical power for experimental research.* Newbury Park, CA: SAGE.

Lipsey, M. W., & Wilson, D. B. (1993). The efficacy of psychological, educational, and behavioral treatment: Confirmation from meta-analysis. *American Psychologist, 48*(12), 1181–1209.

López, O. S. (2010). The digital learning classroom: Improving English language learners' academic success in mathematics and reading using interactive whiteboard technology. *Computers and Education, 54*(4), 901–915.

Lou, Y., Abrami, P. C., & d'Apollonia, S. (2001). Small group and individual learning with technology: A meta-analysis. *Review of Educational Research, 71*(3), 449–521.

Lou, Y., Abrami, R. C., Spence, J. C., Paulsen, C., Chambers, B., & d'Apollonia, S. (1996). Within-class grouping: A meta-analysis. *Review of Educational Research, 66*(4), 423–458.

Lyman, F. (2006). *Think-pair-share SmartCard* [Reference card]. San Clemente, CA: Kagan.

Marzano, R. J. (1992). *A different kind of classroom: Teaching with dimensions of learning*. Alexandria, VA: Association for Supervision and Curriculum Development.

Marzano, R. J. (with Marzano, J. S., & Pickering, D.). (2003). *Classroom management that works: Research-based strategies for every teacher*. Alexandria, VA: Association for Supervision and Curriculum Development.

Marzano, R. J. (2007). *The art and science of teaching: A comprehensive framework for effective instruction*. Alexandria, VA: Association for Supervision and Curriculum Development.

Marzano, R. J. (2010). *Formative assessment and standards-based grading*. Bloomington, IN: Marzano Research.

Marzano, R. J. (with Boogren, T., Heflebower, T., Kanold-McIntyre, J., & Pickering, D.). (2012). *Becoming a reflective teacher*. Bloomington, IN: Marzano Research.

Marzano, R. J., & Brown, J. L. (2009). *A handbook for the art and science of teaching*. Alexandria, VA: Association for Supervision and Curriculum Development.

Marzano, R. J., Frontier, T., & Livingston, D. (2011). *Effective supervision: Supporting the art and science of teaching*. Alexandria, VA: Association for Supervision and Curriculum Development.

Marzano, R. J., & Haystead, M. W. (2009). *Final report: Evaluation study of the effects of Promethean ActivClassroom on student achievement*. Englewood, CO: Marzano Research.

Marzano, R. J., & Haystead, M. W. (2010). *Final report: A second year evaluation study of Promethean ActivClassroom*. Englewood, CO: Marzano Research.

Marzano, R. J., & Pickering, D. J. (2005). *Building academic vocabulary: Teacher's manual*. Alexandria, VA: Association for Supervision and Curriculum Development.

Marzano, R. J., Pickering, D. J., & Pollock, J. E. (2001). *Classroom instruction that works: Research-based strategies for increasing student achievement*. Alexandria, VA: Association for Supervision and Curriculum Development.

Marzano, R. J., & Simms, J. A. (with Roy, T., Heflebower, T., & Warrick, P.). (2013). *Coaching classroom instruction*. Bloomington, IN: Marzano Research.

Mayer, R. E. (1989). Models of understanding. *Review of Educational Research, 59*(1), 43–64.

Mayer, R. E. (2003). *Learning and instruction*. Upper Saddle River, NJ: Merrill, Prentice Hall.

McDaniel, M. A., & Donnelly, C. M. (1996). Learning with analogy and elaborative interrogation. *Journal of Educational Psychology, 88*(3), 508–519.

McVee, M. B., Dunsmore, K., & Gavelek, J. R. (2005). Schema theory revisited. *Review of Educational Research, 75*(4), 531–566.

Means, B. (2010). Technology and education change: Focus on student learning. *Journal of Research on Technology in Education, 42*(3), 285–307.

Means, B., Toyama, Y., Murphy, R., Bakia, M., & Jones, K. (2010). *Evaluation of evidence-based practices in online learning: A meta-analysis and review of online learning studies*. Washington, DC: U.S. Department of Education, Office of Planning, Evaluation and Policy Development.

Mishra, P., Koehler, M., & Kereluik, K. (2009). The song remains the same: Looking back to the future of educational technology. *TechTrends, 53*(5), 48–53.

Mittermeyer, D., & Quirion, D. (2003). *Information literacy: Study of incoming first-year undergraduates in Quebec.* Montreal: Conférence des Recteurs et des Principaux des Universités du Québec. Accessed at www.crepuq.qc.ca/documents/bibl/formation/studies_Ang.pdf on September 3, 2013.

Moskowitz, G., & Hayman, J. L., Jr. (1976). Success strategies of inner-city teachers: A year-long study. *Journal of Educational Research, 69*(8), 283–289.

National Governors Association Center for Best Practices & Council of Chief State School Officers. (2010a). *Common Core State Standards for English language arts & literacy in history/social studies, science, and technical subjects.* Washington, DC: Authors.

National Governors Association Center for Best Practices & Council of Chief State School Officers. (2010b). *Common Core State Standards for mathematics.* Washington, DC: Authors.

Negroponte, N. (2006). *Nicholas Negroponte: The vision behind One Laptop per Child* [Video file]. Accessed at www.ted.com/talks/nicholas_negroponte_on_one_laptop_per_child.html on April 4, 2013.

Newton, D. P. (1995). Pictorial support for discourse comprehension. *British Journal of Educational Psychology, 64*(2), 221–229.

Nielsen, J. (2013). *Usability of websites for teenagers.* Accessed at www.nngroup.com/articles/usability-of-websites-for-teenagers on September 3, 2013.

Noeth, R. J., & Volkov, B. B. (2004). *Evaluating the effectiveness of technology in our schools: ACT policy report.* Iowa City, IA: ACT. Accessed at www.act.org/research/policymakers/pdf/school_tech.pdf on June 4, 2013.

Nuthall, G. (1999). The way students learn: Acquiring knowledge from an integrated science and social studies unit. *Elementary School Journal, 99*(4), 303–341.

O'Donnell, A. M., Dansereau, D. F., Hall, R. H., Skaggs, L. P., Hyhecker, V. I., Peel, J. L., et al. (1990). Learning concrete procedures: Effects of processing strategies and cooperative learning. *Journal of Educational Psychology, 82*(1), 171–177.

Ogle, D. (1986). K-W-L: A teaching model that develops active reading of expository text. *Reading Teacher, 39*(6), 564–570.

One Laptop per Child. (2013a). *About the project: Countries.* Accessed at http://one.laptop.org/about/countries on June 3, 2013.

One Laptop per Child. (2013b). *About the project: Mission.* Accessed at http://one.laptop.org/about/mission on June 3, 2013.

One Laptop per Child. (2013c). *About the project: People.* Accessed at http://one.laptop.org/about/people on June 3, 2013.

One Laptop per Child. (2013d). *People: Nicholas Negroponte.* Accessed at http://one.laptop.org/about/people/negroponte on June 3, 2013.

Ottenbreit-Leftwich, A. T., Brush, T. A., Strycker, J., Gronseth, S., Roman, T., Abaci, S., et al. (2012). Preparation versus practice: How do teacher education programs and practicing teachers align in their use of technology to support teaching and learning? *Computers and Education, 59*(2), 399–411.

Ozgungor, S., & Guthrie, J. T. (2004). Interactions among elaborative interrogation, knowledge, and interest in the process of constructing knowledge from text. *Journal of Educational Psychology, 96*(3), 437–443.

Papert, S. (1980). *Mindstorms: Children, computers, and powerful ideas.* New York: Basic Books.

Papert, S. (1993). *Mindstorms: Children, computers, and powerful ideas* (2nd ed.). New York: Basic Books.

Pearson, P. D., Ferdig, R. E., Blomeyer, R. L., Jr., & Moran, J. (2005). *The effects of technology on reading performance in the middle-school grades: A meta-analysis with recommendations for policy.* Naperville, IL: Learning Point.

Pressley, M., Wood, E., Woloshyn, V. E., Martin, V., King, A., & Menke, D. (1992). Encouraging mindful use of prior knowledge: Attempting to construct explanatory answers facilitates learning. *Educational Psychologist, 27*(1), 91–109.

Purcell, K., Rainie, L., Heaps, A., Buchanan, J., Friedrich, L., Jacklin, A., et al. (2012). *How teens do research in the digital world: A survey of Advanced Placement and National Writing Project teachers finds that teens' research habits are changing in the digital age.* Accessed at www.pewinternet .org/~/media//Files/Reports/2012/PIP_TeacherSurveyReportWithMethodology110112.pdf on September 23, 2013.

Reder, L. M. (1980). The role of elaboration in the comprehension and retention of prose: A critical review. *Review of Educational Research, 50*(1), 5–53.

Redfield, D. L., & Rousseau, E. W. (1981). A meta-analysis of experimental research on teacher questioning behavior. *Review of Educational Research, 51*(2), 237–245.

Reeve, J. (2006). Extrinsic rewards and inner motivation. In C. M. Evertson & C. S. Weinstein (Eds.), *Handbook of classroom management: Research, practice, and contemporary issues* (pp. 645–664). Mahwah, NJ: Erlbaum.

Rideout, V. (2011). *Zero to eight: Children's media use in America.* San Francisco: Common Sense Media. Accessed at www.commonsensemedia.org/sites/default/files/research/zerotoeightfinal2011.pdf on May 21, 2013.

Rist, R. C. (1970). Student social class and teacher expectations: The self-fulfilling prophecy in ghetto education. *Harvard Educational Review, 40*(3), 411–454.

Roschelle, J., Penuel, W. R., Yarnall, L., Shechtman, N., & Tatar, D. (2004). *Handheld tools that "informate" assessment of student learning in science: A requirements analysis.* Accessed at http://people .cs.vt.edu/dtatar/Downloads/InformatingAssessmentFull.pdf on June 5, 2013.

Roscigno, V. J. (1998). Race and the reproduction of educational disadvantage. *Social Forces, 76*(3), 1033–1061.

Rosenshine, B. (2002). Converging findings on classroom instruction. In A. Molnar (Ed.), *School reform proposals: The research evidence* (pp. 175–196). Greenwich, CT: Information Age.

Rosenthal, R., & Jacobson, L. (1968). *Pygmalion in the classroom; Teacher expectation and pupils' intellectual development*. New York: Holt, Rinehart & Winston.

Ross, J. A. (1998). Controlling variables: A meta-analysis of training studies. *Review of Educational Research, 58*(4), 405–437.

Ross, S. M., Morrison, G. R., & Lowther, D. L. (2010). Educational technology research past and present: Balancing rigor and relevance to impact school learning. *Contemporary Educational Technology, 1*(1), 17–35.

Rovee-Collier, C. (1995). Time windows in cognitive development. *Developmental Psychology, 31*(2), 147–169.

Sadoski, M., & Paivio, A. (2001). *Imagery and text: A dual coding theory of reading and writing*. Mahwah, NJ: Erlbaum.

Sanchez, C. A., & Branaghan, R. J. (2011). Turning to learn: Screen orientation and reasoning with small devices. *Computers in Human Behavior, 27*(2), 793–797.

Sanchez, C. A., & Wiley, J. (2009). To scroll or not to scroll: Scrolling, working memory capacity, and comprehending complex texts. *Human Factors, 51*(5), 730–738.

Schmid, R. F., Bernard, R. M., Borokhovski, E., Tamim, R., Abrami, P. C., Wade, A., et al. (2009). Technology's effect on achievement in higher education: A stage I meta-analysis of classroom applications. *Journal of Computing in Higher Education, 21*(2), 95–109.

Schulte, B. (2011). Hybrid schools for the iGeneration: New schools combine "bricks" and "clicks." In N. Walser (Ed.), *Spotlight on technology in education* (pp. 101–112). Cambridge, MA: Harvard Education Press.

Schunk, D. H., & Cox, P. D. (1986). Strategy training and attributional feedback with learning disabled students. *Journal of Educational Psychology, 78*, 201–209.

Shapely, K., Sheehan, D., Maloney, C., & Caranikas-Walker, F. (2011). Effects of technology immersion on middle school students' learning opportunities and achievement. *Journal of Educational Research, 104*(5), 299–315.

Shuler, C. (2012). *iLearn II: An analysis of the education category of Apple's app store*. New York: The Joan Ganz Cooney Center at Sesame Workshop. Accessed at www.joanganzcooneycenter.org /wp-content/uploads/2012/01/ilearnii.pdf on May 21, 2013.

Sitzmann, T., Kraiger, K., Stewart, D., & Wisher, R. (2006). The comparative effectiveness of web-based and classroom instruction: A meta-analysis. *Personnel Psychology, 59*(3), 623–664.

Smith, A. (2000). *Interactive whiteboard evaluation*. Accessed at www.mirandanet.ac.uk/publications /smartboard.htm on May 24, 2013.

Smith, F. J. (1913, July 9). The evolution of the motion picture: VI—Looking into the future with Thomas A. Edison. *The New York Dramatic Mirror, 24*, 42.

Snyder, I. (1998). Beyond the hype: Reassessing hypertext. In I. Snyder (Ed.), *Page to screen: Taking literacy into the electronic era* (pp. 125–143). New York: Routledge.

Snyder, T. D., & Dillow, S. A. (2012). *Digest of education statistics 2011* (NCES 2012-001). Washington, DC: National Center for Education Statistics.

Soe, K., Koki, S., & Chang, J. M. (2000). *Effect of computer-assisted instruction (CAI) on reading achievement: A meta-analysis.* Honolulu, HI: Pacific Resources for Education and Learning. Accessed at www.cs.cmu.edu/afs/cs.cmu.edu/project/listen/dmg/Listen/Proposals/IERI%20 2003/IERI2003%20related%20papers/Effect%20of%20Computer-Assisted%20Instruction%20 (CAI)%20on%20Reading%20Achievement%20A%20Meta-Analysis.htm on June 4, 2013.

Speak Up. (2013). *From chalkboards to tablets: The digital conversion of the K–12 classroom.* Irvine, CA: Project Tomorrow. Accessed at www.tomorrow.org/speakup/pdfs/SU12EducatorsandParents.pdf on May 21, 2013.

Squire, K. (2005). Changing the game: What happens when video games enter the classroom? *Innovate Journal of Online Education, 1*(6). Accessed at http://website.education.wisc.edu/kd squire/tenure-files/manuscripts/26-innovate.pdf on June 5, 2013.

Staples, A., Pugach, M. C., & Himes, D. (2005). Rethinking the technology integration challenge: Cases from three urban elementary schools. *Journal of Research on Technology in Education, 37*(3), 285–310.

Tallent-Runnels, M. K., Thomas, J. A., Lan, W. Y., Cooper, S., Ahern, T. C., Shaw, S., et al. (2006). Teaching courses online: A review of the research. *Review of Educational Research, 76*(1), 93–135.

Tamim, R., Bernard, R., Borokhovski, E., Abrami, P., & Schmid, R. (2011). What forty years of research says about the impact of technology on learning: A second-order meta-analysis and validation study. *Review of Educational Research, 81*(4), 4–28.

TED. (2013). *About TED.* Accessed at www.ted.com/pages/about on June 4, 2013.

U.S. Department of Education. (2004). *Toward a new golden age in American education—How the Internet, the law and today's students are revolutionizing expectations.* Accessed at www2.ed.gov /about/offices/list/os/technology/plan/2004/plan.pdf on June 4, 2013.

van Dijk, T. A., & Kintsch, W. (1983). *Strategies of discourse comprehension.* New York: Academic Press.

Walberg, H. J. (1999). Productive teaching. In H. C. Waxman & H. J. Walberg (Eds.), *New directions for teaching practice research* (pp. 75–104). Berkeley, CA: McCutchen.

Wallace, R. M. (2004). A framework for understanding teaching with the Internet. *American Educational Research Journal, 41*(2), 447–488.

Walser, N. (2011). Teaching 21st century skills. In N. Walser (Ed.), *Spotlight on technology in education* (pp. 37–46). Cambridge, MA: Harvard Education Press.

Wang, M. C., Haertel, G. D., & Walberg, H. J. (1993). Toward a knowledge base for school learning. *Review of Educational Research, 63*(3), 249–294.

Waxman, H. C., Lin, M., & Michko, G. M. (2003). *A meta-analysis of the effectiveness of teaching and learning with technology on student outcomes.* Naperville, IL: Learning Point. Accessed at http://treeves.coe.uga.edu/edit6900/metaanalysisNCREL.pdf on June 4, 2013.

Weare, C., & Lin, W.-Y. (2000). Content analysis of the World Wide Web: Opportunities and challenges. *Social Science Computer Review, 189*(3), 272–292.

Welch, M. (1997, April). *Students' use of three-dimensional modeling while designing and making a solution to a technical problem.* Paper presented at the annual meeting of the American Educational Research Association, Chicago.

West, L. H. T., & Fensham, P. J. (1976). Prior knowledge or advance organizers as affective variables in chemical learning. *Journal of Research in Science Teaching, 13*(4), 297–306.

Wilkinson, S. S. (1981). The relationship between teacher praise and student achievement: A meta-analysis of selected research. *Dissertation Abstracts International, 41*, 3998A.

Windschitl, M., & Sahl, K. (2002). Tracing teachers' use of technology in a laptop computer school: The interplay of teacher beliefs, social dynamics, and institutional culture. *American Educational Research Journal, 39*(1), 165–205.

Wise, K. C., & Okey, J. R. (1983). A meta-analysis of the effects of various science teaching strategies on achievement. *Journal of Research in Science Teaching, 20*(5), 415–435.

Wu, W.-H., Wu, Y.-C. J., Chen, C.-Y., Kao, H.-Y., Lin, C.-H., & Huang, S.-H. (2012). Review of trends from mobile learning studies: A meta-analysis. *Computers and Education, 59*(2), 817–827.

Wubbels, T., Brekelmans, M., den Brok, P., & van Tartwijk, J. (2006). An interpersonal perspective on classroom management in secondary classrooms in the Netherlands. In C. Evertson & C. S. Weinstein (Eds.), *Handbook of classroom management: Research, practice, and contemporary issues* (pp. 1161–1191). Mahwah, NJ: Erlbaum.

Yaakub, M. N., & Finch, C. R. (2001). Effectiveness of computer-assisted instruction in technical education: A meta-analysis. *Workforce Education Forum, 28*(2), 1–15.

Zhao, Y., Lei, J., Yan, B., Lai, C., & Tan, H. S. (2005). What makes the difference? A practical analysis of research on the effectiveness of distance education. *Teachers College Record, 107*(8), 1836–1884.

Zirkle, C. (2003). Distance education and career and technical education: A review of the research literature. *Journal of Vocational Education Research, 28*(2), 161–181.

Zirkle, M. L. (2003). *The effects of SMART Board interactive whiteboard on high school students with special needs in a functional mathematics class.* Accessed at http://downloads01.smarttech.com /media/research/international_research/usa/mennoniteuniversityresearch.pdf on May 24, 2013.

INDEX